THE POSSIBILITY OF ALL THINGS

A STORY OF PARALLEL JOURNEYS

FRANK HEAD

SANTA FE
EL PASO

LAREDO

CHIHUAHUA

COAHUILA

NUEVO
LEON

SINALOA

DURANGO

TAMAULIPAS

ZACATECAS

SAN LUIS POTOSI

NAYARIT

AGUASCALIENTES

GUANAJUALO

QUERETARO

JALISCO

HIDALGO

COLIMA

MICHOACAN

ESTADO DE
MEXICO

TLAXCALA

MORELOS

PUEBLA

VERACRUZ

TILZAPOTLA

GUERRERO

OAXACA

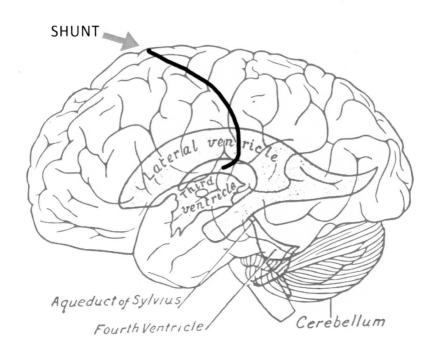

SHUNT

Lateral ventricle

Third ventricle

Aqueduct of Sylvius

Fourth Ventricle

Cerebellum

YUCATAN

QUINTANA ROO

CAMPECHE

TABASCO

CHIAPAS

Yankee Lady Press
Fayetteville, Arkansas

Cover design by Parag Chowdhury

More information at www.frankhead.net

ISBN: 978-0-578-32665-8

Library of Congress Control Number: 2021923607

CHAPTER ONE

DARKNESS AT NOON

February 20, 2011. Coma Day 1.

Dear Friends and Family:

First of all, I want to let you know that my wife Phyllis is still alive, although there were many times today I thought the outcome would be otherwise.

Earlier this afternoon, I came home early from work to accompany her to a doctor's appointment. She's had a nagging stomach pain that's slowly gotten worse for a week and though we didn't suspect anything serious, I wanted to make sure she asked the doctor if it could have any connection to the neurological problems that have plagued her since she was mugged in 2002. I arrived early in the afternoon to find an eerily quiet house, and Phyllis upstairs, asleep in bed. I let her sleep while I ate my lunch, going over her symptoms in my mind—sharp stomach pain several times each day, no other obvious problems. Around three o'clock, I realized it was getting close to time to leave, so I went up to the bedroom. "Hey Phyl! It's time to get up!" I saw that she still wasn't stirring, so I squeezed her hand, but felt no movement. I pulled her lightly by her shoulder—still to no response. A sleep this deep wasn't normal for her, but I still assumed she was okay. Finally, I began shouting "Phyllis! You've gotta wake up! C'mon Phyl!" To my horror, nothing I could do would wake her. She was unconscious.

I didn't allow myself to panic—only to think, and to act. My mind raced for options on what to do, who to call, immediately I dialed Melinda, our neighbor, who was a registered nurse. She came over quickly, checked her breathing, timed her lack of response for sixty seconds and affirmed that it was time to call 911.

I stood by Phyllis's bed, checking her breathing and feeling her pulse. Melinda was calm too, but our eyes locked and communicated how scared we both were. Soon there was a siren and a loud knock at the front door. My heart finally began to race as four firefighters entered our bedroom and began checking her vital signs. I could see their emergency vehicle out the window, blocking the street with blinding flashing lights. They got Phyllis on a stretcher just in time for the ambulance to arrive, another emergency vehicle in the street to add to the mayhem. The stretcher had wheels that folded out underneath her and in a flash, the back doors of the ambulance slammed shut and I was following close behind as they roared and flashed a six-minute ride to Washington Regional Hospital. The gurney was hurtled inside, sheet walls were drawn around her and a doctor shined a flashlight in her eyes.

"My wife had a brain shunt implanted eight months ago in

Little Rock," I told the ER doctor. "She has hydrocephalus. The shunt has worked perfectly till now."

"I'll have to page the neurosurgeon-on-call," the doctor said. "He should be here in fifteen minutes."

By the time the neurosurgeon arrived, two of my sons, Joey and Preston, had joined me, alerted to the crisis by Melinda. "What the hell happened, Dad?" Joey asked. "Why is Mom unconscious?"

I hugged them both, and told them what little I knew.

Just then, the neurosurgeon arrived in a tuxedo with bow tie, having been summoned from a charity event. He only discarded the tie, and slipped on scrubs and gloves over his suit—a combination I might have laughed at had it not meant the time wasted by changing could be fatal. After reading the ER doctor's notes and examining Phyllis, he asked almost casually:

"Anything I should know that you haven't already told the doctor?"

My mind raced to answer as the previous three years raced before my eyes.

"Four years ago, in 2007, Phyllis began dragging her feet when she walked," I said. "Tests were inconclusive and her walking kept getting worse. She kept walking faster and faster until she'd run into something. Last May, in 2010, she was diagnosed with hydrocephalus and had a brain shunt inserted in Little Rock. The first shunt only made things worse. Two weeks later, in June, the neurosurgeon at St. Vincent's in Little Rock put in a second shunt. That cured all her symptoms and till now, she's been just fine." I thought for another moment, then added, "Oh yeah, and for a week, she's had these sharp stomach pains."

"I suspect the shunt is infected; possibly meningitis," the doctor said. "We don't have time for test results or to move her to an operating room. If I'm right and she has meningitis, every minute counts now. I'm going to make an incision in her neck, remove the shunt, and drain the fluid externally. You can watch or you can leave."

We stayed but we felt all the reassurance of the last eight months collapsing as the doctor took a scalpel from a plastic sheath and cut into Phyllis neck where the drain cord from her brain shunt was. There was no time for anesthetics.

"She can't feel anything now anyway," the doctor chuckled. Somehow, the doctor's cavalier attitude was reassuring; surely he wouldn't act this way if he thought she could die on the operating table? Hell, it wasn't even an operating table. No lights, nurses or anesthesiologist, just an ER examining room. I froze all thoughts and emotions and focused on that knife as it cut into her beautiful skin. I held my sons' shoulders as the doctor pulled out the two-foot long plastic hose running from the base of her brain to her abdomen.

Phyllis was moved, unconscious, to the intensive care unit. I prayed that all this wasn't damaging her brain further. My own brain was in crisis mode, emotions delayed so important decisions could be made. I asked myself: *Do you think she's dying now?* My answer immediately was *No, I would know if she was leaving.* Somehow, it seemed we were both shut down until life decided what to do with us.

March 7, 2011. Coma Day 15.

Over the last ten days Phyllis has opened her eyes twice, moved all her limbs on command and showed hopeful signs of wakefulness, then spent the following day going in and out of consciousness before fading completely again. Apparently, this in-and-out is highly unusual and is puzzling. But Phyllis's case has been puzzling her doctors since she started having walking problems in 2007. For three years, her symptoms got progressively worse but didn't exactly match up with a diagnosis of hydrocephalus, the blocked flow of cerebrospinal fluid which causes dangerously high pressure in the brain's ventricles. Since then, I have learned much about her condition.

Spinal fluid is a pristine, highly-specialized liquid which, in a system similar to the body's blood flow, is pumped down the body and circulates back up the spine, soaking the spinal cord and feeding the brain. When the fluid is used up, the ventricles (small receptacles at the base of the brain) collect and recycle it into the body. But when the ventricles don't drain properly, they swell and push against highly sensitive brain tissue. If swollen brain ventricles were the only issue, it should have been fixed by the many spinal taps which were performed on her. But after years of no improvement, in 2010 doctors inserted a shunt which would continually drain the excess fluid.

The brain, when it's working, is a beautifully functioning closed system. The blood-brain barrier keeps any of the nastiness that the rest of your body has to fight off from ever reaching the brain. But putting in the shunt broke that barrier, and it seems that an opportunistic bit of bacterial meningitis sneakily worked its way *against* the current, up though the brain shunt's drain, and into the forbidden territory of her brain. Once the infection blossomed and spread, the shunt ceased to drain. Her ventricles, normally the size of two walnuts at the base of the brain, were now grossly swollen to the shape of two apples, pressing on the most sensitive part of human anatomy. And all the while, infected spinal fluid was carrying the invader to all the parts of her brain.

An infectious disease specialist treated Phyllis's meningitis with a series of strong antibiotics for the first two weeks, with some success. Her neurosurgeon, with the help of a tube inserted into the deep recesses of her brain, attempted to relieve the cerebrospinal fluid pressure, also with some success. Now, another tube inserted in her throat keeps her breathing, and wires seem to flow from every part of her body like the snakes writhing from the head of Medusa, monitoring everything imaginable: blood pressure, blood oxygen, body temperature, heart rate, ventricular size, cerebrospinal fluid pressure, and more. But after all of this, the swelling doesn't seem to be receding.

Now that her infection is gone and there is an external drain of her spent spinal fluid, her brain ventricles should normalize and she should begin to wake up. The expanded state of her ventricles, however, remains unchanged. She will have a replacement *internal* brain shunt inserted this week which will hopefully do a better job of draining the fluid to where it normally should go in the body and allow the swelling to subside. External shunts are always a temporary fix since they expose the brain to potential contamination from outside the body.

Meanwhile, I, along with hundreds of friends and family, are waiting, hoping and praying that she will awake fully this time.

Friday, March 11, 2011. Coma Day 19.

To protect Phyllis from accidentally inhaling saliva into her lungs, which can lead to pneumonia, she's been on a ventilator. It's an oppressive-looking thing, like having a garden hose running down your throat. It was supposed to be a temporary solution, but it's been in long enough that the risk it carries of infection and damage to the vocal cords has become too great. So yesterday they exchanged her ventilator for a tracheotomy hose; less oppressive, perhaps, and with fewer risks, but no less frightening for me. While I didn't watch, imagining the scalpel cutting through her throat was almost worse than watching the surgery. Amazing how easily doctors punch holes in parts of our body we consider inviolable.

Phyllis had a restful day today, enjoying her freedom from the ventilator hose, I imagine. Her heart rate and blood oxygen rate have improved and her breathing seems calmer, her face no longer hidden by a ventilator mask. Even so, it is painful to see her with the newly-acquired trach tube wired to her throat, which would prevent her from speaking even if she were to wake up and want to do so. She cannot speak because her exhaled air travels out the tracheotomy incision and never reaches her voice box.

From the beginning of her coma, everyone from doctors to nurses poke, pry and pinch Phyllis, hoping to elicit a conscious response. When she does display some proof of conscious brain function, like movement or speech, we all cheer like an audience at a circus when the bears dance. If Phyllis really is aware of her surroundings but unable to communicate, all this must be infuriating. I am making an effort not to force her to "perform" for us. Better to let her focus on getting well. Rather than raising our voices when we speak to her, as people often foolishly do when speaking to someone who doesn't understand their language, I just speak to her normally as if I know she can hear me. With the new shunt surgery that is scheduled tomorrow, perhaps she will finally be able to give us the answers we hope for.

Many friends are researching and passing ideas, contacts and leads. Thanks to a dear friend, Barbara, I connected today with an infectious disease specialist at a research hospital in the Midwest to get a second opinion. He has seen a few cases like Phyllis's before, i.e. going in and out of full consciousness after a meningitis-like bacterial infection. He confirmed that the hospital is doing all the right things. He added the comforting assessment that, having seen this kind of rare case before, he thinks she has a real chance of recovery, but that we should expect it to be slow— weeks or even months.

All of her life, Phyllis has had a unique way of embracing every person she's met and leaving them with a better image of themselves, yet she has always seemed totally unaware of having that effect on people. How I wish she was awake now to see the effort so many people have made to offer whatever assistance or connections they can. In this time of silent adventure into her soul, our community of family, friends and strangers have assisted me immensely to continue on the path to help, serve and love her, come what may.

Phyllis's parents, Julia and Louis, live in San Diego, California. Since they are both approaching ninety, they can't travel to see her. In fact, her mother is so fragile, we haven't told her of Phyllis's condition. But I trust in Phyllis's will to survive *because* I know her parents, Louis and Julia, who formed her heart and soul. From her dad, Louis, she got the extrovert's uncanny ability to relate to a whole room full of people and leave every person she meets feeling better about themselves. She also got her survivor's courage from him, Dad having lost a leg to cancer at thirty-five but never having seen himself as a victim. From Julia, her Italian mother, she got her whole nature: beginner's mind, sharp wit, clear intuition, love of food and fierce loyalty to family. From the moment I met them, Dad treated me like his own son and Ma did her best to fatten me up. I never felt anything but loved and respected. They are my heroes and our best teachers. Even though they can't be here, I feel their presence by her side every day.

Sunday, March 13, 2011, 9:32 p.m. Coma Day 21.

Since the day I found her in bed and couldn't wake her, the vast majority of the moments we are with Phyllis her body shows no sign of life other than her breathing. She doesn't blink, doesn't cough, doesn't even move in reaction to all the poking and prodding she constantly endures. So every exception, every occasional tiny movement of her eyes, mouth or muscles fills us with excitement. Which is why today was such a good day. For the first time in weeks, Phyllis opened her eyes numerous times, held them open and was able to follow movement in the room. You can imagine my joy in seeing those beautiful brown eyes staring into my soul once again. But as quickly as the moment came it was gone again, and I was back to watching and waiting.

I take each day as it comes, hoping for more days like this one but pushing away disappointment or doubt on days when nothing changes. I don't think Phyllis's recovery is going to be sequential, one victory building on another. Rather I expect it to be a seemingly random bunch of leaps like this one, followed by setbacks. Even today, although she could see, she couldn't move her face or hands. Her doctors speculate that her inability to move is due to irritation around the surface of her brain. It's like trying to tune a radio with lots of static; sometimes the signal is clear and sometimes it's jumbled. It may go back and forth like this for a good while. Meanwhile, I'll be here listening, waiting to catch my favorite station when it returns.

Tuesday, March 15, 2011. Coma Day 23.

Phyllis is sleeping quietly today, if a coma can be called sleep. I don't know what else to call it. She isn't suffering visibly, but who knows what we can't perceive or measure consciously that the unconscious mind may be seeing and feeling? When doctors come in and test her reaction by sticking pins in her toes, is she really not feeling pain, or is she just unable to react? The surgeon who removed her shunt in the emergency room didn't use anesthesia, but did Phyllis really not feel *anything*? That doesn't ring true to me. Why assume that someone who can't express feelings (or attachments and emotions, for that matter) must not be experiencing them at all—even if it is somewhere deep in the massive enterprise that is their unconscious brain? Is my unconscious lover really just a collection of muscles and organs unable to think, feel or remember? If so, then Phyllis is partially dead already. But if not, she's in there somewhere, aware of everything that's happening and trying to figure her way out of it just as hard as we are on the outside. I prefer to imagine a comatose Phyllis as a traveler in a foreign land, an unknown country where she can't even speak the language. But even though she is lost for now, I still believe wherever she is, she is still the loving, honest, open person she always was. I hope at least it is a peaceful journey.

I arrive most mornings when the ICU opens at 5:30 a.m., and usually have her to myself while the nurses and techs are busy with their morning preparation. We listen to some music, something I know she would like. I read her letters from the website where I'm posting these journals. But mostly we sit quietly, like we would on any early morning. She looks peaceful, her hair freshly-braided by the night nurse. The sun's not up yet; I sing her a few lines of Leonard Cohen's song, "Hey, That's No Way To

Say Goodbye." Poignant, tender lines about the parting of two lovers, ambiguous as to whether theirs is a forever goodbye but certain that love overcomes time and distance.

At 6:30 a.m., the techs come to turn her as they do every two hours to keep her body flexed. This means it's time for me to go—the ICU closes from 6:30 a.m. until 9 a.m. Sometimes, sitting in her darkened room in the early morning, I feel the excitement of a college kid sneaking into his girl's college dorm. Too bad I have to leave; these little moments, as we hold hands with the room curtains closed, feel more intimate than the rest of the day. Sitting in the dark, I feel no separation from her. Touching in silence, I feel as connected to another being as life on Earth allows.

Wednesday, March 16, 2011. Coma Day 24.

Phyllis had her new shunt inserted through the top of her skull today. A lot of our hopes are riding on this new effort. For twenty-one days she's had an external drain, and while the cerebro-spinal fluid *pressure* appears normal now, her *ventricles* have remained grossly expanded to five times their normal size, immediately pressing on the corpus callosum, a bundle of nerve fibers that form a roof over the ventricles. The corpus callosum provides a major conduit between the right and left sides of the brain. If her expanded ventricles damaged any of those millions of nerve fibers, that could explain her lack of consciousness. The actual damage is hard to predict but needless to say, it's not a good thing to have your brain slowly pressed against the skull from inside.

When you are already in ICU, surgery (even brain surgery) is just another part of your routine. Your hospital bed becomes your transportation and all your maintenance systems (oxygen, blood, heart, spinal fluid pressure) are made mobile as well. Phyllis and her equipment rolled away this afternoon with her nurses and techs in tow behind swinging double doors with "no public access" posted on them. Three hours later, she rolled back into her room. Her surgeon came by to say "everything went great." She is resting peacefully now, her and all the equipment back to where it was with one difference—a new brain shunt. Only time will tell us how much of a difference that one change made.

Wednesday, March 16, 2011, 4:28 a.m. Coma Day 24.

So far, on her three-week trip to the underworld, Phyllis has conquered all kinds of scary, horrific dragons: spinal meningitis, bacterial infection in both abdomen and spinal fluid, and brain shunt failure.

But today is a fresh beginning. Her new shunt seems to be functioning well, replacing the external drain with a permanent, internal shunt. The doctors and nurses all have the same mantra: her vital signs (heart, blood, pulse, lungs and all the parts that make us go) are those of a healthy, young body. But now, there is a new diagnosis: ventriculitis. It's less of a cause and more a description of symptoms, meaning that her struggle is focused on the brain ventricles and getting them to function, to again properly flex and direct the flow of spinal fluid to bathe, feed and clean the brain.

Friday, March 18, 2011, 7:00 a.m. Coma Day 26.

I wasn't sure I could write in my journal this morning. I want to give everyone who loves her some kernel of hope but I also need to tell the truth, not to pretend to make myself or anyone else feel better. This is what I decided: to make my best effort to face the truth and in the process, accept that a life well-lived can be joyful from start to finish, even through pain and suffering. But the truth right now is that her condition changes so agonizingly slowly that even the changes, good or bad, are so tiny they seem insignificant. And even the really big changes, like opening her eyes and tracking movement, happen very briefly and then disappear, sometimes for hours, sometimes for days.

Today, if all the paperwork goes through, Phyllis will be moving to a new hospital, the Regency. Sounds like a nice New York City hotel, but it's actually the former location of the Washington Regional Hospital, now converted into a top-notch extended acute care facility. *Extended* acute care means they assume nothing's going to happen quickly and in the meantime, they need to keep you alive.

So here is the blunt truth: she is still unconscious and the doctors have no reason to expect anything to change. After twenty-six days in intensive care, her condition would have been described, had she been someone famous that the media felt compelled to report on, as "serious but stable." Her vital signs are steady but she is acutely ill, unconscious with an uncertain prognosis. She has six different specialists, each with their own guess as to her options for survival, much less her chance of improvement. All agree that the longer her coma lasts, the less chance she has of recovery. Every day you lie prone in bed, unable to consciously move any part of your body, becomes a golden opportunity for vital organs to deteriorate, muscle tissue to atrophy, blood veins to clot, nerve patterns to be disrupted, germs to prosper and inertia to overcome vitality.

I showed up in the morning feeling appropriately blue and prepared to accept defeat. "Pretty non-eventful night," the nurse told me as she finished up, her discouraged tone feeding my mood. I dimmed the lights, drew the curtain against the morning sun, and sat down for my quiet time with Phyllis. As I looked at her and tried to make myself chat normally, I began to doubt that she could hear me. And maybe that she ever would again.

"Phyl, are you still in there?" I said through tears. "If this is too much, you can let go, you know. Are you holding on just for me? You know I wouldn't want that, don't you?"

Suddenly, she opened her eyes fully and looked at me, her cheek and eye facial muscles rippling just slightly. I was so happy I broke out laughing for joy, and then I began to cry, tears of happiness and of relief we were finally *seeing* each other again. Why, I asked myself, had I been doubting this would ever happen again? Why had I wondered if she was *really* seeing me or just involuntarily opening her eyes? The coma has done this to me; I had become so focused on her being *conscious* that I risked missing the real moments of connection. I can't even imagine the strength it took for her to give me this much. Her gaze stayed with me for fifteen minutes, and the whole time we simply held hands and stared into each others' eyes. I had asked for a sign and a sign was given. *She looked at me*. I know now she's in there. I don't think she knows yet if she can find the path back to me, back to her family, back to the world, back to the life she has led. I hope she knows that we stand by her with love no matter the outcome. I do know something no one else does; when we met thirty-nine years ago, I found someone with an inner strength that would not quit. Standing in her darkened room, I thought back to that day, and all that had led me there.

CHAPTER TWO

BORN TO LEAVE HOME

"There is no coming to consciousness without pain."

—Carl Jung

"Our consciousness is a brain-generated neurologic illusion."

—Robert A. Berezin, MD

November 1, 1952

Riding alone, high on the back of a tall, cream-colored Tennessee Walking Horse, I picked my way carefully through the cedar brakes crowding the edges of the balcony-like ledges around Lake Travis in the Texas Hill Country. I was almost five years old. My family was spending the weekend at a guest cabin. The horse, who was old and steady, belonged to the property which allowed guests to ride for free. A blue fog lingered just above the cedars, concentrating their acerbic but sweet aroma. My horse followed a trail around the property and had no need of guidance. I drew back on the horse's reins and murmured "Whoa."

Standing a few feet away, partially hidden by cedars, was a twelve-point buck—a male whitetail deer with antlers. The deer froze in my gaze, pitched up his white-flagged tail, then disappeared up a trail in the brush I hadn't noticed. I guided the horse in the direction the deer had run. There was something up that trail calling me from another time and place. The horse turned his large head to look at me, as if to say "Are you sure?" I was sure but the horse knew better and ignored my dreams, conducting me back to the stables.

Five years earlier, in 1947, I was born in Houston, Texas, the fourth child and only son of Frank and Betsy Head. We lived in a two-story brick cottage home with a side porch near Rice University in Houston. It was an idyllic 1950s American suburb where bottles of milk were delivered daily to the back porch and the newspaper boy threw the paper from his bicycle to the front sidewalk every afternoon. The streets were lined with huge live oaks, evergreen trees whose long branches arched over most streets to form a canopy. Houston's warm, humid air supported well the neatly-trimmed grass yards in front of every house. Neighbor kids and I played in backyards, alleyways and the nearby Quenby Park.

The same year I was born, my dad started his own business. America was awash with surplus equipment left over from the second World War, and Dad would travel to army surplus auctions to bid on used equipment. By 1950, Dad's company began to acquire a fleet of motor cranes, hydraulic-powered lifts mounted on a truck chassis with telescoping steel sections able to lift thousands of pounds. The oil industry was booming in

Texas at the time, and Dad would rent the cranes out by the hour to refineries under construction, then sell them when the price for used equipment was high.

By the time I was ten, Dad had done well enough to branch out into real estate, banking and mining. Financial success in Houston in the fifties was mostly "new money"—men and women who started with nothing and dreamed big, using each other to climb to the top. If you knew the individuals on the county board who would decide the placement of new plants and new freeways, then you knew where to buy investment property. If you knew leading bankers and developers, you were invited to invest in new high-rise buildings sprouting up around the town. It all came down to who you knew and how hard you worked those connections. None of them thought of the system as corrupt. Why would they? Anyone with enough gumption could claw his way to the top—well, anyone who was male, white and sufficiently ruthless. Dad came of age in the Great Depression and he was a strong believer in making his own way. He refused to accept limits imposed by anyone but himself and he could strike like a rattlesnake at someone who stood in his way.

That was one side of my father. But there were as many other times he would let us in on another side, a softer, more adventurous, creative and loving one. From the time I was born, once a year, my father would put aside his obsession with money, power and business connections to take the family on a month-long adventure. It started when I was a year old. Mom, Dad, my three sisters and I left on a rambling trip in our Ford station wagon following the newly-paved Pan-American Highway south into the heart of Mexico. Every year after that, Dad would lead us off in an unplanned adventure, usually camping and frequently in Mexico. He would sing songs, recite poetry and give us his complete attention. He made friends with natives in small towns and took us hiking to remote waterfalls. I dearly loved this humorous, adventurous side of my father and our fearless exploration of old-world Mexico, both secret revelations rarely seen by outsiders. But as soon as we were home again, it was almost as if it had never happened, and everything was back to business as usual.

As I grew up, Dad confided in me his dreams of empire—a growing conglomerate of properties, companies and social connections that he intended for me alone to control some day. He had an entire life planned for me: attend a prestigious high school and college, followed by law school and then a run for elected office.

He took the first step in 1962 by sending me to St. John's School, a college preparatory high school for the children of the wealthy and powerful elite of Houston. It was a small liberal arts school where the academic discipline was rigorous, and the faculty was diverse, creative and excited to be there. My teachers were from a variety of backgrounds, and they all stretched the scope of my understanding far beyond the oil town of my childhood. My geometry teacher had sailed his own tiny boat from England to Nova Scotia, using basic math skills to navigate. My French teacher was Swiss and invited his students to visit him on summer vacation at his home in Geneva. My English teacher,

Mr. Webb, came from Wales, and was open about his atheism—perhaps the most shocking of these new experiences. In his class, I was required to write a daily, free-form journal to which he would always write a lengthy reply. I often wrote about my faith in God, but Mr. Webb never tried to undermine my religious beliefs in his responses. On the contrary, he encouraged me to explore more deeply what I felt to be true, gently articulating the importance of defending my statements in an organized way. By writing about it, I began to realize that I was certain about my personal relationship with God and Christ, but very uncertain about the dogma of the Church.

Meanwhile, Mr. Mercado's World Religion class was my first exposure to faiths other than Christianity. A passionate New Yorker who also coached the school fencing team, Mr. Mercado frequently spoke of the unique character of Buddhism in Vietnam, a place I was hearing about for the first time. He walked us through the ins and outs of Vietnamese history, including France's eighty-year colonial occupation of the country and the remaining post World War II hostilities. He took exception to the American government's portrayal of the conflict as a foreign invasion rather than a civil war. Indeed, he saw American participation in the war as a disguised attempt by Western powers after World War II to keep a controlling political influence in the region. And the same year I began attending St John's, President Kennedy seemed to join the rush to war, increasing the number of American "military advisors" in the area to 11,000. The "peacetime draft" that had started during the Korean war was still in effect, and the increasing number of boys not much older than me being forced into military duty made the class material all the more real.

I went on to attend Vanderbilt University which, after St. John's, felt hopelessly trivial and myopic. But as a sophomore, I escaped Nashville by attending a foreign exchange program in Aix-en-Provence, France for a year beginning in the fall of 1967. At the time, the North Vietnamese Communist government paid for select students to attend college in France. I met several young men and women from Hanoi in class, and in late night talks over wine in French jazz bars we debated the merits of what they called "the American War" in Vietnam. My North Vietnamese classmates showed me that young people from the North were idealists not terrorists. My own education informed me they were also being lied to by their own government. And for the French teachers and students I spoke to every day, Vietnam was a recent national defeat and very much on the public mind. Thanks to these strange coincidences, living in my Mediterranean apartment in southern France I felt more aware of the Vietnam conflict than I ever had in America. Mr. Mercado's lessons had begun my journey of understanding the people my country was asking me to dehumanize, and the more I learned from my new experiences, the less I could support what the U.S. was doing.

In 1968, as I returned from France, the Vietnam War was reaching a previously unknown level of brutality. American troop presence had exceeded 500,000, and American deaths in Vietnam were over 30,000. In February, communist forces had executed more than 2,800 civilians in the city of Hue and, as if in reply, American soldiers killed more than 500 civilians in what came to be known as the My Lai Massacre. Then President Johnson announced that beginning the following year, the draft would include a lottery to "even the playing field" for inductees of different economic backgrounds. While I knew I was exempt for my remaining years of college, I also knew that my mind was made up on the matter, and wouldn't change: I could not serve in a war that I knew was unjust, unwise and that was killing innocent people on both sides. So one of my first actions after returning to the States in the fall of 1968 was to apply for conscientious objector (CO) status which would exempt me from military service.

Anyone who was approved for CO status was exempt from the draft, provided they performed some alternative form of charity or public service. Conscientious Objectors had to prove they opposed participation in war in any form through writing and an interview, and my 10th grade journal exchanges with Mr. Webb had prepared me for the challenge. In essay after essay mailed to my draft board, I maintained that my Episcopalian faith was intrinsically pacifist since Jesus, the Prince of Peace himself, built his entire moral teaching on turning the other cheek and sacrificed his own life by refusing violent resistance. But at that time, only members of religious groups with clearly indicated pacifist beliefs such as Quakers and Mennonites had a good chance of winning CO status. My draft board ignored my arguments and refused to even grant me an interview.

Meanwhile, my attempt to receive CO status meant one thing to my father: I had publicly declared myself "different" by refusing military service and consequently jeopardized the family reputation and his carefully laid out plans for my future and the future of his business.

"Are you out of your mind?" my father asked, when I first told him of my decision to become a CO. "How's that going to look on your record ten years from now?"

"It's going to look like I knew the truth and stood by my principles," I said.

"Horsefeathers!" he shouted at me. "You'll be called a coward and a traitor. A nice resume that'll make!"

By a combination of his years of social-ladder-climbing and sheer coincidence, my father was a member at the same country club as then-representative George H. W. Bush. Bush had assured my dad that I could get into George W.'s Air National Guard Reserve unit, thereby avoiding any chance of my serving in Vietnam. This, Dad thought, was the perfect compromise— the family name would be saved, but I'd never actually have to see combat.

"Will you let the Congressman set you up for it?" Dad asked.

"No, Dad, I won't," I answered angrily. "Is that really what you'd have for your son? Sign up for some safe unit that goes to Florida for two months in the summer, while poor kids get their legs blown off for no reason? Besides, Bush knows better than anyone that the whole war is based on a lie."

"What are you talking about?" Dad asked. "You think someone of his standing would just lie?"

I tried to explain, to walk him through the things I had seen and learned, but with every word I spoke, all he could hear was the end of his dream for me and the family name.

"Who made you so high and mighty?" he asked, both dismissive and angry. "What do you think your great-grandfather, a Texas Supreme Court Justice, would think of you refusing the draft?" he said.

"I don't know, Dad, he's been dead fifty years." I said. "I hope he'd be proud of me."

"So if somebody's dead, they don't matter anymore?" Dad said. "You can just throw away your whole family history?"

This argument played out between us over and over again in the following years, my father, believing only what he was being told by his politically powerful friends, trying to convince me that the family name and honor trumped any "crazy" notions I'd picked up, no matter their source. For the time, it was an argument about what *could* happen—there was no guarantee I'd be drafted, no certainty I'd have to serve in some capacity. But then in 1970, I finished college, and had to draw a number in the draft lottery. I drew a low one, making me immediately eligible for the draft. With my CO status still going nowhere, there seemed to be only one option left for me - fleeing my own country.

I wouldn't be alone in doing so. Young men from all kinds of backgrounds were heading to Canada, including friends of mine. To do so meant a felony charge of draft resistance, the penalty for which was a fine of up to a quarter million dollars and five years in prison. If I fled, I could never return to America—there was no statute of limitations for treason. Although that was a horrendous potential next step, knowing what I knew about Vietnam, how could I possibly become part of a process that I knew was killing innocent civilians, the very kind of people I'd sat across the table from during my time in France? I had no choice but to say no. So, in May of 1970, I said my goodbyes to family and friends and packed my truck to leave for Canada.

But just a week before I planned to leave, I learned that years earlier my dad had partnered in an unsuccessful business with the president of my draft board and, as a result, they considered each other enemies. As a last desperate gesture, I wrote one final essay to my draft board in which I challenged the Board President to recuse himself from the case, arguing that he was too prejudiced to decide whether or not to grant me a hearing. Within a few days, I received a notice in the mail that I was granted CO status and would be working as an assistant to an Episcopal orphanage outside of Cuernavaca, Mexico.

Before I left, I returned to Houston to spend a holiday with the family.

"So, what brings *you* here?" my father asked, sarcastically, when he answered my knock on the door. "Coming home to enroll for law school?"

"No, Dad, I'm not," I said, defiantly. "Law school, and all your plans for me, are BS. I'm making a different life for myself."

"That's how you talk around your mother?" he said angrily. He moved to physically block me from entering the house.

"Oh Dad, really?" I said. "Because I say BS? Get over it. You're really out of another century with all your rules about language and dress and every damn thing. Oh, what would *Grandfather* say?"

"Just get out!" Dad shouted. We were standing face to face. "I won't have a *eunuch* for a son."

So this is it, I thought, as adrenaline pumped and my face flushed. All these years of loving and fearing him, years of pretending to be excited about his dreams of wealth and power, now there would be no more looking the other way.

"Go ahead, hit me," I said, moving closer, my head pounding with our combined years of conflict. "I'm here to see my mother and you're not going to stop me." In my entire life to that point, I had never stood eye-to-eye with him and refused to yield to his power. Something in the power equation changed as I moved past Dad and sat with my mother talking for a while.

"If that's what you want so badly, do it!" he said. "Throw your whole life away!" He glared at me and then stormed out the door. Mom was afraid of Dad's anger and tried to make small talk, but it was no use—I knew that being there could only do more harm than good. I left that day, not sure if my father and I would ever speak again.

Two years later, in May of '72, I finished my alternative service at the Mexican orphanage, completed my CO obligation to the U.S. government and received an official discharge from duty. In June, I traveled from Mexico to Colorado, camped in the woods near Vail and talked my way into a job as a construction helper, though I had absolutely no experience. By August, I had $800 in my pocket and I was a free man. I hadn't spoken to my family in over a year, and I had no idea where the rest of my life was leading, except I knew it wasn't "home" to Texas. I didn't even really think of Texas as home anymore—I wasn't sure I even had a country.

The freedom from everything and everyone I knew felt liberating, but I also felt alone and outcast. As Leonard Cohen reminded me in his song "Sisters of Mercy," when I didn't feel whole, my loneliness said I was lost. There were hints from my time in Mexico as to how I might find my way. In the orphanage where I worked in Cuernavaca, the kids came from villages entirely outside of the modern world, places beyond the electric grid, rural farming communities high in the Sierra. I was fascinated with the possibility of discovering a remnant of the old world civilization. I studied old maps and read accounts of travel in 18th-century Mexico. I took classes at CIDOC (Centro Intercultural de Documentación or Center for Intercultural Documentation), a free university run by a renegade Catholic priest named Ivan Illich. I thought indigenous Mexico might hold the key to unlock my questions on the future of an American civilization I saw as lost. If I had a homing instinct, somehow it was coming from up there in the mountains around Cuernavaca.

The night of August 3, 1972, I camped in the woods north of Santa Fe, New Mexico. I had a companion, a hitchhiker named Larry whom I had given a ride from Colorado. On a whim the next morning, I drove to the Santa Fe Plaza, remembering childhood road trips when my family would stop there. We'd often end those camping trips with a stay at La Fonda, an elegant colonial-era hotel just off the plaza. I decided on the morning of the fourth of August to wash up in one of the bathrooms of La Fonda for nostalgia's sake and to try out my new persona as road warrior. As I walked into the open interior patio of the hotel, standing right in the hallway was my father, smiling at me as he hung up a hotel phone tucked into the corridor wall.

"Figured I'd find you here somewhere," he said. "Thought about Colorado, but I figured you'd be about tired of working and you'd head south."

"Just like that, you show up here?" I asked. "How in the hell did you know where I was working? Or guess that I'd show up at La Fonda?"

"There we go with that gutter language," he said. "Try to be a gentleman. Let's go have breakfast."

To truly appreciate the moment, you need to know more about my father and consider the circumstances of how and why he could just show up in my life. There was a family history of premonitions.

Over campfires on camping trips as a kid, my father told me a story of how his father, Henry, had been on a trip away from their Tennessee farm. Several days into the trip, after crossing the Mississippi River on a ferry with their horse and buggy, Grandpa Henry had a premonition: *go home now*. He reversed course, crossed the river again and rode hard to return to the farm in two days. He arrived home just before the family homestead caught fire and was able to help put it out and prevent a catastrophe. He hadn't known why he needed to return, only that it was imperative. That ability to receive premonitions seemed to pass along to *my* father as well.

Years earlier, Dad had begun a boat trip with business clients in Galveston Bay one Sunday morning. Halfway out into the Bay, he had a premonition: *come home now*. So he canceled his outing, apologized to his friends and rushed home. He arrived to find the neighbors waiting for him with the news that, just minutes earlier, Mom had fallen asleep at the wheel and ran into a telephone post. The ambulance arrived just after he did, and dad was able to accompany her to the ER.

It seemed like a similar premonition had brought him to Santa Fe to find me. We were seated at a table in the open patio of La Fonda. Sunshine streamed in through the clear glass roof. We ordered breakfast, my eyes averted as I avoided even small talk so we wouldn't involve the waitress in what I expected to be a shouting match.

"I just don't get why you're so angry," my dad said, after we were served coffee. "There never was a kid who was given so much or had so many people love him. Why would you throw everything away?"

"I'm not throwing anything away," I answered. "I'm trying to live the way you raised me. *Why am I angry?* I'm angry at my country for fighting a war for no good reason, a war that's killed over a million Vietnamese and ruined my friends who went there. I'm angry at Texas, for being a viper's nest of corrupt politicians who support Nixon. I'm angry at Houston for being a tangled mess of privileged white people ignoring a half-million poor black people living right over the tracks. I'm angry at *you* for sending me to a church that says to believe in Jesus but act like the money changers and 'get as much as you can'." I was out of breath and red-faced. I was expecting another explosion and ready for flight.

Suddenly, sitting in the La Fonda Patio with bright flowers hanging in pots from rails in the open corridors above us, my father smiled.

"Son, look at me," he said. "I don't understand a thing you just said or anything you do. But this is your life. Whatever you do with it, don't do it to please me and for darn sure don't do it just to make me mad. Don't waste your life being angry. I was afraid you'd go to jail over this war thing but that's over for you now. Go find something you like to do and be the best at it."

"I don't know what to say," I replied, after a long pause. "Thanks, I guess. I'll do my best. You're the one who always took me on adventures—to Mexico and the mountains, you know."

"Yeah, I just didn't expect you to *stay* there," he said, with a laugh.

For the rest of our breakfast at La Fonda, I managed to avoid any more talk of war or my future. I told him about visiting places in Mexico that he had taken me as a child. We parted with a hard-gripped, extended handshake. Dad wasn't one to hug; whatever physical signals of emotion he gave were passed through his hand. This one felt like he didn't want to let go.

I walked out feeling pretty good about myself. In spite of making decisions about my life that upset my father, in spite of having rejected the materialism that ruled his world, in spite of having decided *against* becoming a lawyer, *against* living in Houston, *against* pursuing any career he thought socially acceptable, I needed him to know that I was really leading my life according to the principles he taught me *by his example*: treat everyone with respect and humility, do good for others and explore the natural world with awe and wonder. Not that I could say any of those things to him. I knew then how much it hurt him for me to refuse the life he'd planned for me. But by his showing up at this moment, I knew he loved me enough to let me go. It dawned on me that Dad had been acting on one of his premonitions and had come to find me. There were no fires or car wrecks so why did he pick this moment? Did he know that, in spite of my anger, I needed his blessing to find my own way in the world? Was I acting out *his unfulfilled dreams*? Suddenly, all the different paths I had taken in my life, from traveling to Mexico as a child to returning there for CO service, began to make sense.

Freshly washed and feeling newly at peace with the world, I crossed the street and looked for my recently acquired dog, Gringo, who I had left alone in the park. Spotting him sniffing another dog and a young woman, I called him and picked a bench in the center of the plaza to take in the scene. The sun was shining brightly on the adobe buildings on the west side, and as I watched the crowd, I imagined they were all in a parade snaking their way around the trees and monuments in the park.

But out of this parade, the woman who Gringo had connected with caught my eye. She was wearing a blue jean jacket and a brown felt hat pierced with a single white feather, and I watched as she used her hand to push back a few strands of her thick black hair. For a moment, I caught her gaze, and her chocolate brown eyes seemed to smile at me from a distance. As soon as I'd seen her, she was swept up in the crowd meandering around the square again, lost in a sea of bodies. Then, suddenly, there she stood in front of me, smiling, looking straight into my eyes.

Magically, the park was empty and there were only the two of us in the world. In that moment, eye to eye with her, I felt a weight lift off my shoulders like a heavy coat I no longer needed. I waved for her to sit on the bench beside me. It seemed so easy, though I'd never done such a thing before.

"What's your name?" I asked.

"Phyllis," she answered.

"Want some granola, Phyllis?"

"Sure, I'll take some," she said, eyeing Gringo. "That's your dog? I saw him running around in the street. Coulda got run over, you oughta watch him closer."

"Actually, he's only kind of mine. I just met him yesterday up in Colorado. Somebody was giving him away and he just jumped through my window into the seat. So I figured he's on the bus if he wants to be and not if he doesn't. I'll try to watch out for him better though. How 'bout you? What's up?"

There was a sixties way-of-life, a counter-culture I had embraced when I left Houston and took the unconventional step of becoming a conscientious objector, one formed spontaneously by millions of alternative youth around the globe. The culture had its own language code. We didn't use the word "hippie"; that was what the *straight world* called us. We didn't have a sufficiently-cohesive consensus on life to give ourselves a name. But we knew fellow members of the tribe, nonetheless.

You didn't ask, for example: "Where are you from?" If you did, you were likely to get an answer like "I'm from the universe." It wasn't just tribal, politically-correct language; it had a point. It was part of the resistance against the socially-dominant dogma that identified you with where you were from and what you did for a living and limited your worth to that information. We considered it more important to ask "What are you into?"

"I hitched here from South Dakota," she said. "I got in last night and stayed at the convent hostel. That's a riot, huh, staying at a convent? Where are you crashing?"

"Well, I live in an old '49 Chevy truck," I said. "And I'm traveling south to Mexico."

We had a moment of silence, but rather than awkward, it felt good, completely unhurried, and I took the opportunity to bask in her smile.

"Hey, you wanna go get some lunch?" I asked.

"Yeah, there's a health food restaurant a few blocks away," she said. "Let's check it out."

I felt outside of myself as I spoke, so elated to be talking to her that it almost seemed like it wasn't me making the words. We started walking and were joined by my companion Larry and some guy Tom, who looked really young. I paid no attention to him.

From that moment at the plaza straight on through the meal, Phyllis and I never stopped talking. Between bites of avocado sandwiches on whole wheat bread, I learned her story—and felt a new story of my own was beginning. *If we can just keep talking, this could go on forever.*

CHAPTER THREE

NEW HOSPITAL, NEW HOPE

Behold the gates of mercy
In arbitrary space
And none of us deserving
The cruelty or the grace

—Leonard Cohen, "Come Healing"

Friday, March 18, 2011. Coma Day 26.

For better or worse, today is Phyllis's final day at Washington Regional Hospital. Early today, I scheduled a meeting with Dr. Larry, the brain surgeon who so skillfully replaced Phyllis's brain shunt. Between surgeries Dr. Larry made time to meet with me and answer questions. He is a tall, balding man with a long forehead and big ears. His eyes locked with mine in a penetrating look that seemed to be taking my measure. I felt so anxious, I looked at my hands to be sure they weren't shaking. We met in the reception room, not a great location for privacy. I felt frightened by what he might tell me but in need of the truth. He

spoke concisely and loudly but in a tone that implied he needed
to be somewhere else.

"Doc," I said, anxiously. "I have to ask you something. What
do you *really* think of Phyllis's chances of recovery? I don't want
it sugarcoated. I just want to know what your gut instinct is."

"Everybody says they want the truth but most can't take it,"
he said, more quietly than before, but almost smiling. "Do you
really want it straight up, no chaser?"

"Yeah, that's exactly how I want it," I answered.

"Okay, then," he said, appearing to enjoy the chance to speak
frankly. "The numbers are against her. On the Glasgow Coma
Scale, she rates a nine. Optimal is a score of fifteen, and anything
below eight, a vegetative state. The fact that she is opening her
eyes and tracking is, unfortunately, not helpful in predicting the
outcome. It could be the beginning of her waking up or it could
be a sign of a Stage 2 coma where she doesn't progress beyond
eye-opening."

I paused to absorb the information and repress the panic it
caused in me. "I appreciate your honesty. What do the numbers
say about how many people ever make it out of a thirty-day
coma?"

He thought for a moment before answering. "Her case is
unusual," he said. "If she had a stroke or an automobile accident, we'd have more to compare it to. But, in general, patients
at her level on the Glasgow scale have a 30 percent chance of
dying within three months. The fatality rate goes up to 50
percent within six months. At the one-year point, 90 percent
of coma patients have died or are vegetative. That's because the

longer she stays in a coma, whatever the reason, the greater like-lihood of her dying from secondary causes. On the other hand, since we don't know exactly the nature of the injury to her brain, she may have a better chance than most. I wish I had a better picture to give you."

"Thanks, Doc," I said. "Thanks for all that you've done for her."

After talking with Dr. Larry, I needed to escape the hospital walls. It had been a rainy morning but by noon, blue skies were breaking through. I left by a side entrance and found a nature trail outside the hospital parking lot. The trail followed a feeder road of the nearby freeway, then diverted through a short tunnel into a pastoral scene, an overflowing stream noisily rushing nearby. My head was pounding, attempting to absorb what Dr. Larry had told me. I was frightened to my core at the thought of losing Phyllis and the collapse of my world that would follow. The responsibility for finding the best care for Phyllis was going to rest on *me*. Could I really do it all by myself?

At that moment, I looked up at the sky and asked for a sign I was on the right path. Just as I did, I noticed an owl perched to my right on top of a dead tree. He rotated his head on its axis, stared at me blankly, closed and opened his eyes and flew off dramatically. My heart raced and the fear was replaced with exhilaration. I took the owl's appearance as an answer to my plea. We were moving to a new hospital and new staff but Phyllis would arrive there without a clear diagnosis or recommended treatment plan. So being her *advocate* would become even more crucial, and the idea of it energized me, gave me something to focus on other than my fear. I knew I could do it on my own for one simple reason: that's what I had to do, even if I didn't know how. It was the affirmation I needed and I turned back toward the hospital.

As I returned to Phyllis's room, everything was prepared for the move. Numerous friends and family all lined up and escorted her out in something resembling both a parade and a funeral procession. At the front was Phyllis, motionless and lashed down, and me walking beside her, hand on the gurney. Behind us were friends toting paper bags of candy, fruit, books, notes, CDs, Grandma Julia's Padre Pio saint's card and all the little accumulated odds and ends from a month in intensive care. And finally there were the nurses who had treated her for the past month, here to see her off.

As we marched our way down to the waiting emergency vehicle, I thought of how often I'd dreamed of us leaving this place with Phyllis fully conscious and the two of us headed back to our old lives. But instead of coming out of the woods, it felt like we were venturing deeper in. Looking at all the people who were there for her today, friends, family, doctors and nurses, I realized something about Phyllis and myself. I've always relied on her extroverted nature to create friendships and a social life. Without her active participation, my "go-it-alone" tendency had no counterweight and that insight sent a chill down my spine.

Saturday, March 19, 2011, 5:07 a.m. Coma Day 27.

Phyllis spent the first night at The Regency in the Emergency

Observation Section, one of eight rooms with windows both to the outside and to the hallway. From the nurse's station in the middle of those rooms, Phyllis and everything about her is under constant observation. She is wired with hoses, pipes and electrical impulse machines, and connected to an IV post with a monitor whose readout is also relayed to the nurse's station. The ominous, compelling image is the moving line showing the fluctuation of her heartbeat, the digitized graph we've all seen on TV hospital shows with a moving needle that verifies a body's tenuous hold on life. Alarms go off for various reasons about every half hour, compelling a nurse visit, usually just to reset the monitor.

It's hard to start over in a new medical setting. I'm spending our first days here trying to feel my way through their system, to learn when the doctors make rounds, to meet the PTs and OTs (physical and occupational therapists—it's important here to speak in acronyms), to memorize medications prescribed for her, and to apologize for asking too many questions. The Regency has one floor, thirty beds and a fantastic reputation for extended acute care. The doctors and the nurses seem to grasp her condition and are well-trained to keep her healthy while she completes her journey to wakefulness. That this level of care and medical competency exists just ten blocks from my home is astounding; it's a world I never knew existed until we needed it.

At Regency Hospital, as I suppose is the case at most hospitals, not much happens on the weekends; it's more about maintaining the status quo than any bold new moves. I'm okay with that. It gives me time to think and plan and get her comfortable. She seems stable in her new bed but the trip must have exhausted her; neither her eyes nor her body have moved since we arrived. But her temperature and all the vital signs that flicker across the monitor are healthy, and her face somehow looks strong and peaceful.

As for me, I keep thinking I should feel more confident in her support staff. Regency is a top-notch facility and she will be getting round-the-clock attention from a whole squadron of qualified professionals. But instead, an acute isolation has crept in. It feels like I'm the only person able to see the grand picture, constantly aware that she needs to rest in order to heal, but also mentally stimulated to increase her odds of waking up. During the most difficult moments, the pressure of making the right decision brings out a focused, confident side of me, certain of my ability to weigh these options and make the final call. But once the adrenaline is gone and things have again shifted from an immediate emergency to the slow burn of long-term care, my mind has time to worry about how I can keep track of this all, how I can process it all, perhaps whether any one person ever could do all of it by themselves. Sitting in her new room at the close of the weekend, I think about the coming week and all the decisions to be made. And I realize that this is my routine now, this will be my life every week for who knows how long, left alone to fight this fight for both of us, Phyllis and me, until she finally returns. And what if she doesn't? I will have done all this and still be alone.

Monday, March 21, 2011, 4:20 a.m. Coma Day 29.

For a few weeks now, Phyllis has had a nasty skin rash that seemed to be an allergic reaction of some kind. Initially, her doctor had planned to give her Benadryl to stop the itching, a steroid to calm the reaction, and some pain medication. However, I had a theory that the rash was just a side-effect of a medication she had previously completed, and, if so, the rash would eventually go away on its own. I also was worried about the sedative effects of the Benadryl and the painkiller, since the goal is to keep her mind as alert as possible.

This morning, I discussed it with Phyllis's doctor, and he agreed to give her only medicine he deemed absolutely necessary, both of us hoping that if we can reduce all the pharmaceuticals going through her system it might be easier for her head to clear. Some of my fears from the previous night were calmed by our conversation and the feeling that the medical staff at Regency would be responsive, relieving some of the pressure I felt to be constantly present and monitoring things. But that evening as I was returning to Phyllis's room, a nurse I hadn't yet met entered with a cart covered in small bottles of fluid to administer through Phyllis's IV.

"If you don't mind my asking," I said, "what medications is she getting?"

"They're all on the approved list," she said, defensively.

"Okay," I said. "But I'd like to know what they are."

"Whatever," she said. "There's blood thinner to avoid blood clots, Tylenol for her slightly elevated fever, then a strong dose of Benadryl for the itching, and since that rash on her skin has been getting worse, Solumedrol, a steroid to stop the immune reaction. And some Hydrocodone for her pain."

"I'm sorry," I said, "but Dr. Mark and I talked this morning about not using those last three."

"I'm an RN," she said, "and we have a list of allowed medications we can administer. She has an ugly rash, and swelling all over her body so obviously she is in pain."

I recounted the conversation that the doctor and I had earlier in the day, trying to maintain politeness but also be firm in my reasoning. The nurse just stared at me, scowling, obviously not pleased with my interference.

"These are medicines on my approved list," she said.

"And I'm saying I *don't* approve them," I answered. "The blood thinner and the Tylenol are fine but nothing else. I have a medical power of attorney on file, if you need it."

"Fine," she snorted, and briskly exited the room after giving Phyllis only the approved medicines. Worried my wishes might be ignored the moment I wasn't around to enforce them, I waited for the shift change so I could meet with the night nurse. I didn't leave until I had secured a promise from her not to medicate Phyllis without calling. Finally, at 9 p.m., I made my way home wearily, feeling guilty for leaving her alone but badly in need of sleep. I felt as if I'd won a battle, but hoped I hadn't lost the war by alienating the nurses who I needed on my side to get Phyllis the best possible care. I was determined for the nursing staff to see me as a partner in her recovery—I needed them to, so I wouldn't feel so alone in my efforts.

I hit the bed and fell asleep almost before I could get my clothes off. The next thing I knew the phone rang. I caught a glimpse of the clock as I answered—2:30 a.m..

"Mr. Head? This is Annalee, Phyllis's night nurse. Everything's alright; you don't have to come down but I thought you would like to know."

My adrenaline immediately surges, and I am totally calm, awake and ready to bolt out the front door naked to confront whatever hurdles the universe is about to throw at me. "Thanks," I said. "What's happening?"

"Your wife opened her eyes just now. I know she's done that before. But this time, when I asked her if she could open them further, she did. When I asked her if she was able to nod her head up and down, she could. When I asked her if she was in pain, she moved her head left and right, for 'no.' She was even able to move her arm slightly on command."

"Oh my God, Annalee, that's wonderful. Thank you! I'll be there first thing in the morning," I said, my hand shaking as I hung up the phone.

I was elated! Maybe the change in medicine that I'd had to push so hard to get had made the difference I'd hoped for. I fell back asleep, eager for the next day.

Four hours later, I am there waiting for the moment the doors open for visitation. In spite of the nurse's excited call in the night, Phyllis is asleep again. I decide to try playing one of her favorite CDs, and as Joan Baez's crooning fills the room, Phyllis opens her eyes. I speak to her from the other side of the bed. Phyllis turns her head and tracks me with her eyes. She nods "yes" and "no" to questions. The nods are small and take great effort but they show recognition. My heart soars; I know we have connected. She knows I'm there and I won't give up on her.

A half hour later, she is no longer conscious or able to respond to stimuli. In my mind, I know that these moments of recognition, head-nodding and eye-tracking have all happened before, and that they're always followed by hours or days of no response and deep sleep. But in my heart, I need these victories to sustain the long fight still to come. I try to live through the dark spaces that follow these hopeful signs with a deep gratitude for all the joys we have known in the past and an effort to have no expectations for the future. But after a full month of near-constant vigilance, I don't know how I can do what I need to do. Every gain is followed by a loss; every step forward in regaining consciousness is followed by total loss of it. And yet, the doctors tell me she has a chance; who else but me is going to make sure she gets to use that chance?

Wednesday, March 23, 2011. Coma Day 31.

Today I had a visit with two close friends, Ginny and Barbara. Phyllis and I had known them both for twenty years and when they'd asked to meet me at a coffee shop, I'd assumed they wanted to catch up on Phyllis's condition. But to my surprise, that wasn't it at all.

"Frank, we're worried about you," Ginny started.

"About *me?*" I asked, taken aback.

"I've known you for twenty-five years, Frank," Ginny said bluntly. "So I know you're going to try to do this all by yourself. You'll be here every day, every hour that you can, worrying about every decision every nurse makes . . . and you told me before that Phyllis can hear us and her brain needs to be engaged regularly in some way or another, right? I'm sure you'll try to do that all on your own too. But no one can sustain that kind of effort; you'll burn out!"

I wanted to argue with her, but before I could say anything she continued.

"Here's our idea. We'll make a list of all the people who might be able to spend some time with Phyllis. If we can get fifty or so people, and everyone does about two hours, that'd be fourteen hours a day!"

"Fifty?" I asked, incredulous. "How would we even find that many people? And keeping up with them all sounds like a nightmare."

"Barbara and I will do the scheduling. You only need to write out instructions for them. And we'll leave a notebook for the volunteers to write down what the nurses and doctors do or say while they are there."

I started to argue, but a revelation came to me. This could be just what I needed.

"Frank, you can do what you do best. You can observe everything that's going on and try to see the big picture. And you'll be preserving your energy for the long haul. Part of doing what's best for her is taking care of you."

"Ginny, I really appreciate it, but . . ." I struggled with the admission. "I really don't know how to ask for help. That's not in my nature."

"You're not asking, Frank. We're offering."

I looked hard at both of them, fighting with myself over opening this door. Suddenly I was fighting back tears. My nature in a crisis was to work through it alone. I recognized the loneliness I felt in this struggle. Ginny was offering me a platoon of "boots on the ground."

"Let's go for it," I said.

Since Phyllis has been sick, I have been inundated by well-wishing friends and even strangers with suggestions for a "cure." Everything from vitamins to electro-shock therapy. I didn't want to lose my focus but I'd reached the limits of the isolation I'd created.

Over the next few days, I made a list of everyone Phyllis and I knew in town. Every name reminded me of how extroverted Phyllis had always been, of all the social functions and parties we'd gone to, and all the times I'd sat back and watched her work a crowd, make new friends, and recall the name of everyone there we'd run across even just once before. I kept thinking *If only she were here to help me . . .* But remembering how much she loves socializing and company reassures me that setting up these visitations is the right thing to do. Phyllis can't make it to the party anymore, so it only makes sense that I bring the guests to her.

Once I'd finished, Ginny and Barbara began calling them all and asking each person for a commitment to sit with Phyllis once a week and do anything they liked as long as it involves verbal communication: read your favorite novel out loud or sing an aria, recite poetry or gossip about people at work—anything at all to keep her brain stimulated.

A week later, Phyllis now has a packed social schedule, filled with an eclectic mix of every tradition, belief and interest. Ralph recites a Jewish prayer for the sick and catches Phyllis up on the Boston Red Sox; Geshe-la, a Tibetan monk who teaches at the nearby university, comes with several devotees to recite Tibetan chants; Leslie brings her *a cappella* women's ensemble to sing; Rebecca reads *The New York Times* out loud. There seems to be an endless parade of visitors, bringing with them an equally endless outpouring of love. And those who can't make it in person have made their presence known on social media.

One of our friends posted a social media request for a unified moment of prayer, reflection, and general good thoughts for Phyllis. The response was tremendous, and a few days later at 6:00 p.m. my son Preston and I sat with her in Fayetteville, held hands and prayed for her, holding in our minds the thought of so many others doing the same. Love was in the room dancing with tiny dust particles illuminated by a ray of light through her picture window. Phyllis opened her eyes and mouthed a few words. I'm sure she wanted to say thank you.

Thursday, March 31, 2011. Coma day 39.

With all the angels sitting with Phyllis for two hour blocks, I now have a semblance of a normal routine. I see her every morning at 6 a.m. and return in the late afternoon. In between, I have resumed my work duties (I manage a non-profit immigration aid office) and I research Phyllis's case endlessly. I read library books on the brain; I've joined an online listserv for hydrocephalus caretakers; and I randomly search Google using a phrase like "impaired wakefulness solutions."

In spite of the prospective new help, I am overwhelmed at the task ahead. Advocating for Phyllis as she is hospitalized with a long-term brain injury is daunting and frustrating. To begin with, there isn't one single medical professional in charge. However competent her neurosurgeon was, it isn't *his* job to follow up on her recovery. Once she was released from intensive care, a neurologist oversaw her case. But neurologists have more patients than can be seen in a week, so much of the decision-making depends on assistants. Then there are other specialists for all the secondary conditions. Since Phyllis is not responding rapidly to treatment, visiting her is a lower priority for the specialists. In fact, most of the daily visits are from a "hospitalist," a relatively new designation for general practice physicians who do routine rotations in hospitals between visits by the specialists. Care is also provided by PAs, highly-trained physicians' assistants. The problem I must overcome is that no single person in the system is focused on the needs and best plan for healing *Phyllis*. In our case, that falls on me.

By now, Phyllis has been in a non-responsive or partially-responsive state for almost six weeks and no one knows when it will end. Just this week, I had a confrontation with a neurologist making calls as an assistant to the chief neurologist. He was obviously unaware of the unique characteristics of her case and was prescribing sedatives again! Later I met with Dr. Mark, who also happens to be Chief of Staff. I asked him to convene a meeting of all her caregivers: himself, all the neurology staff, hospitalists, head nurse and me. I was ready for him to resist but instead I got a smile.

"No problem, Frank," Dr. Mark said. "It's a good idea. This afternoon is our staff meeting. Are you ready today?"

I entered the staff meeting more than a little apprehensive about holding my own with all these experts. Since I had been working on compiling copies of all her medical records and reviewing her various treatments and the results, I was in fact well prepared. After asking each professional for a review of their participation in Phyllis's care that week, Dr. Mark turned to me and asked how they could help.

"I am so grateful," I said, "for the army of nurses, techs, therapists and doctors who are helping Phyllis. But each of you has only part of her needs to focus on. I want the lead doctor to communicate with me on a regular basis and then to give clear directions to all caretakers what the plan is. I apologize if I seem contentious; I can't express enough how much I appreciate the love and care each one of you gives her. But I am requesting more *coordination* in her case. I want any significant changes in her care to happen for a reason, not just because someone thinks she needs a pain pill or a floor doctor decides to try an antibiotic. I want to be updated, say, once a week, on the results of tests and receive an evaluation of her progress. I don't want to have to *hope* I will accidentally run into the doctor to get that information."

I took a long breath and sat back in my chair. Again, I had that feeling that my hands were shaking, though I could see they were not.

"Sounds like a good plan, Mr. Head," Dr. Mark said, to my great surprise. Everyone at the table nodded in agreement.

Phyllis's new physical therapist spoke next. She asked me to have our team of friends and caretakers work with her to give Phyllis massages and joint movement, something we had wanted to do but needed encouragement, given all the wires attached to her. Among my volunteer caretakers, there are massage therapists, Reiki practitioners, Feldenkrais specialists, homeopathic healers and many more with a loving touch. Most of them have asked to be able to treat her. Now the staff PT was asking to have them *join her team.*

Another doctor at the meeting, Phyllis's pulmonary specialist, suggested that her IV be moved out of her arm into her chest where it has less chance of infection, another of my big concerns. I asked when and what we could do to help Phyllis to talk. When she opens her eyes, she sometimes seems to be mouthing words. He suggested we change her trach device immediately to one which will allow air through her vocal chords and let her speak when she's ready.

You might think that you need to be a medical genius to be able to talk to doctors and coordinate care as I was doing. But that isn't the case. What matters is insisting that you be included on the team. The major effect of my insisting on meetings is that *I got the experts to talk to each other.* I was ecstatic at the cooperation everyone expressed.

Since Phyllis's case is so intractable, so difficult to explain or improve, I'm not willing to just take local doctors' word for it, however. Just this week I finished making six copies of Phyllis's complete medical records so I can send out requests for "second opinions." The records are extensive: two hundred and fifty bound pages of doctor visits, diagnoses, dead ends, evaluations and enigmas, plus three DVDs of CT scans, MRIs, and X-rays. Why second opinions? Do I not trust her doctors? I absolutely do trust them but with all the new brain research out there, I had to make sure we weren't missing something. It's the old Russian proverb popularized by Ronald Reagan: "Trust but verify." I sent a "request for a second opinion" on Phyllis's neurological condition to Johns-Hopkins Hospital today. The cost was generously donated by Phyllis's high-school friend Christine. It will take ten days to get an answer. This is the fourth complete copy of her medical records I've sent to experts and I started today the tedious process of compiling four more.

It's not that I don't trust her medical team. I just want to make sure, given the uncertain nature of her injury, that I have explored every avenue to find a cure. Getting second opinions is part of the decision process as to whether Phyllis should stay here or move to another facility that could help her heal faster. Then I have to weigh that move against the loss of care and support she and I would suffer by leaving this area.

This afternoon, I collapsed on the couch in my office and slept for an hour. So much success after so much frustration was a bit hard. Through all of this, Phyllis has been very quiet, but taking it all in with a wry smile. She continues to open her eyes a lot and convey a strong sense of connection. She isn't moving her arms or legs. She doesn't open her eyes when told to. Maybe she doesn't like performing for the staff; so when they ask her, she keeps her eyes shut. She has a very, very long way to go. She is not conscious and once she is, she will have major rehab to use her muscles. Her condition is improving and now we are working as a team. I have to remember that I am not in control but if it be Thy will, let this be done.

With Phyllis in and out of consciousness, everyone asks— "How is she doing?"—which is the question I want most to be able to answer. We crave some measure, some quantitative scale that we can hold on to in this calibrated, material world. And in Phyllis's hospital retreat, numerical measures abound. She is wired, taped, probed, scanned, counted and studied. Her bodily excretions are saved, cataloged and investigated. *Cultures* are grown in them as if she was an ancient civilization studied by archaeologists trying to know the unknowable: where did her consciousness go, what goes on inside her brain, is it good or bad? Is she functioning at an intelligible level? Does she *see* us when she looks at us? Is she happy or sad? Is she comfortable or in pain? The vast array of modern technology is at our disposal: she has her own computer screen with constant monitoring lines of blood pressure, heart rate, breathing rate and blood oxygen. If she were an ancient civilization, all her archaeologists would agree that her construction is that of a highly functioning culture at the peak of development. And yet she sleeps. Even when her eyes are open, she sleeps.

The nurses banter is, I know, meant to cheer me up:

"Look at that blood oxygen rate, it's almost a hundred, that's great."

"The lady in 410 would kill for that lung capacity."

"She may have had a gram-positive *cocci* bacterial infection but she seems to have fought it off."

Amidst it all sits Phyllis, sphinx-like, her skin color still somehow tan after six weeks inside a hospital room, her high Italian cheekbones more prominent with her hair trimmed on one side from surgery and the other side still long, black and braided tightly. She can't tell us what we want to know and, if she could, she would surely change the subject. Even I, who have made a lifetime career of trying to know her, would be unable to get her to talk long about herself. She would say, "I'm alright. How's your mother? I bet you haven't called her for weeks."

Saturday, April 2, 2011, 5:40 a.m. Coma Day 41.

Today I remind myself it's Saturday, the weekend. Our friends Hamsa and Moshe talked me into going out for jazz and a scotch, scheming to get me to release my hold on routine. Friends on all sides, more than I could count. Bob was there; he had driven twenty-three hours from Boston to see Phyllis, having known her longer than I have. San Francisco blues-man Walter Savage was playing better jazz than this town deserves. If Phyllis had been there, she would have worked the crowd while I marveled from a spot in the corner. With her photographic memory, she would have known everyone and asked about all their loved ones. Louis Petrella's daughter knows how to greet people and how to care about what happens in their lives. But she stayed home tonight, at her new home on the fourth floor of the Regency.

I went home to bed before nine, already out late for my early-to-bed and early-to-rise routine. But I just couldn't stand the thought of her alone in her room. So I drove quickly the few blocks to say goodnight before the hospital locked up. I should have known she wouldn't be alone. My friend Ralph was there. Having finished saying Jewish prayers for her; he was reading out loud the messages friends had left for her in the guest-book. Carole followed soon after. Friends and angels visit her continually. I convinced myself to walk home.

As I made my way on the path through Wilson Park to our house, I spoke to her.

"Phyllis, I need you to make the biggest journey of your life, to wake your brain and make every part of your body start over again. Your muscles aren't meant to be idle; they have to move. Your body needs to be vertical—all the major organs depend on gravity and movement. If you can do that, you can live and prosper, we can embrace life again. In the core of my being, I need you back."

I dozed in a reclining chair and woke later from a dream and all I remembered from the dream was a word: relentlessness. We can move forward if we have relentless optimism, relentless valor, relentless helpers who keep me from being alone in this fight. The word relentless means an "unwillingness to give up" but also "unyielding in severity." At times, relentlessness has a negative connotation, as in the stubbornness of her illness, which like a many-headed mythological monster constantly recreates itself to harm her. But like an Amazonian heroine, she always manages to fight back and persevere.

Relentless in love are our fifty friends as well, sitting with her, reading, praying and singing. Every day more friends write words of encouragement and share memories of Phyllis's wonderful life. Chris, a high school pal of hers, vowed to post a memory of Phyllis every day until she wakes. Pat, another high school friend from New York, calls every Monday to check on *my health*. The community of love grows and grows. I promise my own relentless commitment to pursue every path to healing: we are not in control here but we are also not powerless.

Not knowing where and when I *am* in control and when I *am not* seems at times like a cosmic bad joke. I admire people who are so sure of their faith that they trust divine will. I also envy those who believe their own actions can absolutely determine their destiny. I am caught somewhere in between. I turn to God for help in being a good servant but I do not pretend to know God's will. I avoid using the Name because to name something implies you understand It. All I am sure of is that an infinite force exists around me in a universe I can only sense as a blind man feels the warmth of the sun. I know there is Love emanating from that infinite source if I humble myself enough to ask for it. I have total faith in the ultimate divine outcome of all our journeys and yet I question every single step of the way whether we have any help at all.

CHAPTER FOUR

CHANCE ENCOUNTER IN SANTA FE

She used to wear her hair like you
Except when she was sleeping . . .
                                    —Leonard Cohen, "Winter Lady"

Tuesday, August 4, 1972, 1 p.m.

After our first lunch together ever, Phyllis and I talked our way back to the park bench in the Santa Fe Plaza where we had met a few hours earlier. Her dog Lather and my dog Gringo followed along. Conversation had always felt like a chore to me, but with Phyllis it was intoxicating, and I felt a warm flush working its way across my face as we went on. I had been talking back and forth with this pretty girl for two hours, and I felt liberated from a self-imposed isolation.

"You're from New York, right?" I said. "How'd you get to Santa Fe?"

"I was working in this restaurant in Long Island after I dropped out of university," Phyllis said. "I just couldn't keep studying while this awful war was happening. Then one day I got in an argument with my boss at the restaurant about the war and he fired me. I knew I wanted to head out west, but wasn't sure how. But then my friend Lynn and I heard about this drive-away company that hired you to deliver cars. So long as you pay for the gas and deliver it in so many days, you get to use the car for free. They had one that needed to be delivered to Kentucky, and I thought, 'Why not?' Next thing ya know, I'm on the road headin' west."

"So how'd you get here, then, to Santa Fe?" I asked.

"Linda stayed in Kentucky and I hitched to Colorado, then up to South Dakota, and then here. What about you? How long have you been in Santa Fe?"

"I just drove here from Leadville, Colorado. I've been doing CO alternative service work in Mexico for two years but they weren't paying me at all. So I'd sneak back here every year and get work for a few months. Winter before last I worked as a miner's apprentice in this zinc mine between Leadville and Vail. It was amazing—in the middle of winter with six feet of snow on the ground, I'd ride in a cart with a miner on steep railroad tracks deep down into the mountain and it'd be like seventy degrees down there. This summer I worked construction in Vail. You can live a long time in Mexico on a few months wages from up here. Matter of fact, I'm on my way back to Mexico now."

As we got back to the Plaza, Tom, the guy Phyllis met at the hostel the previous night, seemed eager to get Phyllis to leave.

"We should probably head back to the hostel and tell them

we're staying another night," he said to Phyllis, motioning away from the group. But I wasn't ready to let this encounter end.

"Hey, I've got an idea!" I said quickly. "There's a state park I saw on the map about two hours away called Morphy Lake. Why don't we all go up for a hike? We can take my truck. And I have an address a friend gave me of some folks who live near there. Maybe we can score a place to stay later."

Everyone agreed, though Tom was somewhat reluctant, and we piled into my rusty orange 1949 Chevy pickup. On the back of the truck I'd built a hinged camper frame over which I draped a huge green, Army-issue canvas tarp. It was a wild get-up and was my homage to bedtime stories my mother would tell of Romani gypsy wagons in Germany. I had lived in the truck in Mexico, retreating at night to my own private world where each possession had been carefully chosen. Beside my sleeping bag was a kerosene lantern and an apple-cart shelf which held three books: a two-volume set of the Oxford English dictionary, the Gabriel Garcia Marquez novel *One Hundred Years of Solitude* and Don Blanding's *Vagabond House*. Under the books were a journal where I wrote poems and a sketch pad full of pencil-drawn landscapes. The front seat had seen better days, so I'd replaced it with a wooden bench with cushions. That also allowed me to fit more people in the front because the idea was always to "share the ride." Other modern-day nomads I met had names for their trucks, so I had christened mine the Muleskinner, after the Dustin Hoffman character in the film *Little Big Man*.

"I love it!" Phyllis said, her eyes wide as she took in every detail of my home on wheels. "Can I have it? Oh my God, where did you find this?"

"It was sitting on the side of the road outside Austin, Texas, just waiting for me a couple of years ago. The sign said '*For sale for $200*' and that's about how much I had to my name."

For the ride into the mountains, I took the driver's seat and Larry reclaimed his place as front-seat navigator while Phyllis and Tom climbed in the back of the truck. In two days of slow travel through Colorado and northern New Mexico, Larry and I had caught each other up on a lot of our recent personal histories. Larry was born in Lubbock, Texas, center of the flat plains of the universe, home of the cattle industry but also the birthplace of Buddy Holly. He signed up for the Army to see the world and before he knew it, he was in Vietnam. I told him about being a CO. He came home disenchanted with the war and was looking for someplace to put body and soul back together.

We drove east up a steep pass out of Santa Fe, onto a highway that skirts the high mountain rim, and finally reached the dirt road leading up to Morphy Lake.

"Larry, how 'bout you take the wheel for a while?" I asked, halfway up the mountain. "Think I might like the view from the back. I'll let Tom ride shotgun."

"Mighty thoughtful of you," Larry said with a grin.

Soon Phyllis and I were alone in the back of the Muleskinner with the 10,000-foot high El Cielo Peak towering overhead. Sitting on the piece of plywood that covered the bed, the deeply-rutted road made for a hard bumpy ride, but that did nothing to dampen my excitement.

"This is the life, eh?" I grinned. But before she could answer, the truck hit a deep pothole and we were thrown together. I extended my right arm around her shoulder and kept her from sliding with my right arm. Just as I did, she sneezed and had a hard, long coughing fit. I handed her a clean bandanna and, without thinking, pulled her closer and put my left hand on her chest just below her throat to ease the coughing fit. Her skin was warm and electrifying to my touch. I left my hand there a moment too long but I just couldn't move it. A message passed between us as clear as a ray of sun breaking through dark, gray clouds. *You can trust me.*

"Sorry, I have a bad cold," she said, squeezing my hand and smiling.

I returned her smile, and kept my right arm around her shoulders for the rest of the drive up the mountain.

We reached our destination all too quickly, and I hated having to let go as we felt Larry slow and park the truck. Phyllis and I climbed out together, and marveled at the deep blue mountain waterhole surrounded by alpine forests and high snow-covered peaks. We shook ourselves off, gathered our backpacks and followed a trail around the lake toward the mountains. After a while the trail entered the forest, and there at the edge of a clearing was the ruin of an old cabin surrounded by a disintegrating adobe wall. The cabin was built of huge Ponderosa Pine logs with the chinking gone, leaving spaces for the wind and snow to blow through. The roof was flat and covered with earth.

"Hey," I said. "Somebody could homestead here and do pretty well. Plant crops on the roof and live here forever."

"Yeah, look at these old pots and pans," Phyllis said, peeking her head inside. "You can catch fish in the stream and I'll cook on this old wood stove."

We laughed and Phyllis took my arm as we continued up the trail. We spent the rest of the day hiking under the impossibly blue New Mexico skies. Up the valley, across trout streams cutting through the woods, it felt like we'd known each other forever. As the sun began to make its way down we meandered back to the truck, and when I hopped into the drivers seat Phyllis quickly claimed a place in the front with me.

My friend Mary had given me some rather vague directions to a friend's cabin near Morphy Lake, but in spite of our confusion we found the yellow-painted adobe house with a rainbow-colored bathtub in the backyard. We arrived at dusk just as Bob and his girlfriend, Joyce, returned from a trip into town to sell their hand-made jewelry out of their van. We had never met but they immediately welcomed us to their cabin and insisted we spend the night inside while they slept in their van. I was accustomed to hospitality from strangers in the alternative counter-culture but giving us their whole house was a spontaneous act of generosity. They even made us a spaghetti dinner. It inspired you to pass the love onto others.

I checked out the sleeping arrangements after the hosts retired. There were four of us but only one bedroom with a double bed plus two couches in the living room.

"Phyllis and I could take the double bed and you guys could have the couches," Tom said, making his move in an awkward silence. It was a bold move for this scrawny kid, but I still felt my heart beating and my breath stop as I waited for Phyllis to respond.

"Oh, let's see . . ." Phyllis said. "Tom, why don't you and Larry take the couches?"

I could hardly hide my grin as Phyllis took my hand and we headed for the private room. Up until that moment I had only hoped that my interest in her was shared. Now, I finally knew.

We embraced and so began the sensual journey of the rest of my life. A lot had changed in the sixties about the rules for sexual intimacy but for me, it still meant a commitment to someone for a lifetime. In an instant I made the decision that going down this path meant there was no turning back; I couldn't do this and later say it meant nothing. I had to give it all I had for as long as I lived. Every muscle in our bodies flexed and contracted as we strove to close the heights and depths of human separateness until we were no longer two or even one but weightless. A brief moment followed, spooning our bodies together in an undivided, divine state of peace. I dreamt that her long hair wrapped itself around us, tying us in a bundle.

The next morning, we drove back into Santa Fe and parted ways with Tom, who had decided to move on. Larry, in his mysterious way, had disappeared, leaving Phyllis and me to walk around the plaza again and pause at the park bench where we'd met. We held hands and shared a quiet moment, reveling in what a change a day had made for us. As we stood there, a disheveled man approached us seemingly from nowhere. He offered to trade us some plastic dishes for cash. We told him no. But something about his eyes captivated us, almost as if he was only in the disguise of a panhandler. He looked as if he knew us.

"That's okay," he said jauntily. "You're going to have a long journey. Let me sing you a song." He began to sing: "*Only believe. Only believe. All things are possible, only believe.*"

He smiled and I felt a strange elation. Then he sang it again. "*Only believe. Only believe. All things are possible, only believe.*"

As soon as the song was done, the man shuffled away. Phyllis and I were holding hands and there were tears in her eyes. We looked at each other. Maybe everything is possible if you believe.

"Hey, can I ask you something?" I said to Phyllis. "Why don't you come with me to Mexico? Larry's going too. There's so much to see there, you'll love it." I wanted to say more, to say *trust me, love me, believe in me and I'll do the same*, but all I could do was hope she'd say yes.

"I don't know," she hesitated. "I told some friends in Colorado I'd meet up with them."

"Why don't you call your friends in Colorado and tell them you're not coming?" I pleaded. "Come with me instead. We'll go down the Pan-American Highway through the Sierras. It's this two-lane road they built after World War II that goes through the desert and up into the high mountains. I grew up traveling down there with my family. There's an old hacienda in Ciudad Valles where they had a nightclub in a cave and my parents used to let me ride horseback through the orange groves when I was just a kid."

"*Okaaay*," she said with a smile. "Why not?"

Later that day we were on our way out of Santa Fe for the border. It felt perfect to be making this trek with Larry, a warrior who had done what he was ordered to do, served in Vietnam and got nothing for it but a sense of betrayal by his own country. I, on the other hand, had refused to fight and had no misgivings about my objections of conscience but was pretty sure that none of us was done with the results of that war. Maybe we could help each other figure it out.

Larry, Phyllis, her dog Lather and my dog Gringo, were all packed into the cab of the Muleskinner—it was a full house. With open truck windows and the dogs' tongues hanging outside, we rode slowly across the southern New Mexico desert in the Muleskinner. I drove with Phyllis by my side, her felt hat with a feather in place, while Larry played guitar and we sang Bob Dylan's "Positively 4th Street." It's a song about the hypocrisy of those who betray you when they are supposed to have your back. It was Dylan's genius in the song that he could channel whatever personal bitterness he felt and make it *your own story*. I sang the lyrics to my home town of Houston and all those in it who accused me of throwing away my opportunities for wealth and power. Dylan gave me the voice to tell them that *they* were the hypocrites, not me; they were the ones who "had no faith to begin with." And by God, it felt so good to sing it out to the silent desert, as loud and off-key as we wanted.

Thursday, August 6, 1972

After camping at a roadside picnic area in the New Mexico

desert, we approached the border crossing between El Paso and Ciudad Juárez. Long before the Juárez modern infamy as a vortex of violence, the city was known for 200 years as the crossroads of Yankee and Mexican culture and no safe place for a sucker (or a trio of naive kids). So with that violent, dangerous reputation, why was El Paso such an attractive destination for us? Once again, Bob Dylan gave us a clue in "Just Like Tom Thumb's Blues," a slow lament about being down and out in Juárez, a town that made no pretense about protecting the downtrodden. In spite of that dark picture, the song is about someone, presumably Dylan, who went there anyway. It paints pictures of residents who have their own problems, from the prostitutes to the authorities, a place where, nevertheless, there is an implied "honor code" among thieves but a scene where nobody's going to tolerate your feeling sorry for yourself.

If you think of this song as a sequel to "Positively 4th Street"'s resentment of the establishment, what's the message? Don't be afraid to go out into the world, however dangerous it may be but also don't think the world owes you something; there's plenty of people who don't even dream of the privileges you have. But they might teach you something about survival. If you had a one-day pass to Hell, can you really say you wouldn't go?

By the time we got through Mexican customs and had the Muleskinner thoroughly checked for contraband, it was evening. We headed for the center of town and found a quaint park a few blocks from the main Cathedral. Every town in Mexico of any size offers with pride their central plaza, usually tree-lined with concrete benches and flowers much like the plaza in Santa Fe. But in large cities there are lots of little plazas as well. They are almost always full of people, selling food, hanging out, walking around.

The park we chose wasn't in a tourist area and surely no intelligent tourist would have been caught dead after dark in this place. The cops in Juárez worked for no pay, living on bribes instead. Tourists were told to avoid the "centro" where we camped. Prostitutes worked the streets openly. The streets were also jammed with regular citizens, living and surviving, working, talking excitedly and eating sumptuously from street vendors and open-air markets.

We rolled the Muleskinner into a parking place along the square and proceeded to set up camp. Raising the back of our "covered wagon" always causes a bit of a stir. Picture the bed of a pickup with a four-foot-by-eight-foot piece of plywood hinged on one side, over which is a frame built of one-inch-by-two-inch timbers. By day, it just looks like a pickup with an empty rect-angular frame. But at night, the plywood is hinged up to make one solid side with a *really long* piece of canvas dragged over the whole frame, resembling a close facsimile of a covered wagon. Inside, we unpack the cooking stove and supplies, sleeping pads, bookshelf and other odds and ends. In the country, Phyllis and I would make our own spot outside for our double sleeping bag but in the city, it's bivouac on the floor of the Muleskinner.

Phyllis got out the Coleman stove and began dinner. Larry sat on a nearby bench and began strumming his guitar. Our dogs checked out the scene and set up a safe perimeter around the truck. Phyllis and I went for a walk; she held her arm tightly around my back and we moved as a unit. The square was full of life: kids came begging; men ogled Phyllis and whistled; women offered to sell us tacos and *elotes* (fresh-steamed corn on the cob slathered with butter and chile powder). Passing a theater marquee with an announcement for *Bonnie and Clyde*, Phyllis cornered me against a post and gave me a full-bodied kiss, imitating the embrace Bonnie was giving Clyde in the poster. Oddly enough, we felt safe and accepted, having proved ourselves by having the nerve to stay there. The dogs, who most onlookers assumed were there to protect us, played the part well, obediently staying underneath the truck if they were told, or walking close beside us if we let them.

Our companion, Larry, regaled us with stories about having declared his own "separate peace" and going AWOL in Saigon. He carried a long Bowie knife strapped on his leg outside his pants, for all the honest world to see. He was also the most gentle guy you'd ever want to meet. I only saw him lose his temper once in all the time I knew him and that was when someone threatened my dog. But he was an imposing figure and played a mean guitar. So between Larry's swagger, the protection of our dogs, and beginner's luck, we had no trouble on the square. Next morning we found a local food market and prepared to hit the road for the Chihuahuan Desert. It was August, when temperatures in the desert could exceed 110 degrees, but we had no worries.

The *mercado*, a many-blocks-long collection of market stalls covered by canvas strung in every direction giving the appearance of an Arabian tent convention, had at its center a large metal roof, covering the meat section. Carcasses of every domesticated animal known to man hung there, theoretically slaughtered recently enough to not be rotten. Phyllis was strictly vegetarian and after smelling the fly-covered meat hanging in the market, I decided I had no problem with that.

We discovered that morning what was to become our mainstay throughout Mexico: the fondas—little restaurant stalls in every market with a few tables and chairs. The food was so cheap that even with our limited resources, we could eat like kings if we could figure out what we could safely eat. What we discovered was a mainstay of the ancient Mexican Indian diet and always safe to eat. Some lady at the market would have a charcoal fire going with a pot of beans that had been cooking all night; no way any bugs could live through that. I'm not talking about refried beans; this is a large soup bowl of beans with broth: just say *frijoles de la olla* (beans from the pot).

In the market, you find ten to twenty different kinds of beans and each fonda has their own recipe. Maybe beans don't sound like much of a meal but ancient Mexicans had that covered a long time ago. You complete the protein with a kilo of fresh tortillas. But don't get them off the machine at the tortilleria or worse at the supermarket; find a woman kneeling Zen-style on the ground with a charcoal fire and comal, hand-forming and cooking them from a pile of masa dough—the source of which is a corn field in the mountains growing corn from seed her family has saved for generations. Finish off the feast with some super-black Mexican *café con crema*. We were out-of-pocket about a U.S. quarter.

August 7, 1972, 12 noon

"Hey, can we get going already?" I said to Phyllis and Larry, with obvious irritation. We had lingered all morning in the Juárez market, the Muleskinner was freshly supplied and I was anxious to hit the road for the desert. Phyllis withdrew her arm from mine and gave me a smirk.

"Crank, cranky Frankie," she replied.

Finally, we were packed and rolling down the road, through miles of slums with ditches serving as open sewers. Before too long, though, the irrigated fields of desert maguey soothed me and the distant blue haze of mountains on both sides offered adventure to come.

There was of course no radio in the truck, no stereo and definitely no air conditioner. The music we covered by singing to ourselves. I carried a song book in which I wrote down the lyrics to every song we knew. Of course, a lot of Bob Dylan. Larry knew a lot of Texas folk-country: Willie Nelson and Jerry Jeff Walker. Janis Joplin was naturally on the bus with us. The songs closest to my heart were from Leonard Cohen whose lyrics I had memorized. Phyllis added Motown girl groups, the Shire-lles, Gladys Knight and the Pips, and Martha and the Vandellas. She had seen The Who play *Tommy* live at a New York concert.

To the sixties generation, music was much more than

entertainment. As we stumbled our way through the tangle of questioning every facet of our parents' way of life, musicians were our leaders, our elders and our mentors. A release of a new album by Dylan or Cohen or the Beatles was a reason for celebration—a coded set of directions in an unchaperoned but shared search for freedom. The breakup of the Beatles was a personal tragedy: did you side with John or Paul? Leonard Cohen's song "Nothing to One (You Know Who I Am)" was a gentle reminder that life wasn't just up and down but a spiral that took you from nowhere to oneness with everything to gain. I had sung those songs alone for so long; now there was a live person to sing them to.

The air conditioning in the Muleskinner was taken care of (in my opinion) in an ingenious way: a bucket of water on the floor and a dipper. If you were really hot, you just doused yourself; moderately hot, you soaked your bandanna in the water, and put it on your forehead, letting the wind cool you. Phyllis and I were always side-by-side, her leg touching mine. We laughed as we splashed water on each other; it seemed as if we had been together forever.

Riding in the Muleskinner taught a kind of meditative patience because the truck tended to overheat in the desert if we pushed it much past forty. So we poked along slowly, hardly seeming to move at all from landscape to landscape. It all seemed dreamlike, Phyllis by my side, showing someone all the scenes I loved like they were paintings by masters in a museum. All her senses absorbed the moment, entering into and amazed by the great Chihuahuan Desert. I couldn't believe there was someone in the world who *got* me, someone who shared what I thought was beautiful without having to explain.

The Muleskinner followed the dips and rises of the mostly empty Chihuahuan Desert highway as the sun reached the middle of the sky. It seemed to go on forever and by late afternoon, we were alternately boiled by the desert heat and cooled by continual dippers-full of water from the bucket. The desert is starkly beautiful if you can accept its harshness. The plants that survive are monuments to the adaptability of living organisms on Earth. The desert, contrary to common wisdom, offers one of the most diverse plant ecosystems on the planet. Although the invasive creosote bush proliferates as a result of overgrazing, the landscape still shines with fire-barrel cactus, rainbow cactus, agave and a proliferation of insects and animals.

But at that moment, we were thinking more about our own ability to survive through the heat. The Muleskinner struggled up a steep rise; laid out below us were pure white sand dunes, unbroken by any living thing. We were mesmerized by the beauty, the feeling of finding the perfect, completely private, white sand beach (minus the ocean, of course). We felt strangely tempted to jump out of the car and run to play in it, except that the sand burned with the heat of an oven.

Soon after we topped the hill, a miraculous thing happened. A large, dark cloud appeared, seemingly from nowhere, and darkened the sky. Within a few minutes, the temperature dropped to a delightfully comfortable ambiance and we felt the sky spitting at us. Rain in the desert is rare and can be dangerous; flash floods are frequent. But this rain seemed to be made for us; it was light and cooling, not harsh or pounding.

We quickly pulled off the road and ran like children into the dunes, shedding our clothes as we ran. At first we tried barefoot but the sand was still much too hot. But by leaving our sandals on, we could run through the sand, slide, fall and rinse off in the rain. It was exhilarating and magical and seemed an auspicious sign for the beginning of our journey. Larry, as was his wont, disappeared and spent several hours exploring by himself. We were out of sight of the highway and didn't see another living soul as we romped and played. Phyllis and I found ourselves alone at the top of a tall, clear sand dune.

"Look," I said. "I'll race you. Lay down here and we'll see who rolls to the bottom first."

"Obviously, I'll get there before you," Phyllis said, as she quickly started rolling down. I followed and we ended up at the bottom covered in sand and in each other's arms. The contest was quickly forgotten. We were all alone in paradise: sand, sky, and naked bodies, covered with sand, all blended into ecstatic connection—with each other and with the universe.

"If the sun was out, we'd be fried by the sun out here, you know," she said.

"Yeah but I know magic and I called in the clouds," I said. "Let's explore a little farther. Maybe we'll find an oasis with fig trees and Turkish wine."

"Maybe you're a devil leading me to my doom," she said.

"You won't know till you've tried me."

At dusk, we made it back to the Muleskinner. Just as we began to worry Larry was lost, he returned. We were spent and subdued as the sun set just beyond the clouds, a blood-red ball on the dunes and we made camp in the desert. The dogs, who had hung out throughout the rain under the truck, came out and set up as sentries at the perimeter of camp. We slept under the stars, at peace.

August 9, 1972

Heading south from the Chihuahuan Desert to Mexico's heartland with no known destination or timetable we rattled slowly along the high, central valley of Mexico with the spine of the Sierra Madre Occidental ascending on our right toward the Pacific and the Sierra Madre Oriental with valleys leading to the Gulf Mexico falling to our left. The desert is stuck between these two ranges, robbed of rain most of the year by both of them. From Chihuahua City to Durango to Zacatecas and finally to Queretaro, we wandered from village to city with frequent dirt road side trips.

If we weren't camping in the wilderness, we'd direct the Muleskinner into a town, find a suitable park for the Muleskinner and spread out our camp around the truck. Larry would play and we would sing along. With Phyllis and I as lead singers on Bob Dylan and Leonard Cohen songs, it must have sounded as foreign as Tibetan throat singing to those villagers, but we didn't care.

In Queretaro, we sat in a park and Larry took off his

straw cowboy hat to cool off as he played guitar. A very short, elderly native woman, her long black hair braided and carefully wrapped around her head with ribbons—on her back a woven basket with vegetables to sell at the market—stopped to hear us sing. We performed a heartfelt rendition of Leonard Cohen's "The Stranger Song," about a man who trades a life of chance and imagination for the shelter and safety of intimate love, only to discover that we are all strangers to each other but that in that isolation lies the key to our humanity and our connection. The native woman put a peso in Larry's hat! Our first fan! Or maybe she took pity because, like Leonard, she knew that it was *we* who were the strangers and that we had *no chance* of earning a living this way.

August 13, 1972

After days of holding each other all night, playing and traveling by day, singing and laughing with Larry, exploring the landscape, both external and internal, we arrived in Celaya, Guanajuato. We stopped to visit Phyllis's relative, Alfredo Gonzalez, later to become a university professor and Cornell Ph.D. in agronomy who married Phyllis's cousin Rosann. What he thought when this scraggly band of three arrived I'll never know, but he was the first representative of Phyllis's family I met and he treated us royally, taking us to dinner and insisting on paying for two hotel rooms. Rosann was away on a visit home to New York. At dinner, Phyllis and Alfredo talked about family back in Bethpage, New York. He explained his fascination with the life of plants and how man manipulates and changes them. But somehow, seeing Phyllis back in her family circle left me feeling lonely. I wasn't part of that scene and our little adventure, cruising down the high plains of Mexico in an old truck seemed diminished. We stayed up late, had shots of tequila and toasted Mexico but something had shifted, something I couldn't explain.

The next morning I awoke unsettled. We were meeting cousin Alfredo for breakfast and as much as I liked Alfredo, he dispelled my traveling-gypsy-circus fantasy.

"So, what are your plans from here?" Alfredo asked me, in his perfect English pronounced with the cadence of an educated Spanish-speaker.

"None, really," I said. "Except to work our way down to Morelos, where I used to live." I hated talking about plans. As soon as I made a plan, I would hear my father's voice questioning my judgment.

"Did you say you graduated from the University of Texas?" Alfredo asked. "What degree did you receive? Will you look for work in that field?" Alfredo couldn't have been more friendly or more gracious, but suddenly I had a past again and I was being forced to talk about my future, neither of which were pleasant thoughts that morning. Since meeting Phyllis, I had felt elated with the adventure of living every day in the present, especially a present-day reality that included a lover at my arm and sharing adventures day and night together. The past I didn't want to remember was the dream my father had of me entering the world of business and law—to take my place in the civilization

I now saw as fatally flawed and intent on preserving its exclusive hold on the world's resources.

On the other hand, I didn't have a Plan B. I didn't know how I should live my life and what I should do for a living nor where to look for the answers to a meaningful life. Meeting my dad in Santa Fe had liberated me from the tyranny of his judgment but it also meant I had to make my own way and find my own answers. Since I was a young teenager, I had struggled with feelings of loneliness. My parents provided me with every opportunity to socialize, from dance cotillion in junior high to enrolling me at an elite high school. None of it mattered; I always felt like an outsider. Some nagging voice kept whispering *you don't belong.* Although my military obligation was now complete via my CO service, my future was totally muddled, having burned all the bridges I could possibly burn with my family, friends, career and country.

"I got a bachelor's with a double minor," I said, "in Comparative Government and American Literature. But that seems like a long time ago."

"Hey, Frank, why don't we go into Mexico City?" said Phyllis, changing the subject. "We could look up the Mena family, where I was an exchange student in my senior year of high school. They have this incredible mansion with swimming pools and gardens."

What? I didn't say anything but my thoughts were dark. We hadn't talked about a change in direction and she brings this up at breakfast with Alfredo? *Really?* I asked myself. *Go from wandering troubadours to bedraggled suppliants at a rich Mexi-can's house full of peasant servants?*

So began our first fight as we told Alfredo goodbye and began to load up the truck.

"I don't know why you put me on the spot back there," I said. "Why do you want to go to the city to meet some upper-class rich people? I could have stayed at home and done that!"

"Well, *excuse me*," she said. "Guess you get to decide where the truck goes. And they're not *just some rich people.* The Menas are a family that took me in as an exchange student in high school. They have kids my age. Yeah they live in a mansion but so what?"

I didn't know what I was afraid of by giving in to her. Somehow, I felt I was living in a magic bubble and going back to a modern city instead of wandering in the wilderness was going to break the bubble and send me crashing to earth.

"If you don't want to go with us, I could buy you a bus ticket to the city," I said, regretting my words immediately.

"Thank you very much, I'll buy my own," she said, curtly. Before I knew what had happened I'd backed myself into an impossible corner and I headed to the bus station to drop her off.

Maybe this is for the best, said one voice in my head. *Suddenly she has to make the plans and she doesn't think that what we're doing is important enough . . . I could use more time alone to write and draw.*

Are you crazy? thought the other side of me. *This has been magical. Everything's been perfect for days; I haven't had a bad thought. Now it just goes to hell in the blink of an eye? Tell her you're sorry; tell her you'll go anywhere she wants. What are you doing?*

We reached the bus station. I tried to speak but nothing came out. We parted without even a kiss.

"Hey," I said, still frozen. "You wanna meet up in Cuernavaca next week?"

"Sure," she said, without meeting my gaze. "Maybe in a week or so."

As she left, my head was pounding. I wanted to go back. What had I done? Just like that, she and her dog Lather were gone, with no phone numbers, no address, nothing. No way to ever see her again. Why was I so stubborn? I was hurt that she would leave, hurt that she didn't want to follow my lead, and suddenly it hit me what I had done. But the bus was gone. A moment earlier, I was telling myself that Larry, Gringo and I would have a better time without her. Then there I was, alone again, lost on a trail, heading for the hills. This didn't feel magical at all.

CHAPTER FIVE

EXCURSION TO THE BASE OF THE BRAIN

They say that every man needs protection
They say that every man must fall . . .
—The Band, "I Shall Be Released"

Sunday, April 3, 2011. Coma Day 42.

Today, Phyllis peeked out at us from the inside of her brain's universe and let us know she was there. It started with my usual 6 a.m. good-morning kiss in her hospital room. Her eyes were open, staring blankly. Then, upon the touch of our lips, something happened in her face that made her *Phyllis* again, like a scene in a movie when someone is viewing a portrait and the facial muscles move just slightly or the eye winks.

Her eyes *looked at me* and the muscles around her eyes moved. It must have been a long, long journey from the swollen folds and valleys in the depths of her brain down all the rivers of nerve clusters through the caves of her eyes and out into the world, all so I could have a kiss.

Later in the morning, my daughter Julia's in-laws, the

Chowdhurys, came to visit and Peri, the father of the clan, greeted Phyllis. Just as he said hello, she opened her eyes, tracked her pupils to where he stood and gave him a smile. She was only able to hold that smile for a second but it meant everything. She did the same thing a little later for Dr. Mark as he made his rounds. Then throughout the day, she was able to keep her eyes open and use her face, however slightly.

Most likely, tomorrow she will be exhausted and sleep all day. This is the first time Phyllis has been able to do this much and I long to see her make the next step. We are still living with the possibility that this is a Stage Two coma, in which her eyes open but there is no further development in consciousness. Stage Two patients can linger tantalizingly close to wakefulness for months without improvement. But I can't let fear stop me from encouraging her further; I must try to stay open to the outcome I want, but not be attached to it.

When neurologists try to explain to me the workings of Phyllis's brain, it isn't easy to follow. Not only are the place-names of brain geography totally unknown but the concept of how it works is hard to grasp. But I am determined to try. *If I can't visualize the mechanics of consciousness, how can I know how Phyllis's is blocked?* Without that understanding, I feel disoriented, trapped in the isolation of my ignorance. So I keep searching for clues.

In our three-year search for a diagnosis before the decision was made to insert a brain shunt through Phyllis's skull, only one physician was willing to be specific as to her illness. Dr.

Jankovic, a renowned brain surgeon at Baylor Medical Hospital in Houston, had a very technical explanation.

"Phyllis has an obstruction," Dr. Jancovic said, "in the Aqueduct of Silvius, a very small tube running between the third and fourth ventricles of the brain. I believe that the blockage of the flow of her spinal fluid is causing her *lateral ventricles* to swell and push against highly-sensitive nearby parts of the brain."

From the beginning of Phyllis's illness doctors have talked about her *lateral brain ventricles* and the possibility she suffered from a condition called hydrocephalus, or "water on the brain." As I've studied maps of the human brain, here's what I've found so far: Brain ventricles come in four parts, the first two of which are the *lateral ventricles*, two C-shaped chambers, each surrounded by a respective half of the brain. It is these two ventricles at the base of her brain that have expanded and precipitated her coma. There is also a third small ventricle at the very center of the brain connected by a tube with the exotic name, *Aqueduct of Silvius*, which leads finally to the tiny fourth ventricle. This is where Dr. Jancovic suspects a blockage.

According to recent research, brain ventricles begin as empty spaces in the fetus, around which the brain is built as we develop in the womb. The walls of the ventricles are literally formed by the brain itself as it grows. Brain ventricles, moreover, are a central component in the brain's evolution; they are both the laboratory which produces the all important cerebrospinal fluid—a highly-filtered form of plasma that bathes, protects and feeds the central nervous system from the spine to the brain——*and* the plumbing system that controls the circulation of that fluid. The point is that Phyllis's swollen lateral ventricles caused a major disruption to the incredibly complex system of neural pathways we experience as consciousness.

I close my eyes and imagine myself as a tiny traveler in Phyllis's brain. As I reach the bottom of the brain (the equivalent of Antarctica on the Earth), I encounter two semi-circular lakes (the Lateral Ventricles) on either side of which rise high peaks. One shore is created by a huge mountain (the Corpus Callosum) carrying 200 million nerve fibers connecting the two halves of the brain. On the other shore rises an equally imposing range (the Central Lateral Thalamus) which among its many functions is the *regulation of sleep and wakefulness*. The two lakes empty into the same river (the Aqueduct of Silvius), which forms two successive deep pools (Third and Fourth Ventricles). Along the way, the pools are filtered and the water (spinal fluid) is reabsorbed into underground rivers—*unless, as in Phyllis's case, the river is blocked, the pools back up and the lakes overflow and flood.* Phyllis apparently picked a pretty important place for things to go wrong.

Even though Phyllis is unconscious and not fully responding, I know that her brain is not a lifeless bowl of Jell-o sitting in the skull's bowl. Though unconscious, all indications are that Phyllis's brain remains very active, an evolved universe carrying on millions of electrically-connected synapses racing through thousands of feet of sensory cells, connecting to an unimaginable quantity of data storage and muscle memory, organized by departments of nerve cells governing her organ functions, movements, emotions and memorized responses. I know that *she* has to find the path back to consciousness by herself but I believe that *we* (the entire community of volunteers and professionals treating her) *can communicate with her unconscious mind through love and awareness.* I believe her brain will sense our inquiries and together search for a new path around her damaged ventricles. Then she can gather her memories and lay down tracks for a new trail through her brain to consciousness.

Tuesday, April 5, 2011. Coma Day 44.

Amazing day! Phyllis had a huge breakthrough. In the afternoon, I met with Dr. Mark, Phyllis's physician at Regency Hospital, who gave me some *very* good news. Her most recent CT scan shows a dramatic *decrease* in the size of her brain ventricles compared to a CT from three weeks ago. This is the news we've been anticipating for six weeks—the first concrete physical evidence we've had that the new shunt is working and that her brain can begin to heal. The change in her scan is phenomenal— from large, swollen ventricles two weeks ago to a tiny, normal H on the X-ray. The "before" slide shows her ventricles as huge dark spaces pressing on her brain matter; the "after" slide shows her with the ventricles of a normal brain. Finally the breakthrough we've been hoping and praying for! The new shunt has begun to work as it should and the ventricles have returned to normal size. Although the effects of the expansion may linger for months, I am speechless with gratitude at the effort of so many people to get to this moment. I feel hopeful that her healing can begin.

Wednesday, April 6, 2011. Coma Day 45.

Phyllis moved down the hall this morning to a new room at Regency Hospital. Dr. Mark decided she could make an internal hospital move out of the Emergency Urgent Care to Long Term Urgent Care. While it's good news that she is stable enough to *not* be considered an emergency risk, the bad news is in the phrase "long term." It means that she is expected to stay in her current unconscious condition for an unknown period and the hospital's task is to keep her alive. The words of Dr. Larry, her neurosurgeon at Washington Regional echoed in my mind: "Most coma patients don't die from their underlying disease; they die because the body can't stay still that long." Also, since Regency Hospital is designed to help patients with a positive prognosis, if Phyllis does not continue to improve, there will be pressure to move her somewhere else.

Phyllis's new room is much bigger, quite a large suite with a private bathroom and a comfortable extra bed. Out the window, the hospital park grounds are even prettier here, with flowering trees and abundant green gardens. The outpouring of love from everywhere continues to surround and bless us. Volunteer helpers, in two-hour rounds, not only entertain and stimulate her but record every action of any medical personnel, report any new information from staff and document any communication from Phyllis. Every night, I read and review the notes.

I decided to celebrate and stay over with Phyllis at Regency. The medical staff has disconnected the monitor that showed constant fluctuations of heart rate, blood pressure and blood oxygen. All those medical measures are still taken periodically by staff but are no longer considered a matter of life and death. There's new staff to get acquainted with at this end of the floor—a friendly, happy bunch. This will be the first night we've spent together in a month and a half.

Phyllis's room has a decent personal bathroom attached with shower. It doesn't appear, however, to have been used in some time. The nurses were using the shower stall to store extra bedding. I moved everything out and waited for the water to turn to hot. I waited and waited but "hot" never happened. So I ended up using the shower down the hall in the bathing room where nurses take Phyllis every day in a special bathing wheelchair. Only problem is, it's not exactly private and the door doesn't lock. Anyway, I jumped in and bathed for two minutes before the next orderly popped in.

Freshly washed and ready for bed, I kissed Phyllis goodnight without any response. I tucked myself into my bed and fell asleep immediately. That didn't last long however, because I discovered the nurse always switches on the light when she comes to turn Phyllis every two hours. Aleesha, the night shift nurse, was very polite and each time she turned on the light would apologize and ask if I needed anything. By morning, I hadn't slept at all and I was miserable. So much for sleepovers at the Regency.

Thursday, April 7, 2011 8:00 p.m. Coma Day 46.

Phyllis and I have six children, the oldest born in 1974 and the youngest in 1988. I met with two of them today, Julia and

Preston, to give an update on their mother and to assess her treatment. I told them that Dr. Mark is excited at the return of her ventricle size to normal.

"Does that mean her brain function is normal now?" Julia asked.

"No, it doesn't," I answered. "Nothing changes that fast in the brain. Dr. Mark is cautious in predicting the future. I asked him about a timeline, an educated guess on how long her recovery of consciousness could take. 'Ugh, I wish I knew,' he said. So our job is to keep patient and protect her health until she wakes up. Will she wake up? My instinct says yes. But you know your Mom, she'll do it on her own timetable."

There was more good news today. Phyllis's medical team believes she is becoming more self-reliant and are close to acting on several changes to her treatment that have been under consideration. Her pulmonologist is considering removing the trach tube from her throat, letting her breathe on her own, thereby eliminating a potential source of infection. Similarly, her internal medicine specialist hopes to remove her IV line, a direct portal in her chest used to administer medicine. Both the trach tube and the IV are places where bacteria can enter the body and compromise her recovery. The fact that her pulmonologist thinks she can live without a breathing tube is great news but the final decision hasn't been made and the team doesn't universally agree that it should be done. She also continues to be fed by a tube inserted into her abdomen.

I agreed today to let Phyllis's medical team start giving her Ritalin. This has become a common treatment lately for non-responsive neurological patients with no other known compromises to their health. Ritalin has the opposite effect on adults with neurological conditions than it does on kids with ADHD; if it works on her it would speed up her brain reactions. I've read up on it and I don't see any terrible side effects. It excretes from her system rapidly, in eight hours or so. I've been weighing this option for some time and was planning to wait a while. I know Phyllis would want to heal on her own as long as possible and I intend to respect that. But acute care means there has to be a treatment plan, so I made the decision to move ahead. The trial will take about two weeks. It's not a panacea; I don't expect too much. The doctor describes it more like a jump start for your car battery; not enough on its own to bring consciousness, but maybe a catalyst. If it doesn't, we'll go back to letting her control the timing.

Tonight I'm back in our home bedroom where for the last twenty-eight years, we've ended the day. It sits on a hill that falls away towards the north, with a view of the park and, just above the treetops, the outline of Phyllis's hospital. We added this third-floor, high-in-the-treetops room twenty years ago; it has windows on three sides, open tonight to the breeze. I've been so incredibly lucky to have one person to grow and change with; memories of Phyllis permeate the room and this house.

Saturday, April 9, 2011 6:43 a.m. Coma Day 48.

My kids have been planning to get me out of the house and hospital scene. So, Friday, they succeeded. First, there was play time with Maddie and Hayden, my magical grandchildren. Three-year-old Maddie provides a hilarious running commentary on her world; whatever the subject, she has lots to say. One-year-old Hayden is walking and it is a marvel to see. He's so happy to walk that he lunges forward like a football linesman, ready to hit the ground in a second. I fell asleep on their couch.

Later we had dinner with my daughter Julia and her in-laws, the Chowdhurys. We talked a lot about Phyllis's condition. They are all curious about progress in Phyllis's health and discuss clues to her recovery. Peri, the father, and sons Parag and Pritham are all Ph.D. scientists. The consensus of an evening's brain review, discussed over several courses of curried fish and Indian vegetables, was that modern medicine, with all its technological advances, favors the precise over the intuitive, often at the expense of the patient. Lots of experts work diligently on Phyllis, observing, measuring, and treating all the individual parts—but none understanding the whole. I do feel that Phyllis's current medical team is the best yet; the lead doctor is flexible in his approach and open to suggestions. Nevertheless, I have to advocate for her; no medical staff person has the luxury to focus just on her and it's so easy to miss something. The constant focus on the ever-changing goal of her recovery is exhausting and I appreciated the relaxing evening with a loving family.

Monday, April 11, 2011 7:21 a.m. Coma Day 50.

Monday morning. The daunting task of what Phyllis and I have to do weighs on me. If she was talking, she would be telling me how hard things were and I would be the one *reassuring her*, reminding her of all that we had done and how far we had come, softly murmuring that all we ever really have is this moment and how blessed we are to have it to share, no matter how hard things are. Harder to tell it to myself.

I've been reading a fascinating book called *My Stroke Of Insight* by Jill Bolte Taylor, a neurological research scientist. As a result of having had a stroke herself, Dr. Taylor has been on the other side of that consciousness mountain and lived to write about it. She explains how the two halves of our brain take the same information and process it in diametrically opposite ways: the left brain categorizes the data according to all previous information, adjusting your reality according to past and present memories; the right brain, on the other hand, takes exactly the same information and processes it as if there had never been anything other than this present reality, looking for connections to all your other sensations of the moment. All this is done for you almost instantaneously and, depending on your own individual brain, synthesizes them into one thought process experienced as *you*. When Dr. Taylor had her stroke, her left brain was immobilized and she was forced to evaluate her experience only with the right brain. She felt a great euphoria, a sense of being connected to all beings and all time. But she also felt a great frustration and isolation because she could not put together all the memories of who people were and how she knew them.

Phyllis has not suffered a stroke, nor is there reason to think she is experiencing a similar incapacity in her ability to assimilate right and left brain. But Dr. Taylor's insight helps me to see how Phyllis's brain is working to repair its ability to relate to the outside world. In her case, at various times her brain ventricles expanded grossly and remained so, pressing on the center of her brain, compacting it and interfering with the very complicated electrochemical process that informs consciousness. So perhaps what happens when Phyllis is able to open her eyes, see someone and even smile but then relapse into unconsciousness is a momentary success by the brain in opening a path to the outside world. Her brain is hard at work repairing the millions of synapses and chemical connections which enable consciousness. Even though she hasn't yet made those new connections permanent, we can still celebrate these early steps toward wakefulness.

Tuesday, April 12, 2011. Coma Day 51.

Several weeks ago, our friend, Anita, contacted me about wanting to do "Feldenkrais work" with Phyllis to help her regain conscious awareness and movement. I had no idea what Feldenkrais therapy was but I was sure Anita must not realize how *un*conscious Phyllis was. I invited her to visit anyway and allowed her to work on Phyllis.

I was impressed that Anita spoke to Phyllis continuously as she moved her limbs.

"Phyllis," Anita said, "I'm going to try to move each bone in your hand and your arm. Is that okay with you?"

Phyllis opened her eyes. We took that as permission.

Does that mean Phyllis is *awake* and *aware* of what she sees, or is this another Stage 2 dead end? The answer is I have no clue.

"Phyllis," Anita said to her, "as I move your bones, I am trying to help your brain repair impaired connections between the motor cortex and your body by simulating skeletal movements that the brain recognizes. I am going to move your jawbone too. Soon you will be able to open or close your own mouth, not on command but at your own choosing."

Anita is a very gentle soul with very wise hands. She seems able to communicate with Phyllis at conscious and unconscious levels; the former by talking quietly and asking permission, the latter by helping Phyllis's autonomic brain *register movement* and thereby activate synapses it memorized long ago. Many of her caretakers speak loudly to Phyllis or physically try to stimulate her; Anita has a way of subconsciously instilling Phyllis's confidence in her own control of herself.

Phyllis's doctor came in during the session and Anita looked up to see if she needed to stop her interaction with Phyllis.

"Keep doing what you're doing, Anita," Dr. Mark said. "I think it makes good sense."

Thursday, April 14, 2011. Coma Day 53.

BULLETIN: Phyllis woke up and talked tonight! Not just "yes" and "no" but real conversation. We attached her new breathing apparatus to her trach tube to allow her to answer a question! It leaves the trach tube in place but has a valve that allows her to speak by exhaling. This afternoon, I spoke to her as I always do as if she could hear me.

"Where have you been?" I asked when her eyes opened, never expecting an answer.

"Mostly sleeping," she answered in a forced whisper.

Yes it really happened today, a true miracle, the combined will of so many prayers, so much love, so many devoted friendships, loving caretakers, concerned doctors, dedicated nurses, Ritalin, intentional treatments, Feldenkrais—it all came to fruition today as Phyllis woke up, truly woke up, moved her head from side to side and carried on conversation after conversation. She talked in a very slight, quiet manner but she talked! Even with her trach still in place, she talks. She looks puzzled when anyone in the room hugs each other every time she speaks.

"Phyllis," I asked, "do you know that you've been unconscious for seven weeks?"

"No way!" she said.

"Do you remember anything or have you been pretty much asleep?" I said. "Everybody wants to know."

"Pretty much asleep, I guess," she said.

Our conversation ended with this exchange. I was exhilarated and beside myself with joy at having received words from Phyllis that showed self-comprehension. I've been warned by her doctor not to get too optimistic when this happens. She is very unlikely to remember this conversation or repeat it tomorrow. But we have to start somewhere don't we?

Our daughter Julia says Phyllis even moved her arm slightly, another huge step in coming back. Anita will continue her Feldenkrais treatments three times a week. No doubt this step forward will be followed by renewed unconsciousness. We must be patient. I will try to sleep tonight, knowing that she is there, awake and alive. I will try to sleep. I will try . . .

Friday, April 15, 2011. Coma Day 54.

Phyllis did wake and talk again today but weakly and only for an hour or so.

"Where have you been?" she greeted me this morning.

"I've been at home," I said. "Do you know where you are?"

"In bed?" she answered.

"Right!" I replied, laughing and grinning. "Do you know what hospital?"

She closed her eyes and went silent. Did I ask a question that caused her brain to shut off consciousness, for lack of a pathway to that memory? Whether she is physically weak or whether her brain is still recovering or both, is impossible to tell but, either way, she has a very, very long way to go. Of course, I am anxious for her to awake at least several hours a day, so she can begin physical therapy. So far, her "awake" periods are more like windows into her journey than a real exit into conscious life. The hospital where she now lives is focused on acute care, which means keeping her alive and away from infection. But "acute" assumes forward progress, which we got yesterday!

But a frequently sleeping body unable to move on its own is not a healthy one. Does that mean we have to move to a new facility? If so, where and how soon?

I needed to get out of my head this morning, so I came at 5 a.m. to be with Phyllis. Her room at Regency is very bright, filled with flowers from friends around the country, and has a beautiful window-view of spring in full blossom. I have set up a small shrine for her with Mother Mary and Padre Pio, icons I brought from our house, plus a rose crystal and many blessings and intentions. There are CDs to play and stacks of books to read to her. There are pictures of family and friends. Her nurses are angels who drop by to see her even when they aren't assigned to her. The only thing missing, the only thing we need more of, is a fully awake Phyllis, my New York girl. So hard to let her decide what *she* needs to do, instead of what *I need* her to do. I hear Mother Mary calling: "*Let It Be.*"

Tonight I lay in bed, alone and unsure. We have made so much progress; why am I filled with doubt tonight? The shunt has finally worked and her ventricles have returned to normal size. She has begun to talk and recognize me and others. I know she is in there somewhere. But she has so far to go. She is still unable to move most of her body, eat and drink normally or remember what happened an hour ago. How do I keep hope at the same time as I stay vigilant on everything that has to happen for her to recover? The clock is ticking: we need time for her to create new paths to consciousness but time is also her enemy, as her basic body functions wither and decay from lack of movement. *Only believe, all things are possible, only believe.*

CHAPTER SIX

LOSING OURSELVES IN MEXICO

Living on the road my friend
Was gonna keep you free and clean . . .
                        —Townes Van Zandt, "Pancho and Lefty"

August 14, 1972

If everything was supposed to happen for a reason, I saw no reason for having had to part with Phyllis in Celaya the day before. I saw only darkness, a waking nightmare of isolation I knew well. So I quit listening to my mind, rolling slowly along the highway, hour-by-hour and step-by-step through small cities built by Spanish conquistadors on top of ancient indigenous temples in the 1500s.

Larry and I drove in a weeklong, meditative journey southward across the high plains of Guanajuato to the rugged mountain state of Michoacan, circling around the volcanic rim surrounding Mexico City and ultimately stumbling by back roads into the state of Morelos and its capital, Cuernavaca. Rather than take the quick, direct route by freeway through

Mexico City, we followed small backwoods highways, weaving our way through snow-tipped peaks, dipping down into the tropical zone and once again rising into highland forests.

We drove slowly through Acambaro, Guanajuato, first settled in 1426 BC and reconstructed by the Spaniards in the 1500s. Down the road to Valle de Bravo, with its emerald-green high-mountain lake, waterfalls and Monarch butterflies. Repression of the natives there didn't start with the Spaniards. Two centuries before Columbus, the Aztec Empire brutally conquered indigenous natives, a continuous tradition of subjugation enforced in modern times by the criminal cartels. Somehow, though, native Mexicans survived and thrived. I hoped to find their secret.

We camped in a forest outside Valle De Bravo, down a dirt lane leading to a clearing that looked over the lake. Clouds settled in as dusk turned to night. Sitting by the campfire, I studied the glowing embers as Larry played Kristofferson's "Sunday Morning Coming Down," as we both recalled dreams we had lost along the way. What was I to do? The month before I met Phyllis I had this idea to go on an adventure and live life spontaneously but live it as if each event was a clue to your next step. Every unusual encounter in the wilderness and every urban rendezvous would be a clue to my progress on a pilgrimage. Make no plans, have no agenda, be open to signs and let the universe direct you. And indeed, since then, magical things *had* happened to me, from picking up Larry as a hitchhiker to a serendipitous meeting and reconciliation with my father and on to a chance encounter with Phyllis in the Santa Fe Plaza which began a full-blown passionate affair that had kept us together every moment of the previous ten nights and days.

And then came that short conversation in the morning in Celaya, a misunderstanding about what to do next, and suddenly we had gone our separate ways with just a casual comment from her about meeting in Cuernavaca. So what meaning was I to see in this? How was I supposed to get back to living spontaneously? Does everything really happen for a reason? If I wanted to finish this vision quest, I had to believe it. I sent my thoughts silently over the mountains to Phyllis and rolled up in my sleeping bag for the night.

I knew this way across Guanajuato, Mexico State and Michoacan; it was one of two routes from my childhood that my father preferred on our family trips to Cuernavaca. The patch-work-quilt route of small, barely paved roads revealed a rural Mexico unchanged for centuries. The eastern and western ranges of the Sierra Madre, which we had been driving between for ten days, collide near Mexico City with an east-west mountain range known as the Cordillera Neovolcánica. This is the geological division between North and South America and contains some of the most dangerous volcanoes in the world, massive peaks that frequently erupt with ash plumes spiraling tens of thousands of feet in the air. The ground is *alive* with volcanic soil, the fertility of which, over the centuries, gave birth to some of the oldest civilizations on earth.

"Larry," I asked, as the fire dwindled, "how did you know, back in 'Nam, when you just couldn't be in the war anymore? How did you know what to do?"

"I don't know. I'm not sure how much of it I even remember. My platoon sergeant was a crazy son of a bitch; we all knew he was going to get us killed. One day we went into a village that Charlie, the Viet Cong, had burned down the day before, killing women and kids as they went. We were supposed to be looking for tunnels where the Cong might be hiding. We didn't know who the enemy was and who was friendly. Then the firing started and that's all I remember. There's a long gap in my memory after that, maybe some rehab, until I'm living in an apartment with a woman on the outskirts of Saigon."

"There was so much nobody told us about how we got in that war," I said. "I think I had some kind of waking dream of what would happen if I went there and I just couldn't. You found the best path out of there you could, Larry. I'm sorry you had to live through it."

We retreated back into our silences. I couldn't stop myself from wondering where Phyllis was. The highway to Cuernavaca from Mexico City, the way Phyllis would have to come if she was planning to find me (which didn't seem likely), was a grand entrance on a modern air-conditioned bus charging down directly from Mexico City on a super-highway. The route was surgically cut out of the high mountains, dramatically topping the peaks and dropping precipitously into Morelos, a state which calls itself *La Primavera Eterna*, land of eternal spring. If it was paradise I was entering, I felt it was best if I slipped in, unannounced, in case the gods of chance recognized me as one who couldn't follow clues. I wasn't following a map, just going by impulse as to which road to take.

August 20, 1972

Larry and I rolled into Cuernavaca a week to the day after I let Phyllis slip away. For days, my darker moments told me it was stupid to even hope to see her in Cuernavaca. After the way we parted, she probably wouldn't come anyway. And if she did, how would I find her? It was a sprawling town of 200,000 people. I made up my mind that if it was meant to be, it would happen. And I fervently hoped it would. I'm sure Larry did too because I hadn't exactly been a barrel of laughs since she'd left.

We drove into town and were quickly drawn into a swirl of traffic, beeping horns, buses, donkeys with heavy burdens and winding one-way streets. As in most Mexican towns built with native slave labor by Spaniards, the streets are small and turn in unpredictable directions. In order to accommodate modern automobile traffic, one-way avenues are carved out of the cities from the outskirts to the center in concentric circles, forcing you into a river of cars headed into a whirlpool, out of which you were ejected into the plaza at the heart of town.

I let the Muleskinner comply, slowly leading us through the winding, narrow streets to the two main Cuernavaca plazas, one bordered by the Governor's Palace and the other by the Palace of Cortez. As the Muleskinner came to a stop in traffic at the junction of the two plazas, there stood Phyllis and her dog Lather, about to cross from one side to the other!

My dog Gringo starts barking, I am honking and yelling, Larry is grinning and before I know it, Phyllis is back on the bus. I have to block traffic to let her and Lather in but I don't care. We all crowd into the front seat, the dogs squirming and trying to jump in our laps. It forces Phyllis and I to wrap ourselves around each other just to fit all of us and the dogs in the front. For me to be able to drive, she has to drape her arm around my shoulder and lean her head on my neck.

"Hey, so how was Mexico City?" I asked, testing her mood.

"Great," she said. "I saw my host family from high school, the Menas. They're really nice people; you shouldn't have been so stubborn."

Phyllis had a way of saying things directly that, coming from anyone else, would have made me uncomfortable but with her hugging me and rubbing my neck while she spoke, it was music to my ears. She managed to dismiss our separation with a simple statement and do it while I was feeling intoxicated with her unbelievable appearance. Miracles do happen. I promised myself to never again let her out of my life without a fight or at least a plan to get her back. If only we all kept our promises.

"So where are we going?" Phyllis asked.

"I don't know," I said. "I'm just following the traffic. We could park here by Cortez's Palace. This is the neighborhood where I lived for the last two years, doing my Conscientious Objector service. Later on, we can look for a camp up in the hills outside of town."

After an afternoon of being tourists in the ancient heart of Cuernavaca, we drove up the mountain and out of Cuernavaca to Santa Maria Ahuacatitlan, a wooded village above the city, just at the edge of town. It was founded in the 1500s when natives fled the approach of the invader Cortez and it felt like a refuge to me as well. Tall pine trees make a canopy under which tropical flowers grow as two climate zones embrace each other. There are no villas in Santa Maria, just peasant adobe homes connected by donkey trails. I parked on a deserted side street and told Phyllis and Larry to wait a few minutes for me.

Within a block of where we parked, I encountered a middle-aged native woman with tortillas stacked high on her head, secured by a rebozo, a long scarf tied under her chin.

"*Disculpe, Senorita,*" I said to her. "*Sabe usted donde hay una casa que puedo rentar por unas dias?*" Excuse me, Ma'am. Do you know of a house I could rent for a few days?

"Sure, young man," she answered in Spanish. "My brother-in-law has one but there is no furniture."

Perfecto.

Within an hour, we had moved into a small two-bedroom adobe cottage with a dirt floor and a wood roof. Larry was happy to have his own space and Phyllis and I could play house.

"Tomorrow," said Phyllis, "we should make an excursion into Cuernavaca to buy a mattress and some small chairs."

In the space of one day, my world was restored to a magical journey. We spread our sleeping bag on the dirt floor of our bedroom with a view of the valley below. The flickering light of a kerosene lamp played off the adobe brick wall, occasionally showing her beautiful skin, black hair and happy smile.

The early morning sun hit the volcanoes in the west first, so, although the sun's rising in the east was obscured by the mountains behind us, the morning view from our bedroom was of a brightly-lit Popocatepetl, a giant volcano rising above a sea of fog in the arms of the Sierra Madres. To the south, we could see a V-shaped pass in the Sierra Madre leading to Guerrero and the Pacific Ocean. I knew we had to go into those mountains. The warmth of Phyllis's body spooning me as she slept would keep me balanced for a while and even give me momentum for a few days but I was anxious to make our next move. Then I remembered something.

"Are you awake?" I asked, quietly in the dark.

"Yes," she answered.

"I own a house across the valley. I kind of forgot. We should go there."

"How do you *forget* that you own a house?"

"Well, two years ago, when I started my Conscientious Objector service here, I heard that you could buy a house in a native village nearby for a thousand dollars. So I did. I haven't been back there for more than a year. I really didn't expect to ever go back. One Christmas, my parents, knowing how broke I was, had given me a present of just that much money; so, on a whim, I bought this house with an acre of land and a plum orchard. But every time I went there with my lousy Spanish, I felt out of place and unable to communicate. And it didn't help that there were these mobs of little kids that would follow me around like I was a freak of nature. So I finally told Augustina and Don Lauro, the older couple who live there as caretakers, to just run the place like it was their own. Really they have more right to it than I do."

"You own a house in a village in the mountains and you just forget it?" she said. "You never checked on them to see how they were doing? You are so *strange*. We are definitely going there."

Even though Phyllis was excited about my house, we were having too much fun to leave too soon. We decided to stay a week in Cuernavaca and then head to Tilzapotla. Cuernavaca has been an oasis of rest and relaxation for two thousand years and several civilizations. Founded by the Tlahuic people some 3,200 years ago, it became a weekend retreat of Aztec emperors in the 1400s. Cortez conquered it in 1521 and built his own weekend getaway castle there. As recently as 1910, 90 percent of Morelos residents spoke only Nahuatl, the native language; now Nahuatl is almost a forgotten language, except in the wilderness mountain areas. So, settling in with kings and conquerors, we made the scene.

In the morning, Phyllis and I would wander through the tangled streets of town, arm-in-arm, alive and happy to be together. Cuernavaca, like so many Mexican cities built by Spaniards, is a study in contrasts: the bustling noisy streets lined with high walls covered with bougainvillea, the purple-flowering vines imported by ancient kings from Peru, behind which are quiet elegant gardens and courtyards. Walking the streets was a visual adventure, sneaking around corners and peeking in open carriage doors, expecting to see a *conquistador* removing his armor. Inside the walled driveways and houses, we'd find court-yard gardens cultivated for hundreds of years and watered by aqueducts predating the Roman Empire. For lunch, we'd eat in small restaurants tucked into courtyards, imagining ourselves as an elderly expatriate couple; afterwards we perused tiny markets tucked away in centuries-old corridors hanging off the sides of vine-covered hills.

Naturally, we gravitated to the *fondas* of the giant Cuernavaca market for our frijoles de la olla and homemade tortillas. Finding the market fondas was a challenge since the market encompassed the entire hillside neighborhood below Cortez's palace. There were blocks of woven straw goods (petate mats and baskets and hats), followed by cookware and pottery, surrounded by flowers (several hundred stalls of every conceivable flower), invigorated by fruits from all over the nation, enticed by the edible-cactus vendors, enveloped by a plethora of all the vegetables known and unknown to man, and finally fed at the center, by the fondas with their aroma of bubbling cauldrons of hot chocolate and rice *atole* with cinnamon and sugar.

One morning at the mercado, several days after our reunion, as Phyllis and I held hands and dipped a *bolillo* (fresh roll with the taste of French bread) in our hot chocolate, I saw something that transported me back to my childhood family trips in Mexico. Lumbering slowly up the steep cobbled-stone street behind us was an older man, the white hair of his long mustache showing under his sombrero, leading an equally ancient burro loaded with charcoal. *Indios* were a frequent sight, of course, but what struck me about this man was that, like us, *he was not from here.* He must have walked many miles to bring his charcoal here, and they weren't *highway* miles.

I jumped up and asked him:

"*Disculpe, Señor, de donde eres?*" Excuse me, sir, where are you from?

He told me the name of the village, a word in Nahuatl I couldn't pronounce.

"*Y de donde vienes, llegan coches ahí, hay carretera?*" Where you come from, do cars arrive there, is there a road?

He laughed deeply and responded.

"*No joven, es ocho horas de puro camino.*" No, young man, it is eight hours of only trails.

I knew it. Memories of coming to Mexico on vacation with my parents flooded over me. Native people who move quietly with an ancient grace that sets them apart from the hustle and bustle of modern Mexican towns. I was convinced that around Cuernavaca and in the mountains above Tilzapotla where my house was, there must exist a network of trails and villages, accessible only by foot, free of cars and electricity. It must be a land, I imagined, unknown and unseen by all the rich Mexicans, American tourists and expatriates who took so greedily and gave back so little. I imagined a trail leading up the mountain. I expected that somewhere up that trail was the world out of which we all originated, before technology sped up time and made us all, rich and poor—workers on a giant treadmill without knowing who or if anyone was in charge. It was a dream I had been following since my childhood, the scenes filled in by nights of studying the *National Geographic* magazine I got every month as a child.

August 22, 1972

After a week in Cuernavaca, the relentless magnetism of the land before time calling from just over the mountain began to build momentum. I felt the need to get back on track—even though I couldn't say to what or where. So finally we packed up camp, folded the canvas tent cover on the truck, stocked up on basics and pointed the Muleskinner toward the village of Tilzapotla—where I owned a house.

If you know where to look, you can see Tilzapotla across the valley from Cuernavaca. From our rental house in Santa Maria, I had seen the "V" in the mountains on the southeast horizon just east of Tilzapotla. That "V" is an ancient geological cut in the Sierra Madre, and it leads to Paso Morelos, a route which for thousands of years gave entrance and exit to those fleeing danger or seeking shelter. It was the exit of choice for Mexico's most revered revolutionary (or terrorist, depending on your politics): Emilano Zapata, a guerilla fighter from Morelos whose bands raided government forces in Cuernavaca from 1910 to his death in 1919. Using horse-mounted raiders who were farmers by day and soldiers by night, Zapata would attack and retreat, leading government troops on a merry chase out through Paso Morelos into the wilds of the neighboring state of Guerrero from which his *compadres* would ambush the pursuing *federales*. Zapata, by most accounts, was one of the few Mexican revolutionaries who did not fight for personal gain. He kept his demands simple (return of stolen lands to peasants and liberty for them to farm their property) and within the territory he controlled, Zapata did just that. He refused to take a position in the revolutionary government, other than general and he was, in the end, assassinated by his fellow revolutionaries who objected to Zapata's insistence on honoring his promises to the peasants.

The trip from Cuernavaca to Tilzapotla in a modern vehicle with heavy use of the horn can be made in an hour; Phyllis,

Larry and I took most of the day. The valley of Morelos has many springs, rivers and natural watering holes used for centuries to irrigate ubiquitous sugar cane fields. Sugar cane, planted eight centuries earlier by the Aztecs in Morelos, was always a tool of domination since it required cheap heavy labor and paid its bosses handsomely. Along the way to Tilza, we paused for a swim in Lake Tequesquitengo, a collapsed volcanic cone flooded by a Spanish *hacienda* owner to create a deep turquoise oasis. The road continued on through cane fields to Tehuixtla, a farm town on the Rio Amacuzac and battled seven more bumpy miles on a dirt road to Tilzapotla.

The backdrop to Tilzapotla is a steep mountainside looming 3,000 feet above the town. In the *mojados*, the rainy season, which lasts from May to September, a waterfall careens off the top of the mountain and crashes its way through the canyons to join the Amacuzac River and water the fields of Morelos. Tilzapotla was home to almost 10,000 but it felt much smaller, partly because so little was done to change the topography. Homes were built out of the red clay soil, trees grew tall for shade and yards were large enough for horses, burros and chickens.

On a late afternoon in September of 1972, the three of us and our two dogs in our post-World War II vintage truck bumped over the cobblestone streets of Tilzapotla and arrived at the wooden gate of the house I had bought two years earlier. We rattled the gate, shouting *"Bueno?"* by way of announcing our arrival, and waited in anticipation as I took in the bright, white adobe walls, the blue sky above and the cobbled street below.

We waited for quite a while at that wooden gate for *Doña* Augustina to answer our call. Out she came, dressed in pants and tennis shoes with a *rebozo* wrapped over her head. She must have felt she needed to do *something* to greet us properly. We were, after all, *los patrones*, the owners who had the right to just drop in out of nowhere and turn her world upside down, even order her to leave. Doña Augustina, was a very short, very strong lady in her seventies and caretaker of her husband, Don Lauro, an eighty-two year old survivor of the Mexican Revolution, a farmer-soldier in Emilano Zapata's ragtag army.

Phyllis and I were, in her estimation, *los ricos*, rich people who had resources beyond her imagining, so who knows what might happen, maybe something good, maybe something disastrous. And there we were at the gate with an entourage of dogs and a tall *hombre* with a knife strapped to his leg. If I could have told her that, no, we were just three relatively impoverished travelers, it wouldn't have changed anything. We had *access* to resources she could never hope to reach.

"*Bienvenidos*," she welcomed us, avoiding our gaze and speaking respectfully. "*Pase*," she said, opening the gate.

"*Ola, Doña Augustina, soy Phyllis, mucho gusto conocerte*," said Phyllis, passing the gate and enveloping Augustina in a hug. I'm Phyllis and I'm so glad to finally meet you.

There was no awkwardness in their embrace, Phyllis greeting Augustina, a complete stranger, as she would her own grandmother. Before leading us onto the open porch of the adobe house, the floor of which was raised a few feet and made of hard, smooth clay, she splashed water from a plastic bowl on the floor and cleaned the dust with a homemade broom. We were seated and served water and *pan dulce*, sweet bread.

Augustina barked commands to a young girl: "Veronica, *llévate las ciruelas del árbol*," pick some plums from the tree. This sent her eight-year-old granddaughter scurrying for one treat after another to serve us. It was late afternoon—not their mealtime—yet she was obviously bustling to prepare food for us. Phyllis assured her she did not have to feed us, only for Augustina to look offended and assured us that indeed she did.

So began a long negotiation over what our relationship with Augustina would be. I was determined to treat her as an equal, which meant I didn't want to be served or catered to. Phyllis however understood that was impossible. Coming from different worlds, our resources were never going to be equal. Phyllis also knew grandmother-types like Augustina from her New York Italian extended family, where even casual family friends are addressed as aunts and uncles and instantly made a connection with her.

Our future in Tilzapotla would have to play out over time. The issue at hand, as the sun set over the valley below, was sleeping arrangements. The house had three rooms laid out in a row along an open porch. The nearest room was where the chickens slept at night covered by baskets and blankets. At the far end was a bedroom which, I surmised with a quick tour, Augustina occupied with her granddaughter Veronica. In the middle room, lying in bed, was her husband, Don Lauro (*don* and *doña* being terms of respect, like mister and ma'am). Don Lauro had a portable IV bottle on a rolling rack by his bed and greeted us with a grin from an ancient leathery face framed with snow-white hair. With much negotiation, it was settled that the chickens would move in with Don Lauro, Phyllis and I and the dogs (surely we didn't want dogs in the house?) would have the third bedroom (after much splashing of water and sweeping), and Larry would get the hammock on the porch. His offer to sleep outside in the Muleskinner was not even considered.

Tucked in our places like so many of Augustina's chickens, we soon learned that sleeping there would take a bit of adjustment. The roof of an adobe house is made of a resilient frame of tough wood branches tied tightly together and covered with rounded clay tiles. Air passes freely, water is repelled and sounds are magnified. And what sounds there are! Night sounds of crickets, birds, radios and town drunks stumbling their way home. Then as one group of sounds settle in, another begins: the donkeys bray to each other, horses answer, pigs snort, dogs bark and roosters crow. Roosters may crow at dawn elsewhere, but in Tilzapotla, they crow all night.

That night, as I tried to simultaneously cuddle close to Phyllis and bury my head deep enough under a pillow to escape the concert, Phyllis asked, "Why does Don Lauro have that IV thing?"

"I don't know," I replied.

"Do you think Augustina is upset we are here?" she asked.

"Shall we try to sleep?" I pleaded.

"Maybe we should sleep in our tent in the orchard so the chickens could have their room back," she said.

"Good luck telling that to Augustina. Shall we sleep?" I replied.

"Why can't we talk?" she said, pulling away from me. "You're trying to control me again."

"Hey," I said, gently. "I'm sorry. I was just tired. Talk."

I embraced her tightly again and her back muscles softened.

"You were right about the Menas, my host family in Mexico City," she said. "They're very nice to me but they have servants, young girls from towns like Tilzapotla, and they treat them like dirt. I don't know, like, *inferior*."

August 23, 1972

Waking up in Tilzapotla after our first night in Augustina's house, having finally overcome the cacophony of sounds from the village to embrace the joy of sleep, with Phyllis in my arms and new adventures waiting all around, I felt like my life was just beginning. Leaving her asleep in bed, I dressed quickly and slipped outside. Augustina was already awake, starting a small fire outside to heat up the frijoles and warm up the *comal*, a fired-clay griddle for making tortillas. Don Lauro had moved out on the porch sitting upright on a tiny, straight-backed child's chair with his IV bottle beside him. He greeted me with his silent, full-toothed grin.

The morning sunlight was already filling in the canvas of the valley below. It was a patchwork quilt of adobe houses with red roofs, green, yellow and orange foliage and walled yards, connected by trails leading to a small blue lake suspended over the valley below. I could just make out men on small, wooden boats casting nets for fish. Enough food to feed Tilzapotla was grown within a few miles of the village. Corn grew in every conceivable nook and cranny for as far as the eye can see.

Electricity only arrived in Tilzapotla a few years before we did. For the most part, it was used to power a few bare lightbulbs on street corners. There was only one telephone in town (in a store on the plaza) and television hadn't made it yet. No police appeared on the streets and the *juzgado*, a single-celled town jail, had to all appearances, been abandoned for years. An old-world town with just enough of the *new world* to remind me what century I lived in. Modern buses departed hourly on a three-hour trek to Mexico City.

On the southern end of town, loomed the dark and monumental mountain, whose peak marked the border of the next state, Guerrero. The top of that mountain—from which flowed the source of Tilza's water—was the apex of the Sierra Madre, and beyond it lay descending rolls of mountain ranges leading ultimately to the Pacific. I felt a battle in myself between the warm, safe glow of comfort (a woman, a house, a family, a friend, a village) and the need to climb mountains, to go into the unknown, to find life more primitive than this safe place. If I slowed now, I knew the darkness of my isolation would soon catch up to me; it always had. But the key, I somehow knew, was to be in the right place when it did, a place with a well-worn trail leading out of the banality of life and into a universal connectedness.

Meanwhile, I saw Phyllis was awake and I moved to join her

on the porch. A man was at the front gate with a bucket, selling *queso fresco*, a creamy, tart, non-aged cheese crumbled over beans. Augustina shook her head "no" to him but Phyllis nudged me to buy some, which I did and then gave it to Augustina. Veronica appeared with a pail of fresh-soaked corn to take to the *molino* for grinding. She came and took Phyllis's hand by way of inviting her to come along.

All over Tilza, little girls and old ladies who had no grand-daughters were heading for the molino, the village mill, where for a peso, your pail of corn was fed into two giant, slowly-turning granite plates out of which appeared fresh ground masa dough which was then covered with an embroidered cloth and rushed home to the now-heated comal. The people were fed and life was good.

September 4, 1972

Some days were taken up just exploring the streets of Tilz-apotla with Phyllis, my dark-haired beautiful girl, whom I called the "*Buenos Dias Señorita*" because she insisted on greeting everyone with a bright, cheery "*Buenos dias!*" even the *borrachos* lying on the street in a mescal-induced drunkenness. Some-times the drunks who were able to stand would try to follow us after her acknowledgment but the handicap of their inebriation kept them from being a threat. In spite of my warnings to ignore them and not to meet their gaze, Phyllis believed in treating each person she encountered as fully human and deserving of a greeting.

One day in Tilzapotla, Phyllis decided we could use a cold drink of *pulque* from a local *pulqueria*, a street-side storefront saloon with an unpainted wooden bar and a few tables of macho cowboys. Pulque is the distant relative of tequila, fermented rather than distilled (think warm beer made from tequila). The pulqueria serves its beer with a dipper from a clay jar. A pulqueria doesn't have a sign saying "no women allowed" but it was a given and I was pretty sure we'd run into some interesting situations as I reluctantly followed her in. Four men slouched in the corner of a dark room and the pulque jar sat on the counter. No bartender in sight. Definitely a B movie setting.

"*Buenos Dias*," she said to the dark. "*Hay servicio?*"

"*Si, Señorita*, I buy you a drink. Come sit with me," said one of the four, without moving.

"No *gracias*, I'll buy my own. *Cuanto cuesta?*"

"Me or the pulque?" he said.

"You? I'm definitely not buying!" said Phyllis with a snort.

The other three laughed at him in derision and a bartender appeared to serve us our drinks. I was playing the strong silent type, counting the steps to the door and wondering if I could get her to leave when the fighting broke out.

"Hey, Gringo, your woman is okay! *Bienvenidos a Mexico!*" said the guy and the ice was broken.

Within a few weeks in Tilzapotla, we were old news. The crowds of young kids didn't even follow us around the streets anymore. We were just *los gringos*, the only foreigners in town. Life in a Mexican town was all about food. Even a small town like Tilzapotla had a *mercado*, a market with fifty or so stalls, selling an astonishing array of fresh vegetables, fruits and herbs. We walked every day with Augustina a few blocks to the mercado to buy vegetables. In Tilza we learned to add the *licuado*-stands to our list of safe places to eat. Basically the original "smoothie" shop, the counter was piled high with fresh pine-apple, oranges, lemons, grapefruit, bananas, papayas and fruits unknown. Armed with a blender and clean bottled water, the licuado lady could work miracles.

September 16, Mexican Independence Day, was fast approaching and every day was a *fiesta*. September was also the time of *las cosechas*, a less formal but more deeply felt ancient country ritual of celebrating the harvest. Corn is harvested continuously from July to November as variously-timed plant-ings mature but September is the peak of the harvest. Ripening along with the corn are beans, squash and pumpkins grown in the same field, fixing the soil's nitrogen and completing the protein. Every family who can work was allotted a field of ten acres or so a few miles from town and everyone has a little extra to share at harvest time.

Each day Augustina would make a different treat from corn; that morning it was *tlaxcales*, a treat resembling a *gordita*. Gorditas, in Tilzapotla anyway, are a smaller, thicker version of a tortilla, hand-formed from fresh masa and roasted on the comal with the intention of breaking them open on the side and filling them with *queso fresco*, or beans or anything your heart desires. Tlaxcales, on the other hand, are made from ears of corn picked at exactly the right stage, part way between fresh corn and dried corn. The kernels are cut off the cob and ground into a paste which is used instead of *masa* to make a mind-altering sweet corn-cake and eaten around the comal on little chairs in the yard.

Here we were: Augustina, bent over the fire; Don Lauro, still tethered to his IV but somehow able to carry it to the yard; Veronica, scrubbed clean and dressed in a threadbare blue cotton dress; Larry, sharpening his Bowie knife; Phyllis, hair now properly brushed and tightly braided by Veronica; and me, long hair washed and pulled back in a ponytail. The dogs were given bowls of yesterday's tortillas with bean broth. Augustina was in control of her universe.

Phyllis was content with learning from Augustina the way of *her* world. I, on the other hand, was locked into my contradictions, glowing with the miracle of this new family the universe has sent me (Phyllis, Larry, Augustina, Don Lauro, Veronica, and our dogs) but tugged by an invisible cord toward the misty mountain above.

CHAPTER SEVEN

FINDING A WAY TO WAKEFULNESS

"If our brains were simple enough to be understood, we wouldn't be smart enough to understand them."
> —David Eagleman, *Incognito: The Secret Lives of The Brain*

A sunny day
With hopes up to the skies
Not one that comes and dies
> —Nina Simone, "That's All I Want From You"

Sunday, April 17, 2011. Coma Day 56.

After intense physical therapy on Friday, Phyllis has not been conscious much this weekend. She has spoken both days but not as easily or as clearly as earlier in the week. If I ask her about anything that happened the day before, she just goes silent. We will have to wait for her next wave of energy and hope for more progress.

Looking ahead to Phyllis's next step in treatment, my daughter Julia and I visited a Neurological Rehab Hospital in

Tulsa this week. It's only a two-hour drive from Fayetteville and is a great facility with lots of talented staff and a small patient load. They offer an intensive six to eight hours a day of physical, occupational and other kinds of therapy to neurological patients. But the downside is that, even for a motivated spouse like me, they only allow for very limited visitations—no more than one hour per week. That wouldn't be easy. In any case, at this point, Phyllis is not even close to being able to move to rehab because it requires that she be both awake and participatory. As of now, she still cannot move most of her body and cannot be woken up on a regular schedule. Even so, we will soon have to make choices.

Monday, April 18, 2011, 10:33 p.m. Coma Day 57.

Since Phyllis lapsed into a coma eight weeks ago, I have tried to keep a balance between optimism and honesty. Here's the thing: Phyllis and I both are having a harder time now than we were back when her coma first started. Why is it harder for her? Because every once in a while she's awake now! She must see how things are, and from her view, they likely look pretty hopeless. She can hardly move a single muscle. She can't turn to her side or scratch her nose. She can't speak unless someone attaches the talking tube to her trach for her. But, Catch-22, she can't let us know when that is. Every exterior body function is handled by a machine or a nurse. Even the ability to stay awake and focus on a conversation is out of her control. So although she can talk sometimes, it's not like waking up and having her body back.

Why can't she use her body? Just like before, we really can't be sure. Doctors know that anyone immobile for eight weeks loses a lot of muscle tone. Therapy can get it back but you have to reach a certain level of consciousness to be able to do therapy. Oops, Catch-22 again: therapy helps you be awake but you need to be awake to do therapy. So while we wait for her brain to regroup, her muscles are weakening, and bacteria, the garbage collectors of the universe, are looking for a way to break down tissue. It's their job: eliminate excess, digest the weakest. Then there's the brain.

Remember the brain ventricles, the mysterious spaces most of us never heard of? Well Phyllis's ventricles are still deciding what the right beat is. I say "beat" because it turns out that not only do the brain ventricles create the precious spinal fluid that feeds, bathes and cleans the brain; not only do the ventricles contain stem cells that *create* brain cells and regenerate them; but *the ventricles, it turns out, have a pulse like the heart.* Its beating is a diastole/systole cycle of advance and withdrawal, sending fluid down the spine, and then drawing it back up. That same cycle sends spinal fluid out over the brain in one direction, then back the other way. That system has to work perfectly in sync with her shunt as it drains the fluid so there is no extra pressure on the folds of the brain that contain all the memories of how to do things, like scratch your nose or walk. So the core of Phyllis's brain is trying to learn a new rhythm in sync with her shunt while also trying to rebuild damaged synapse connections all across the brain. And both have to happen for her to do even the smallest thing, like move a finger.

This morning I caught myself wondering, *Why does it seem*

harder having Phyllis partially awake than completely unconscious? Shouldn't I be thanking God for the miracle of her return to the speaking world and have faith that it will all work out? I should and I do, at some level of my consciousness. But I can't stop thinking that I also have to be a participant in the process. The whole creation and maintenance of life is a miracle of which I am in awe, and I know that decay and death are just as noble a part of the process as healing and life. But in feeling and keeping a passionate connection with one human being, Phyllis Rose Petrella Head, I need to know the nature of every impediment to our connection at every level. My conversations with Phyllis now are like a chess game where I have to guess which of the rules she knows.

"Would you like to hear some music?" I asked this morning, when I saw her eyes were open.

"Sure," she mouthed.

"Would you rather I read you a book?" I said.

She gave me a blank stare, as if I had uttered a complete absurdity. Then she closed her eyes and went to sleep.

Wednesday, April 20, 2011, 2:55 a.m. Coma Day 59.

I woke up thinking there has to be something we've missed. I say "we" because there are so many more people than me that are involved in Phyllis's healing: her primary care doctors, the nursing staff who see her 24/7, all the friends and family who sit with her, chanting, praying and reading, plus the medical experts around the country reviewing her files. Two "second-opinion" reports came in a few days ago, one yesterday, a fourth is due in a few days. None of them found a "smoking gun," but they did ask a lot of questions. One question everyone raises is why her brain ventricles stayed swollen for a month after her shunt failed. Her failed shunt had been immediately replaced by an *external drain* which is supposed to do everything that a shunt does, with the bonus that the doctor can observe the pressure of the spinal fluid and calibrate the rate at which it's drained to achieve the right balance of pressure. I was pestering the neurosurgeon at the time to vary that pressure and he did, but *the adjustments didn't help*. This was the period Phyllis was in her deepest coma. Then on March 28, after a month on an external drain, a new *internal* shunt was inserted and two weeks later, presto, the ventricles were down to normal size. Had the external drain been inserted in the wrong place? Or was the brain just feeling "insulted"—as the doctor speculated at the time—and thus too traumatized to return to normal balance? Maybe the reluctance of her ventricles to shrink is a clue to the mystery of her lack of improvement. One of the researchers thought so; he recommended a more extensive MRI now that the ventricles are back to "normal."

Everything in this field is imprecise. Even the term "normal" is a misnomer. Your expanded ventricles might be the size of *my* normal-sized ventricles. All we can really say is that Phyllis's ventricles are dramatically smaller than they were a month ago. But the researchers agree with me that it's important to know *why*.

Confused? Welcome to my world. I know I'm an obsessed husband but I have to go over it all in my head to make sure

I'm giving Phyllis every chance to exercise her will and wake up fully. I trust and admire her medical team but they don't have the luxury of focusing just on *her*. I'm the only person here looking exclusively at *one* patient. They have many, and Phyllis changes so slowly that they don't have a sense of urgency. We talk about doing a test and a week goes by before someone reacts. Her neurosurgeon has perhaps been called to another hospital or is busy in surgery. I would love to have all her team together for a weekly meeting but they are too dispersed.

Then there's a huge issue of the trach tube, the device in her throat for breathing. Everyone's afraid to take it out but not really able to justify leaving it in. She seems able to breathe on her own and very likely would be able to swallow with no problem. I have the authority to make them take it out but I'd rather they be convinced it's the best medical decision. When the trach tube is removed, Phyllis will be able to start speaking normally, and eating *food* again instead of industrially produced "food-like liquid" inserted through a hose into her stomach. But if it is taken out too soon, we could precipitate a breathing or swallowing crisis, which can lead to pneumonia.

Phyllis is on a journey and she will make the decision how and when to come back but I'm not willing to just let her wander around out there by herself. I'd much rather get lost in the wilderness with Phyllis than know exactly where I am and be alone. So I try to put myself where she is. It's hard to do.

The Feldenkrais Method helps me feel like we're closer to taking that walk together. It's a way I can have a physical conversation with her that feels more meaningful than a spoken one for now. Of course I'm a complete novice at Feldenkrais, but I do know about physical contact with Phyllis as a spiritual connection. On that subject, I'm an expert. From the first moment I touched Phyllis's shoulder in New Mexico to all the nights we have chased away each other's demons in loving intimacy, I have experienced a higher connection than words can explain: it is spiritual; it is sexual; it overcomes physical pain and it soothes suffering. It told me when she fell into a coma that she was not ready to leave her body. I am convinced I would know if she was ready to give up.

So I'm learning as I go how to use this new connection with Phyllis. Feldenkrais seems to be about skeletal awareness as opposed to muscular. We tend to experience our bodies as muscles: the visible forces that do work for us. But the bones are what makes us whole; remember the child's song "The leg bone's connected to the ankle bone?" We are really just one bone connected by joints and held up by muscles. So Feldenkrais seems to emphasize the awareness of your skeletal nature; the beginning exercises I've learned to do with Phyllis are about gently rocking her bones so her brain registers the movement, remembers that specific previously-recorded brain pathway, and begins to renew its control of the muscles. My hope is her brain then uses that information to build thousands of new connections which is what we absent-mindedly call consciousness.

Where is the path for her out of this wilderness? As much as I want to rescue her, she must literally lay down new neural pathways to create her own new trail to consciousness. All I can do is to try to send signals that help her on her journey.

Thursday, April 21, 2011. Coma Day 60.

Wow! Sometimes you get what you ask for. For the last two months, I have looked for a specialist who could focus intensively on Phyllis's case, and three days ago, I got exactly this. Phyllis has a new neurologist, called in as a consultant by her physician Dr. Mark, the hospital director. The new neurologist, Dr. Rob, stayed up late the first night reading the "second opinions" I had requested and then ordered some advanced MRI studies and EEGs. He visited Phyllis before and after the tests, reviewed the results and met with me immediately to discuss the results. That's about a month's worth of attention in three days!

"Here's my thoughts, Mr. Head," said Dr. Rob. "I am, of course, looking for an explanation of her continuing coma, even though she has some capacity for speech. The bottom line: she has none of the *visible* signs of brain injuries: no lesions or abscesses, no tumors or hematomas. I know you've heard that already from various doctors but the new tests confirm it. *Guillame-Barré syndrome* could explain her muscle weakness but the spinal tap showed no sign of it. *Locked-in syndrome* and *catatonic depression* are out because she is now showing a slight response to pinching her toes. And finally there is no evidence of a stroke."

"What's left, Doc?" I asked. "Why isn't she able to stay awake longer, remember anything short-term or move any of her limbs?"

"Well, I have to preface my analysis," said Dr. Rob, "with the possibility of some unknown rare syndrome but otherwise,

I would narrow the explanation of her symptoms to three possibilities, in no particular order of probability. The first explanation could be intermittent silent seizures which are caused by an electric short-circuit in the brain even though she has no convulsions. The second possibility is a condition called slit ventricle syndrome where the brain ventricles become *over*-drained and too small. Obviously she began with her ventricles too *large* but slit ventricles could be an over-reaction to the draining of the ventricles. The third explanation is the least satisfying. We call it brain insult, for lack of a better term—generalized damage to the brain caused by the original infection and the swollen ventricles. It's least satisfying because it's really just an admission that we know there is damage but we don't know how or where."

I bit my lip and tried to not show my frustration. "So what do we do now?"

"I think we should find a specialized research hospital to confirm my evaluation, probably Washington University's Barnes-Jewish Hospital in St. Louis, one of the top neurological research facilities in the country."

Amazing, I thought to myself. A doctor who doesn't think his analysis is the ultimate word.

"Barnes-Jewish can confirm or rule out slit ventricles by observing the shunt closely. They will check for silent seizures," said Dr. Rob, "with continuous EEG monitoring which we can't do here. And of course, they'll be in position to find an altogether different explanation and cure. It will mean a stay of up to two weeks for tests."

All this input has my head spinning: *finally* we get a smart guy who compiles all the work of two years of Phyllis's medical records, compares it with the "second opinions" and comes up with a plan of action. Sometime in the next week we'll have another EEG test, and the most comprehensive "second opinion" from Johns-Hopkins Hospital should have arrived. Maybe it will give us some new clues. At least we have a plan.

Friday, April 22, 2011. Coma Day 61.

For sixty-three days, friends and family have traveled with Phyllis and me through a labyrinth of pain and resolve, sorrow and hope, fear and faith, setbacks and improvement, as we weaved through a crooked path of darkness into the light. When I could not imagine going further, friends, by their compassionate sharing of faith, experience and love have allowed me to keep going. When everyone wanted to celebrate victory, I held back out of an abundance of caution. Today, I just want to give thanks to everyone and to God for the moments of Phyllis's return to consciousness, whether they last a day or forever. This Sunday will be Easter—the day we celebrate the rebirth of darkness into sunshine and I humbly say *thank you.*

The staff members at Regency Hospital are old friends now. They know my regular volunteer support team and greet newly arriving ones. There are no secrets here. If one of the staff doctors has information about Phyllis, he shares it with whoever is sitting with her at the moment, who writes it down in the yellow notebook. Some of our friends come when they can, while a special few have been coming at the same time every week. One nurse is from our church parish and brings greetings from old friends at St. Joseph's School which our children once attended. Another nurse is from Kenya and likes to hug everyone. The shift nurse always greets me with an update like: "She's feeling warm tonight, I took her blanket off," or "Phyllis said hello to me when I turned her!" So many patients seem to have no one to call on them at all; I feel truly blessed that Phyllis is attended by a cast of angels!

Saturday, April 23, 2011. Coma Day 62.

For the first time in two months, I slept eight hours! In spite of all my internal dialogues, I have a deep sense that we are making order out of chaos in understanding Phyllis's condition. I am up early and arrive at the hospital at 6 a.m., just as visiting hours begin. Phyllis has been talking some the last two days, usually when a new person comes in. She moves her mouth and we know to attach the speaking device. Now that we know she's capable of speech, the question is what it will take for her to stay awake, recover her memory and regain control of her muscles? She makes gains in speech, greeting a friend, for example, then for a while recognizes no one. She has no short-term memory. When I asked "Do you remember seeing Judith yesterday?" she replied "Who?" and closed her eyes and slept most of the day. It's not supposed to happen this way, they say. Comas don't just come and go. But then, Phyllis never did follow the beaten path.

Easter Sunday, April 24, 2011. Coma Day 63.

Hundreds of friends, family and strangers will be praying for a miracle for Phyllis today, this Easter Sunday. But this morning I'm filled with the miracle that has already happened, though not in the way we imagined. The love and support so many people, both friends and strangers, have sent to Phyllis through prayers, gifts, concerns and unwavering compassion for one person's suffering in a tormented world have changed us all.

Phyllis has always struggled with the torment of feeling insignificant in the face of so much pain in the world, wanting to make a difference but unsure how to do so. But just by sleeping for sixty-three days, she has introduced all of us to each other and let us share her successes and failures on her way to becoming fully awake. So perhaps her Easter miracle has been to help so many people through this ordeal to *wake themselves up*, to live life fully and to open up to the everyday opportunity for compassion and joy. If she can inspire this much love and devotion by just sleeping, how much can each of you do by being fully awake and aware of the suffering of those around you? I wish for each of you that today brings great joy and a renewal of passion.

Monday, April 25, 2011. Coma Day 64.

Last night I had a very direct dream with a simple message: "Accept what is." These words came clearly to me as I awoke in the middle of the night, painfully aware of being alone in bed. Immediately I caught myself fighting the message. I resist accepting Phyllis *as she is* at this moment because I fear that doing so means surrendering to the inevitability of losing her. The reality is that she is alive, that her brain and body are intact, that all our loves and adventures of the past are intact but that she is in a semi-sleep-like state. Friends frequently tell me to "let go and accept what happens," and I struggle against it in a similar way. *Letting go* sounds like *letting her die* and I fight that with all my heart and mind. But the dream's instruction was not to let "her" go; it was to "let go." So if I combine the two, I have *let go and accept what is.* Let go of my attachment to what the future will be and accept where she is with love and joy. Then I am suddenly free to give her what she actually needs and what I so crave: a loving, present connection free of fear and attachment. Isn't that all we can ever give another human being?

For those who knew Phyllis before all this, the reality of being here and seeing her in a hospital bed with wires from every orifice and almost unable to move a muscle is a physical shock. All my kids have been through it, and now Phyllis's sister Rosalie is suffering from it, coming from California to sit with her. All the words in the world don't prepare you. You want to change her condition as soon as possible. You want to do whatever you can to keep her awake as many hours as possible. In reality, all you can do is *be with her as she is.*

It has been a month since a nurse called me at 2:30 a.m. to say Phyllis had opened her eyes and answered questions with a nod. It has been a week and a half since Phyllis started talking every day, however haltingly. "Let go and accept what is" frees me to celebrate those victories without needing them to lead to an inevitable outcome. It frees me to have an intimate physical conversation with her through Feldenkrais-informed touch. It frees me to remember what a life with her has meant to me. It frees my spirit to go walking with her in the night as Billy Joel sings me a lullaby: "I know I'm looking for something, Something so undefined, That it can only be seen by the eyes of the blind."

Tuesday, April 26, 2011. Coma Day 65.

This evening, I awoke as I dozed in a reclining chair in Phyllis's hospital room to the sounds and sights through the picture window of an electrical storm, one unlike any I remember, a magnificent hour of interminable flashes of light and sound, indeed a loud, thunderous cacophony.

Instead of lightning bolts and thundering cymbals, this maelstrom sent random electrical synapses *horizontally* across the sky for minutes on end, accompanied by drum rolls building to a crescendo, fading to a moment of quiet, then returning again in staccato light flashes and rolling thunder. Suddenly I imagined myself a tiny traveler sailing across Phyllis's brain, caught out in a similar electrical storm, as brain synapses rocketed across the surface in passionate search of nerve receptors. Light trails of energetic explosions snapped from gyri peaks to sulci arroyos, mountain to valley, ventricle to aqueduct, bouncing rhythmically off the internal sky of her skull. Sound and light drew ever closer together until the two were united in an indistinguishable fury of sensation, the dual senses becoming one in a glorious connection which held for a full minute of vibration and then dissolved slowly and peacefully into a thought. The storm passed and Phyllis, as well as I, slept peacefully.

Wednesday, April 27, 2011. Coma Day 66.

Today, I went with Phyllis for an MRI to get a closer look at the upper part of the spine. Her neurologist, Dr. Rob, wants to eliminate any chance of the *spine* as a source of her problems. Meanwhile, the Regency Hospital team is working on the mechanics of a trip to Barnes-Jewish Hospital.

True to form, Phyllis has been talking less and sleeping more since her breakthrough, although she has spoken some every day for ten days. My concern is not so much for the waxing and waning of her ability to talk but rather that the limited degree of her wakefulness has stayed the same. I suspect the novelty of saying a few words but not being able to fully communicate has worn thin for her. Sometimes when a question is too hard, she just looks at me then shuts down and sleeps for hours. I fear the extreme effort required won't continue to be worth it to her. It begs the question of how she might become *more* wakeful and that is what everyone is working on.

My resolve to "let go and accept what is" is being tested by the approaching move to Barnes-Jewish Hospital. While I'm breathing deep and enjoying my time with Phyllis, I want to be an active participant in this new adventure in St. Louis. The modern medical treatment of neurologically-compromised

patients, dependent as it is on an uneasy alliance between neurologist and neurosurgeon, seems oddly disjointed. The neurologist
sees his job as diagnosis and is more of a generalist. He proposes
options for treatment but refers the neuro-patient to a surgeon
for treatment. The neurosurgeon is at the top of the heap in
status and tends to belittle the neurologist's lack of hands-on
experience. The trouble comes when the diagnosis is uncertain—
neither the neurologist nor the surgeon wants to take responsibility. In an ideal world, there would be a neurological *team* to
diagnose, treat and follow through until the outcome is clear. I
want to make sure that happens at Barnes-Jewish Hospital but
I realize we will be one small cog in a huge machine. Call me
obsessive. Once a path presents itself, I have faith that a destination will appear.

The move to Barnes-Jewish Hospital in St. Louis continues.
Calls are being made, contacts established, doctors' notes passed.
It's impossible to say if this will be a short visit of a few weeks or
a longer stay. I'm excited and nervous at the same time: excited
at the prospect of a new, highly-qualified neurological team and
nervous at leaving the incredible support of local friends, family
and attentive, supportive hospital staff. My insurance company
approved the transfer, and Barnes-Jewish has accepted Phyllis
as a patient and has a bed waiting for her. Dr. Rob spent an
hour on the phone discussing her case with the doc in St. Louis.
The hospital's compiling her records to send with her. The "Life
Flight" paperwork is in process. They haven't told me that I can
tag along but they'll have a hard time keeping me off that flight.

Thursday, April 28, 2011. Coma Day 67.

Dr. Rob met me early this morning in Phyllis's room to tell me that the Life Flight is happening *today*, in a few hours, and we both have a ticket to ride! Preparing to leave feels a bit like I've been stranded by rising flood waters and suddenly, there's a rescue boat with two oarsmen at my front door and they're saying "grab what you need and go."

I'm feeling a bit distracted. Not by the "organizing to leave" part; that's easy. It's keeping Phyllis's needs at the center of this. Whatever is preventing her recovery (silent seizures, slit ventricles, garden-variety brain insult or something else), I don't want to lose the progress she's made as we rush to move to a new facility (new room, new tests, new doctors, new life). I want her to feel supported and to know we'll get through this together. Having said that, we plan to load her into a flying rowboat and see where we land on the other shore. We're outta here at 1 p.m. today on a jet flight. As Judy Garland used to sing, "*Meet you in St. Louis, Louie.*"

CHAPTER EIGHT

UP THE MOUNTAIN AND INTO THE WOODS

There is a road, no simple highway
Between the dawn and the dark of night
                    —The Grateful Dead, "Ripple"

September 10, 1972

After almost three weeks of village life in Tilzapotla, Phyllis and I rose each day at sunrise with Augustina, who had by then created a place for us in her daily routine, giving us chores. Sometimes we ground the masa in a hand mill instead of carrying it to the molino; sometimes we tended the small fire that heats the comal. Larry was assigned heavier-duty tasks like stacking adobe bricks needed for wall repair. Don Lauro watched us from his tiny straight-backed chair, smiling and wanting to talk.

One morning, I woke up before everyone else and thought I'd make myself useful. Looking out in the yard between the cobblestoned courtyard and the orchard, I saw lots of weeds growing up to eye level and assumed Augustina hadn't cared enough about aesthetics to cut them. I set myself the goal of clearing the yard before the household awakened. But after removing a six-foot swath of plants, I looked up to the sight of Augustina barreling her way towards me.

"Why are you tearing up my *sorgo* brush? How am I supposed to make brooms if you kill it all? And look here, you've pulled up my *epazote*!" She was holding up some green leaves with jagged edges. "I thought you wanted mole sauce today!"

"Augustina, I'm so sorry. I was trying to help. Can I get epazote at the market?"

She made a snorting sound and looked down sadly at my destruction but then sighed and returned to her own tasks.

Soon Phyllis and I were off to the mercado for epazote and a few other herbs to add to her special mole dish. More than ever I felt like a bull in a china shop. How was I to know that all the "weeds" in the yard were carefully planted herbs? On the other hand, I'd given Augustina an opportunity to assert control of her domain; so I ended the incident feeling less like the *patron* and more the ignorant grandson.

The metal staples on our leather sandals clicked on the cobblestones as we made our way uphill to the town plaza, passing open courtyards. Along our route, several men unloaded freshly-dried adobe bricks for a house under construction. All the materials needed to build this house were *free* if you were willing to do the labor: mud by the nearby lake for drying into adobe bricks, clay tiles to be fired in a mud oven, and wood beams from the mountains for roof supports. Tilza was a country town, so unlike Cuernavaca where everything was hidden from the street by high walls, courtyards in Tilza were only partially closed in by eye-level fences which let us peek over and see inside. Horses were being saddled and burros loaded for the day's labor in the fields. *Caballeros* in tall cowboy hats herded a few cattle through the streets toward the open range. As we approached the plaza, native women from the mountains in colorful blouses and long braided hair were unfolding their wares on straw *petate* mats.

Towering above the plaza, ten or twelve blocks south, was a steep mountainside, bathed in lush green foliage watered by four months of intense seasonal rains. Although the mountain rose some 3,000 feet above us, it was only a foothill of the Sierra Madre, a continent-spanning volcanic outburst known in the North as the Rocky Mountains that reach for the heavens from Canada to Central America.

"Have you heard Don Lauro's revolution story?" I asked Phyllis as we stopped at the market for a cup of steaming hot chocolate with cinnamon.

"I can't quite understand his stories," she sighed.

"I know—me neither," I said excitedly. "Until yesterday morning, when something clicked. I think I get it now. He's old, right? Like eighty or something. So he keeps telling that same story over and over."

"Old people do that. Something about some horses and the *soldados*, federal soldiers?"

"Yeah, it's hard to make sense of it, right? Whenever he gets to the part about his brother, he starts looking sad and the story gets confusing. But yesterday, the Spanish words came more clearly to me. The story is about when they fought with Zapata in the revolution; it would have been around 1914. He and his brother were Zapatista guerrillas fighting the federal forces who supported the hacienda bosses. One afternoon, they were returning to Tilzapotla from a raid when a bunch of federales gave chase. Instead of heading for Paso Morelos, the usual escape route across the valley below our house and the one the federales expected them to take, Don Lauro made a fast turn with his horse up a trail right here by the plaza. They rode up the mountain, trying to escape into the orchards up there. Just as he did, he heard a shot ring out, and when he looked back his brother was on the ground, bleeding. His brother died there."

Phyllis broke out in tears. "I never put it all together like that. He talks a lot about crossing barrancas and something about papayas."

"I know!" I said. "I figured out that part, too. He keeps pointing across the valley toward Paso Morelos and then gesturing up toward the mountain. You see that papaya grove? Look, it's that green and yellow patch a little ways up the mountain. This must be the place where he turned to escape, and up there is where his brother died. We have to go up there soon."

September 12, 1972

Nighttime meals in Augustina's world were more ceremony than substance. The mid-afternoon meal provided most of the calories; at night, we might eat only bean soup, *frijoles de la olla*, with tortillas, maybe with some rice. After the light evening meal, I sat with Don Lauro as he finished an after-dinner cigarette and offered me a sip of mescal.

"Don Lauro, *cuando subiste ese camino hacia la montaña y te alejaste de los federales, ¿hasta dónde fuiste?*" I asked. When you took that trail up the mountain and got away from the federales, where did you go?

He flashed a wide-toothed smile. "I was so scared I was gone for three days," he said in Spanish. "I went up the mountain and crossed into Guerrero; then I made my way through the brush to Coaxitlan and came back through Paso Morelos."

"Are there still people living there?" I asked. "Up the mountain, past the papaya groves? I want to go there, to Guerrero. I think I always wanted to go there. Am I crazy?"

"Go there," said Don Lauro, smiling. "The trail is not easy to follow, it's easy to get lost. People live there but they're hidden. You'll find your way."

A fully-formed idea entered my brain; it was already decided. I had to go there.

When I shared this plan with Augustina, she replied disapprovingly: "*Van a matarles alla*," she said. They're going to kill you there.

"*Why?*"

"*Because you're foreigners. They will think you're rich.*"

"*How far away are these bad people?*"

"*Three days' walk.*"

"*How far have you walked in the mountains?*"

"*Two days.*"

I agreed I would walk for two days and check things out very carefully. I knew that her warnings of danger were not idle chat. But I also knew that people assume the worst about people they

don't know. The way people at home were sure they hated Vietnamese rebels without ever meeting one. Or maybe Augustina
was right and we would get shot. Either way, I was going. *We*
were going. I knew Larry would go along but would Phyllis want
to leave the relative comfort of Augustina's world for some crazy
adventure without an end game?

Phyllis and Larry didn't try to stop me or complain *directly*
about my plan.

"How long are we going to be gone?" Phyllis asked, in bed
later that night.

"Who knows? I've been learning from Don Lauro how
people travel back there. We'll have to learn how to recognize
the trails so we can find our way. At some point, there's this really
big river to be crossed to get to the wilderness I'm after."

"Oh, so just climbing a mountain with no map and no
roads and no equipment isn't *wild* enough?" she said, playfully
but with just enough sarcasm to warn me she had *issues*. "Why
isn't it enough to live in Tilza?"

"Once we figure out what we're doing, we'll be going back in
time," I answered, ignoring her implied worry. "Imagine a place
people have lived for several thousand years without phones or
TVs or armies."

"Oh my little *bandito*, you are out of your mind," she teased.

September 16, 1972

At dawn the sun lit the valley below Augustina's hillside
orchard. Firecrackers exploded all over Tilza, announcing *El Dia*

De Independencia, Mexican Independence Day. Loudspeakers mounted on trucks blasted *Gritos* from loudspeakers followed by *Ranchera* music from popular Mariachi bands. The Mexican *Grito* repeats the cry that Father Miguel Hidalgo issued to his rural congregation in 1810, proclaiming Mexico's independence from Spain. *Ranchera* music, also born in the country and also during the Independence era, is less *sung* than loudly *shouted* with accompaniment by guitars, strings, accordion and an occasional shot of tequila, somehow weaving together romantic themes of lost love and hopeless bravado. The day had arrived: "*Independencia!*"

Phyllis, Larry and I were up at dawn, ready to leave for the mountains of Guerrero. Augustina's neighbor, Tere, had used her sewing machine to make saddlebags from our truck's canvas sides and small backpacks for the two dogs, Lather and Gringo. With Don Lauro's help, I had bought a horse from a farmer outside of town. We didn't intend to ride the horse, just use him to pack our gear, as I had seen *indios* do as they walked into the market from the mountains with heavy loads. Don Lauro had painstakingly shown me how to tie a Mexican saddle, which is just a crude wooden frame wrapped in a blanket. This Mexican steed—whom we named Colonel Sanders or more briefly *the Colonel*—was no Palomino show horse from a Colorado rodeo. No, he was instead a member of a wiry, surefooted breed that, like the people who raised him, had navigated the Sierra for twenty generations. He was very old and tired but also true and cheap.

Before we could leave, Augustina had to finish cooking

gorditas for us, a special recipe of hers with lots of oil in the masa to keep them soft for traveling, stuffed with refried beans and wrapped carefully in a cotton cloth. Veronica filled our two water gourds and hung them on the saddle, the gourds sweating slightly, cooling the water. Augustina had given Phyllis her *rebozo*, a long, handwoven shawl, and showed her how to wear it across her face to keep out the dust. We were all outfitted in new leather-and-rubber-tired sandals which Don Lauro had trained us, when we first got them, to wear into a stream and leave on our feet until they dried and shrunk to fit, after which they were forever exactly molded to your feet. I wore *blancos*, the baggy white cotton pajamas worn by men in Tilza. They keep you cool in the heat and dry easily after you wash them. If we were going to die in the wilderness, at least it would not be because Augustina and Don Lauro let us leave underprepared. They both repeated their instructions about the unexplained dangers of traveling to the wilderness. The mountain dwellers we would encounter in the first two days would be hospitable but beyond? Who knew?

I led the horse through the gate Augustina's young grand-daughter, Veronica, held open for me and everyone followed. She stared out of her almond-shaped eyes, looking both sad that we were leaving and excited at our adventure. Augustina shook her head, a tear in her eye, and Phyllis hugged her. Don Lauro leaned on the gate, smiling broadly. In a few short weeks, we had become the prodigal children who came home, and now we were leaving again. We never spoke of the ownership of the house but it was clear that Augustina was in charge and that was how I wanted it. My emotions were a mixed stew of pride and joy to be finally starting this quest and also apprehension at my complete lack of experience, exacerbated by my need to carry out this trip exactly as I had imagined it for years, without any complications or revisions from anyone, including Phyllis. *Only believe.*

It was late morning and we avoided the plaza since it would be packed with holiday revelers and mescal-laced borrachos. Instead, we took the cobblestone street beyond the plaza up to the edge of the village, then doubled back on a path Don Lauro had directed me to. Soon the cobblestones stopped and the road became a mountain trail. We gained enough height to see the plaza, the lake, and the valley of Morelos below, Augustina's house now but a small blur in the green trees. But as the town faded behind us, for some reason the sounds of Independencia celebrations began to get louder.

"What's all the noise?" Phyllis wondered aloud.

"Sounds like a rodeo," I said, taking what turned out to be an accurate guess.

As we rounded the bend, we realized our path had taken us on a rise immediately above the Plaza de Toros, a natural bowl on the mountainside where the town bullfights took place. The bowl was packed with Independence Day spectators, horses and bulls. The Tilza version of the bullfight did not torture or kill the bull. This was not done out of compassion but practicality; no one could afford to sacrifice such a prize possession as a bull. So instead the toreador taunted the bull from his horse, and tried to jump from horse to bull and ride him. Many attempts, never successful, were first made by the town borrachos, who are quite drunk but also excellent riders—the equivalent of rodeo clowns—followed by the true contestants.

As luck would have it, Phyllis, Larry, the dogs and I had appeared on the hill facing the entire crowd of spectators just after the inebriated clowns and before the introduction of the true competitors. With nothing else for them to focus on, some of the crowd turned their attention to our motley crew. So much for my charade of slipping quietly out of town. A cheer went up from the crowd as Phyllis waved her felt hat, and we proceeded in glory, gleefully playing our part in the day's entertainment. But as we rounded the next bend, now out of sight of the stadium, all that glory came crashing back down. The Colonel, our affectionately-named, ancient horse, was already rattled by the crowd's attention and the concentration of adrenaline-charged horses and bulls. So when the canvas bags slipped a little on his back, startling him, he shook from side to side and took off running, dragging the bags behind him and spreading our gear on the ground. Fortunately we were not humiliated in front of the whole town, and the only witness was a barefoot kid who retrieved the horse and a few passers-by who helped re-tie the load.

And so we began our long, slow ascent, switchback by switchback, through orange groves, over the creek, and up through the papaya groves. We continued along corn fields, across rocky bare ground, and up to a patch of pine trees where we took a moment to look back at the view behind, then bent our necks to see the mountain above. We kept going to the top of the next rise, only to find another hill. The path was not hard to follow; although it broke into multiple choices, all paths eventually converged, and they all led upward, forever upward. I was ecstatic. The dogs, Lather and Gringo, ran ahead, behind and around us, sometimes seeming lost, and then appearing in a moment when called.

Stopping for a late-afternoon meal by a creek, we were surrounded by swarms of tiny yellow butterflies.

"Look at this," I said. "They're all over my arms! What are they?"

"I saw them once when I was picking nananche berries with Augustina," Phyllis said. "She says they're good luck; they stand for hope."

The view was majestic: looking north, the volcanoes Popocatepetl and Iztaccihuatl appeared at one end of the valley below and the city of Cuernavaca at the other. Judging by our height above the valley, we were perhaps halfway up to the peak of the mountain, heading south toward the Pacific Ocean. The sun was resting on the horizon, and Phyllis cradled her head in my lap to take in the view as we nursed our sore feet.

After the sun came to rest beyond the mountains, Phyllis suggested we just make camp where we were. I favored pushing on, but eventually relented, and we began to set up our first campsite of the trip. I staked the horse for grazing, his only sustenance. For tents, we brought along two large pieces of the Muleskinner tarp and some rope. Larry set his tent on a rise a little ways off, while I made a bed of pine needles for Phyllis and me. We scavenged for wood and started a fire, and before we knew it, it was dark. Though the dogs rested while we built camp, at nightfall they became sentries, growling at unseen intruders.

Larry played Leonard Cohen's "Bird On The Wire," a song that had become one of my closely-held prayers, a repentance for those you had betrayed along the way and a promise of renewal if you kept true in your search for freedom. The darkness of the mountain wrapped around us and we slept.

September 17, 1972

Stirring the coals of the fire the next morning, I heated water for coffee and prepared the comal, a small metal travel version of the clay griddle Augustina used to heat tortillas. If you treat the comal every morning by heating a paste made of lime and water on the fire, then brush off the lime, you have a perfect lightweight cooking griddle. Corn cakes, coffee, oatmeal, and some oranges conscripted from trees along the trail—a breakfast of champions! The dogs ate leftover tortillas and beans, the horse had grazed all night. I figured we had enough food to last several days, then we'd be on our own. Don Lauro had advised me it was common practice to pick fresh corn from fields along the way for a backup meal but so far we hadn't seen corn fields. Eventually, I assumed we would find the village of Coaxitlan. Mind you, we were not on the direct trail to Coaxitlan; that trail went around the mountain. But I wanted the big view, the one you could only get from going over the top. I also needed to *disappear* into the forest, so I could see if my childhood intuition about being at home in the wilderness was a true one. Then I could get started with the minor details—like figuring out how we would survive.

"Are you sure you know what you're doing?" Phyllis asked me over breakfast. "We could get completely lost out here."

I crossed my arms, annoyed at the question. "I know exactly what I'm doing."

"Sure he does," Larry said with a wry smile, rolling his eyes.

Phyllis looked at me with an intense gaze. "You want to clue us in?"

"It doesn't matter if we get lost. We'll go over the top of the mountain and ask anybody we meet for directions to Oaxaca." I thought my plan was obvious to everyone. I didn't want to know where I was; I wanted to stumble through a gate into another time and place.

"Oaxaca is three hundred miles away and you know that no one we'll meet will have ever been there," she said with resignation.

"Exactly my point," I said. "They will know it's somewhere to the south but not how to get all the way there. Then I'll ask for the best trail to go in that general direction and they'll give us the way to the villages they know, which is what I want anyway."

"You really are out of your mind," she said, with admiration and concern.

"Your worst nightmare," I said, astonished but exhilarated that I was finally taking the path that had beckoned me all my life. "Sealed with a kiss."

September 18, 1972

When Phyllis and I, along with Larry, the Colonel, and the dogs finally made it close to the top of the mountain above Tilz-apotla, the trail had become almost indistinguishable from the brush. After a while, the path entered a grove of Palo Blanco trees with peeling white bark and hanging green parasitic plants. The grove was eerily quiet and the animals seemed reluctant to enter, but it was clearly the only way up. With one final look at the valley below, we took the narrow path up the steep hillside through the trees. Deep in the grove, sheltered from the noonday sun, we came to a ramshackle fence and a large wooden gate hanging on a tree across the path. It seemed strange to encounter a gate—there were no animals grazing at this height and, since leaving Tilza, there had been no other gates on our trek up the mountain. We had come this far, so we swung open the gate and followed through. The gate creaked eerily and closed with a loud crunch behind us.

We soon came to an open glen with a spring and a clear pool. There were pipes leading away from the spring headed down the mountain toward Tilza. Apparently, we had come to the source of the town's water at the very crest of the mountain. We could no longer see the valley of Morelos to the north but instead had a spectacular southward view. The state of Guererro lay before us in descending waves of blue-green mountains, sealed in under-brush. And somewhere stupefyingly far below the clouds on the southern horizon was the Pacific Ocean. It was impossible to tell if the turquoise blue patches we saw were ocean or sky but the sensation of flying was almost dizzying.

Phyllis took my hand and we gazed in awe. *This was it; this is what I was meant to do*, I thought. Something had *always* felt a little misplaced in my life, like I was accidentally born into the wrong family or the wrong century and was living someone else's life. When I was five years old and my dad put me on that old horse to wander alone in the cedar brakes of the Texas Hill Country, I felt the tug of a memory of an earlier time when people lived closer to the earth. For years, I had felt lonely and isolated, trying to find direction, not able to adapt to the domestic suburban American life I was born into. Then I had decided to give up control and let a new life happen. I had walked onto the square in Santa Fe, met Phyllis and been swept away in a desert wind to this mountain top.

Phyllis ran her hand through my hair and gave me a kiss. I felt she could read my mind. "There's a whole new world out there for you to explore. Where do we go from here?"

"Yeah, there must be a thousand ways down the mountain," said Larry.

"I don't know," I said. "We'll have to see."

After filling our gourds with fresh water, we started down the mountain into Guerrero. Gradually the trail disappeared—or rather, it turned into numerous animal trails leading from a water source down to hidden shelter. Once we led our elderly and ever so slight-of-build horse down into the barrancas and arroyos that twist their way past creeks and boulders, we no longer had the perspective of the grand view. Even though we were going *down* the mountain, much of the time we were climbing *uphill* as we reached minor summits, only to confront another valley, the longer view hidden by more trees and boulders. Strange tropical orchids hung from oak trees and thick brush gave way to pine forests.

That night we made camp by a roaring stream, muscles strained and feet sore. The dogs' footpads were sore and scratched, and the Colonel had no grass to graze on. What firewood we could find was wet and when burned yielded a smoky mess, so we gave up on cooking and ate cold corn cakes. I was sure there were established trails here but I wasn't finding them, and I had no idea where we were. I thought of Don Lauro having camped here sixty years before us, fleeing the federales. I felt his invisible smile encouraging me to persevere. I felt the presence of Nahua warriors who had traveled these paths for a thousand years. Larry's harp led us into Kristofferson's "Me and Bobby McGee" at day's end, giving us solace, Phyllis singing her part like Janis Joplin did it—with both despair and joy, the perfect antidote to feeling lost and helpless, bravely displacing anguish with camaraderie, song, and a warm body next to you at night. The dogs even howled a bit in sympathy.

The next day was long and equally frustrating, with continual switchbacks and dead-ends. The awful truth, which, in spite of my bravado, I didn't want to face, was that we were truly lost. At dusk, we came to an outcrop of solid rock hung out over a high precipice. Three ledges were connected to each other but suspended over nothingness. The view was breathtaking, but as good as it felt to get some perspective on the valley far below, all we saw were more ridges and gullies, a seemingly endless green carpet descending into the fog with no clear path forward. The prospect of being shot by bandits was sounding better all the time. Nevertheless, we managed to get a fire going on the middle ledge and Phyllis surprised us with a hot meal of sorts, using up the last of our supplies and coffee. Larry whistled through his harmonica to play Leonard Cohen's "Tonight Will Be Fine," which fit my mood perfectly. It's a sparse but sensual song that transports you to a lonely and almost empty room with bare whitewashed walls, a high window and only one bed. Soon it has you listening for footsteps on the stairs, waiting in anticipation of the person you most desire in the world, and by that act embracing the present with ecstasy.

Because the ledges were narrow, we camped on separate boulders by tying our tarps to the rock wall behind us on neighboring precipices. Just above, the Colonel was tied tight to a tree. The fire went to embers; Larry retired to his ledge and Phyllis, the dogs and me to ours. We slipped off our clothes and melted into our army-issue sleeping bag, a world unto ourselves, snug against the harsh reality outside. Tomorrow would be a new day, but tonight, Cohen assured me, "will be fine, will be fine, will be fine, for a while."

The rain started gently enough that night, smoothly pattering on our tarp as we lay sleeping peacefully in each other's arms. Then the patter turned to a strong, steady downpour. We snuggled more tightly, confident we could ignore the outer world. Then the bottom of the bag began to feel wet. It took a lot to soak through that bag, so by the time it did, I knew we had a problem. I put my hand on the tarp below us and felt a stream of water several inches deep moving through the tent. With some difficulty I woke Phyllis and we dressed hurriedly into our now soaked clothes. Larry was stirring too although he had made peace with his wet bag and voted for sleeping. Our picturesque ledge had turned into a dangerous hydrant, focusing all the water running off the mountain and out of the rock wall onto our ledge and into infinity below. In a mad rush, we had to gather up our kitchen gear, tarps, packs and clothes, carefully extricating ourselves, the Colonel and the dogs from the rock without slipping or being swept over the ledge.

The rain was coming in sheets now, as if some angry mountain god had discovered our arrogant intrusion into his paradise. We formed a chain to pass gear from ledge to ledge and onto solid ground. Except even the ground wasn't entirely solid; the mountain was moving in a torrent down every open trail it could find. The Colonel was frozen in place. It took all I had to make him move but our lives depended on it. Finally, he consented to having the saddle strapped on and the bags packed and stumbling back up the mountain in search of safer ground.

We couldn't go far in the dark. With ground-water rushing around us, we were unable to see beyond the next step. Finally, we stumbled into a rock wall with an overhang of a few feet. The small shelter the overhead rock created was dry, punctured by a web of dead roots sticking out, as if a piece of the mountain had previously fallen away making a small cave. If we stood single file, with the dogs huddled under the Colonel (now beyond humiliation), we could at least avoid the insult of more rain stinging our faces and running cold down our backs. There was no comfort, just the hope of numbness. The path below was a muddy flooded river.

"What time is it?" asked Phyllis.

"I don't know, maybe three hours till sunrise."

Larry leaned close. "I could start a fire."

"Yeah, right."

"No, really, these roots break off and they're dry."

Against all odds, Larry, quiet companion and troubadour, created fire. Coughing from the smoke, blowing on the tinder, we all set ourselves to breaking off enough roots to keep it going. There was no heat generated and we were all smoked like barbecue, but it worked. The fire became our light against the assault of the elements. Huddling on our heels and watching the fire to keep awake (if not warm), we survived until dawn. The fire finally sputtered and went out just as the sun was born again in a clear sky.

Fog filled the valley, with only the mountaintops breaking through and we began a new day. Each ray that hit my face reminded me that I had been here before (when? how?) and that we had lived to face a new day. The Colonel stamped his feet and shook his coat, spraying us all with cold water. He knew when we bought him that his dreams of retirement in a corn field full of harvested stalks were shattered. A Mexican horse works hard all his life, carrying heavy loads from field to home. But the key

words are *field-to-home*. There is supposed to be a home. He is
not expected to camp in the wilderness in a rainstorm next to the
end of the world. These gringos would be his undoing.

September 24, 1972. Guerrero, Mexico

Though our clothes were soaked in the rain all night,
walking in the morning sun soon dried them. But even being
dry didn't make it much easier to keep moving down a trail that
we all knew might just lead in circles. Without a map, I used
my best judgment with the angle of the sun to head southeast,
but when you're lost in a labyrinth judgment can pull tricks on
you. Around mid-day we met someone on the trail, our first
encounter with other humans in three days. He was a young man
on a burro, as surprised as we were at our encounter. Augustina's
warning of *mala gente*, bad people, made me apprehensive.

"*Disculpe, joven, sabe donde va este camino?*" I asked. Can
you tell me where this trail leads? He gave no sign of recognition.

Phyllis tried as well. "How many hours to a town?"

The boy answered not in Spanish, but in a language I didn't
recognize, full of sounds made with his tongue on the back of
the roof of his mouth.

"*Kwa-seetch-laan* (Coaxitlan)?" I asked in a one-word
phonetically pronounced plea of desperation, remembering the
village Augustina had pointed us toward, the limit of safe travel.

Smiling broadly, the boy spoke rapidly with more words
we couldn't fathom and pointed excitedly down the trail ahead
of us. With this encouragement, we parted ways with him and

walked a while longer. I say "a while" because none of us had watches, nor did anyone we met. The sun made it pretty clear what part of the day we were in, as did the moon at night if there was one visible. That didn't stop Phyllis from asking.

"What time d'you think it is?" she asked.

"Dunno," I answered.

"Well how many hours do you think it'll take to get to that village?"

"Dunno."

"Can we make it today?"

"Not sure."

Phyllis gave me a dark look and seemed to limp a little as she walked. "Well I would like to get *somewhere* soon."

"Okay."

We did indeed get *somewhere* about mid-day. The trail exited the deep canopy and we began to spot corn growing along the trail and on the steep hillsides. Remembering Don Lauro's advice to take corn from a field whenever we wanted, we each grabbed an ear of corn and tore off the husks, hungrily devouring it raw—pretty tasty if you're starving. We crossed a creek, swollen and muddy from the rain. The trail then led deep into fields of corn, beans, wild grasses and yellow-flowering chamomile, the intoxicating aroma encouraging us on.

Before our spirits could soar too high, however, Phyllis screamed.

"Ow! What the hell?" she yelled.

"Damn," Larry shouted. "They got me too. They're all over my legs!"

I began screaming in pain as well, dancing crazily in place as we tried to brush off our attackers. Even the dogs howled and barked. In our exuberance at the sight of human endeavors, we had failed to notice the trail was covered with an army of red ants which were stinging our bare, sandaled feet with great gusto. The trail was narrowly bordered on both sides with high corn, so there was no clear avenue of escape. All we could do was keep going, hoping to outpace the tiny red predators.

After a short painful sprint, we saw a wooden gate and a wisp of smoke over the rise. Not pausing to announce ourselves, we quickly opened it, escaped the ants and, following the smoke, came upon a man having lunch in a *casa del campo*, a field house consisting of thatched roof, adobe oven and no walls. I had no idea how this white-haired man in blancas would react to the rapid approach of three gringos. "*Buenos dias*," he said and motioned for us to join him. The Colonel shook the sweat off his back as we removed the packs and saddle. The dogs licked their ant bites and we took the cold water offered us and poured it on our abused feet. Our host introduced himself as Don Agustin, and graciously offered us tortillas and frijoles.

Looking outward from the clearing, corn grew in every direction, up every hill, covering every spot that was not rock or tree. It was indeed *las cosechas*, harvest time. Don Agustin explained he was the *viejito* of his family, the elder who was sent to guard the field from animals in the last days before family and neighbors would come from his village, Coaxitlan, to harvest the corn.

September 24, 1972

We began the day well-rested, having camped overnight at Don Augustin's *casita*, bucket-washing and sun-drying our clothes, repairing our gear and recharging our spirits. With clear blue skies and a hot sun above we continued the trek to Coaxitlan. The path was clear and wide and we could see the village below us most of the day. By mid-afternoon, however, we were uncharacteristically exhausted. The town was clearly visible at the base of the large mountain we were descending, stretching from one side of the valley to the other, but it felt like the village was moving away from us at the same speed we approached it.

At least we had a clear destination close by with water, food, and people—some of whom were coming and going on the same path we were on. Phyllis, of course, wanted to ask each one how long it would take to reach the town. The answer, if the traveler understood Spanish, was always *dos horas*, though "two hours" is a relative term to people who have no instruments to mark time. When Phyllis showed consternation at the village's retreating distance, most travelers were polite enough to change the estimate to "*una hora*" to accommodate her obvious chagrin with the first answer. The long walk began to wear on us. Our leg muscles aching as we silently descended the back-and-forth spiral of the trail, a green valley below began slowly moving up to our view, then the leg of an angry-looking brown, frothy river appearing from nowhere behind the village and disappearing again into the hills behind, the village itself a glimmering patch-work quilt of thatched-roofed, woven reed houses connected by various trails.

At twilight we limped into a clearing by a house in Coax-itlan. This was our first opportunity to follow an instruction from Don Lauro on traveler's etiquette in the old world. He had told us that once we were hungry or ready to stop for the night, we should approach the gate of the first house we saw, rattle it, and shout a greeting. "*Bueno?*" I said loudly, shaking the rickety gate—the first sounds I'd made in the hours since Phyllis and I had gone silent. Soon enough a man who looked my age but with black hair, dark brown skin and a large smile greeted us and beckoned us to enter. He led the Colonel to a stall behind the house and brought him a bundle of dry corn stalks and water. Phyllis, Larry and I were directed to a conical, open-aired thatched structure with a swept floor and no walls. Burlap bags of dried corn still on the cob were pulled to the side to make room. A kerosene lamp was lit. Woven straw mat petates were unrolled for us to sit and sleep on.

Dinner was served in the main house, which was about the same size as our corn-crib structure, with an elaborately thatched roof descending in a cone to woven reed walls two feet off the ground. We ate sitting on the floor as his wife and their three curious children wanted to feel Phyllis's long hair. After dinner, Phyllis and I sat outdoors, frogs croaking somewhere in the bamboo forest surrounding us.

Phyllis paused and turned toward me, her eyes staring directly at mine, her mouth forming a forced smile:

"We need to talk."

"Why does your tone make me nervous?"

"There's something important I need to tell you."

"I'm here; go ahead," I felt my stomach muscles contract.

"Lather is about to have puppies. I think she's due any day. We've been lost for days, and now just because we found a path you think everything's wonderful."

I did think everything was going great. The dogs were part of our team. How could I not even know that Lather was pregnant? No doubt that my dog Gringo was the father but puppies hadn't entered my mind. "Wow! Okay, so what do we do? We could camp and let her have them here," I said, answering my own question.

"I have to take her home. She can't be on the trail with nursing puppies. They'll need a month or two before I could even find someone to take them."

"Home" was a conversation stopper. It just hung in the air. Where even *was* "home" for either of us? At the very least, Phyllis's words implied "home" wasn't on the trail with me and Larry in the remote mountains of Guerrero, Mexico. I said nothing, and we sat silently together, the question of what we would do lurking like an intruder in the dark. Go *home*? How? Where? Why?

If I had a thought of looming change, I suppressed it. Tucked into my sleeping bag with Phyllis wrapped around me, the distant drum-roll of the Rio Amacuzac lulling us to slumber, I slept without a care in the world. I was happy; I was living in the moment; I was doing what I always dreamed of; I had a beautiful girl snuggled close to me. What else could anyone need?

September 25, 1972

At dawn, Phyllis and I were awakened by the vibration of the ground and the unmistakable whine of a diesel engine and grinding gears. My unconscious brain identified the sound I'd heard as "truck," but then my conscious mind asked, "What the hell?"

We had walked for days from Tilzapotla to get here over the mountains from Morelos, and hadn't seen any kind of vehicle nor any sign of a road since then. So what was that sound? It grew louder as I went outside, stepped to the fence, and caught sight of a huge dump truck with five-foot high wheels lumbering up the path from the river. Was I dreaming?

Our host was awake, feeding the animals. I asked him about the sound.

"*Vengan cada semana para llevar el cal de la mina*," he said. They come every week to carry away the cal from the mine.

Cal, I knew from Tilzapotla, referred to limestone mined in the mountains to make slaked lime in which corn is soaked to make tortilla dough or *masa*; it's also used as a building material in bricks. Phyllis had joined us, slipping her hand under my blousy white peasant shirt and stroking my back lightly with her nails. Her mouth had a forced smile but her eyes looked as if she might cry.

"How does the truck get here?" she asked our host. "There's no road."

They follow along the river from Tilzapotla on a road of broken stone.

We gathered our belongings and ate a breakfast of beans, cream and fresh tortillas as we sat on our petate mat. After breakfast, Larry knew something was up and made himself scarce.

Phyllis made eye contact and spoke commandingly. "I'm taking Lather home to have her puppies."

"Home to the house in Tilza?" I asked.

"No, home to New York," she replied. "I'll hitch a ride out of here on one of the trucks."

"Can I talk you out of it?" I asked.

"No," she said, as my neck muscles tightened. "Lather has to go home and you have to go further into the mountains."

Before I knew it, she gave me a kiss and climbed up into the cab of the giant truck. I handed Lather up to her. Larry held Gringo who wanted to go with them. This time I had her parents' phone and address, but New York was in another universe. The noise of the truck was deafening and the driver was waiting. I had that feeling again that life was making plans without me.

The door shut and the truck hammered slowly out of sight. When that door shut, I went into crisis mode. I wanted to stop her but I couldn't. The noise of the truck was too loud to soften her with words. The loner in my brain jumped into the breach. "Maybe this is for the best?" it said. "You can explore and you won't have to explain everything to her all the time." No. No.

No. I need her here to even *have* feelings. Seeing her staring at me through the glass window of the huge vehicle, time was frozen again and my lonely heart screamed at me. "You fool, she was there for you but you went off in your own world. Now look at what you get!"

As the truck pulled away, I went in my head to a very familiar place: no emotions allowed; make all movements strategically; move toward the wilderness. I could see the mountains behind the town leading south beckoning to me. Within an hour, Larry and I were packed up and leading the Colonel south of town, down an unknown trail southward. Clearing the first mountaintop, the voice of my heart spoke clearly: "You didn't lose her, you *pushed* her away. You let her in when you needed her, but you never asked her what *she* needed. You should have let her know she could trust you. You *have* to get her back if it means following her all the way to New York City."

CHAPTER NINE

LIFE FLIGHT TO A NEUROSURGERY HOSPITAL

"Any man could, if he were so inclined, be the sculptor of his own brain."

—Santiago Ramon y Cajal, *Advice For A Young Investigator*

Thursday, April 28, 2011. Coma Day 67.

After much uncertainty all week whether it would ever happen, I was told this morning that I had *three hours* to prepare to leave on a life flight with Phyllis to Barnes-Jewish Hospital in St. Louis. No problem, right? Not knowing if I was to be gone for days or months, I threw all the clothes I could stuff into one bag, grabbed my checkbook and unpaid bills, and before I knew it I was in the ambulance with Phyllis arriving at Fayetteville's private airport, Drake Field, looking for our plane.

When I caught sight of a sleek, long Lear Jet ready to tear the clouds apart, I assumed it must be our ride. But alas, the ambulance passed the shiny Lear and pulled up instead to a 1988 Cessna 2-banger prop plane. Two attendants and a nurse strapped Phyllis to a stretcher, passed the stretcher sideways through the plane's tiny door and transferred her to a gurney waiting inside. The attendants waved goodbye to us. The nurse sat beside Phyllis and relegated me to a corner seat. The ascent from Drake Field was by necessity very steep, as the airport is couched between two precipitous Ozark mountains. The engines roared and we were off to the skies, and Phyllis made a groaning noise as the plane banked skyward to the East. None of us was very comfortable, but somehow getting some distance from the Earth and from all the hospitals in which she had been imprisoned for two months was comforting. I felt both ecstatic and frightened.

"Will we be back for you soon?" the nurse asked.

"I have no idea," I said, realizing how much this trip meant to me and how little I knew about its outcome. "I think they'll be running tests for a month or so. Hoping for a miracle, I guess."

As we approached St. Louis, I spotted the Gateway Arch on the Mississippi River. I felt the thrill of watching a city exploding toward us as we descended from the sky in a small plane—an experience I grew up with, accompanying my dad on business trips. The thrill quickly dissipated into concern about Phyllis, strapped down on a stretcher in the plane as it made a quick descent to a small municipal airport. Before I knew it, we had landed and Phyllis was loaded into a waiting ambulance for the trip to Barnes-Jewish Hospital.

My Fayetteville friend John had insisted I stay with his brother Glenn and his wife, Mary Kay, in St. Louis. My new angel-hosts picked me up later at Barnes-Jewish, fed me and gave me a bedroom in their house. I would have been tempted to spend the night with Phyllis but all three of the beds in her room were occupied by patients.

It's late at night now and I stare out my open window at the lights of St. Louis. In better times, Phyllis and I might have come here to visit. We share a love of urban spaces as well as wild ones. We would scout the city for bagel shops, city parks and good music. My shadow goes out the window and walks hand-in-hand with Phyllis along the wide boulevards under the canopy of oak trees.

Trying to sleep, I began to rethink my understanding of Phyllis's condition, especially after re-reading Jill Bolte Taylor's book, *My Stroke of Insight.* I thought I had gleaned from it what lessons I could, given that Phyllis did not have a stroke. Now I realize that I had read it with tinted glasses, thanks to my desperation to find some medical procedure that was going to make Phyllis wake up and be herself again. What I failed to absorb the first time around is Dr. Taylor's insight, the one for which she named the book. In her words: "Peace is only a thought away and all we have to do to access it, is to silence the voice of our dominating left mind."

According to her explanation, being inside your brain with no requirements to act in the world is a very peaceful, loving, delightful experience. The question for her, as she lay unconscious in a hospital bed, was "Why would I want to make this huge effort to go back into a world of conflict and pain?" Certainly doctors and nurses who yelled at her, pinched, poked and prodded her to move did not convince her to try. What *did* convince Jill was the loving support of her mother and other caretakers who believed in her ability to heal and had the patience to wait. Dr. Taylor was also motivated to come back to share the peace that she found within herself, the peace that she had spent a lifetime looking elsewhere for. It sounded like it could work for someone I knew.

Phyllis's biggest challenge, in other words, may not be to relearn the use of her entire body, daunting as that task is; it may be the will to leave a place in her head that is calm and harmonious in order to make a painful return to a world where nothing is certain. As her family and support team, our biggest challenge may be to make a case for "peace and tranquility" being *out here* in the world too, the reward of having a purpose to be alive in spite of the cruelty and suffering in human existence. We never know until we try.

Friday, April 29, 2011. Coma Day 68.

Since our arrival at Barnes-Jewish Hospital Neurology Clinic, it's been a whirlwind. This is the opportunity I've dreamed of for two months: the best experts in the world looking for the answer to Phyllis's cure. Already today, she has had three lab tests, a CT scan and an MRI. She's resting peacefully now on an air-motion bed, a device that reverses flow of air back and forth across her mattress to keep her blood circulating and prevent dangerous blood clots. Phyllis had a good landing yesterday but has *sooo* far to go.

I'm determined to get the most information possible about Phyllis's condition from the Barnes-Jewish doctors, but to do so takes some planning. Standard procedure will be to put

Phyllis through all the neurological testing every new patient must endure. I say "endure" because, as Dr. Taylor says, much of it is repetitive, inappropriate and even barbaric in a case of loss of consciousness, but I have no standing or time to make that point. Doctors, nurses, technicians, they all try screaming at Phyllis to wake her up, pinching her to elicit an involuntary response, moving her sore leg to see if she will pull away, and prying open her eyelids to shock her with very bright lights. *No, they really do.*

But she's been through it so many times before and each time they try to force a reaction, the farther she seems to withdraw. What if she can hear and understand everyone but is unable to move or speak, feeling that everyone is treating her like a freak in a carnival show? Wouldn't she hide as far inside herself as she could?

Avoiding overly aggressive evaluations is just one of many negotiations I'll be having with the medical staff so Phyllis can feel safe enough to work with us to become more conscious. The next is medication. The temptation is to medicate her for each and every symptom, both the neurological ones (impaired wakefulness, possible seizures) and the maintenance issues (fevers, UTIs, allergic reactions). Even though each treatment might be medically appropriate for that symptom, the aggregate direct effect of the treatments and their subsequent side-effects are the opposite of what we are here for: they drive her further from wakefulness. When I confronted numerous medical personnel in the past, from her day nurse at Regency Hospital to various staff physicians, I was uncertain about these conclusions; now

I am totally convinced. Phyllis would insist on being a partner in this return to consciousness; she would not be forced into it. My challenge when I first meet the doctors and their students, which the hospital calls the "Green Team," will be to gain their confidence without alienating them. Phyllis's case is a mystery and I'm hoping the challenge of finding a solution will motivate them.

Saturday, April 30, 2011. Coma Day 69.

I woke early and arrived at the hospital before dawn. The Green Team arrived in Phyllis's room at six-thirty in the morning, led by Dr. Will, the Washington University Chair of Neurology, followed by an entourage: a case doctor, four interns and six students. A tall man with a broad forehead and military-cut short hair, Dr. Will dictated notes to his students in a monotone.

"Patient is a fifty-nine-year-old female with impaired consciousness as a result of bacterial meningitis due to an infected brain shunt." Appearing to notice me for the first time, the doctor continued. "Mr. Head, how can we help you?"

I cleared my throat and presented her case. "Unlike all of you," I said, "I have no credentials, but I *am* the world's most interested observer of my wife. I'm here to find out what's preventing her from staying awake. I'm sure you've all seen her history. Doctors in Fayetteville have been unable to find a clear explanation of the damage to her brain that prevents her from being conscious. She's been unable to communicate consistently for ten weeks—and what's worse—she often seems to withdraw further when she's forced to respond."

Dr. Will took it all in, paused for a moment and addressed me in a professorial but compassionate tone. "This is how we'll proceed," he said, speaking to his team more than me. "Draw cerebrospinal fluid—CSF—from her shunt immediately to test for any continuing bacterial infection. Check CSF *pressure* to see if, in spite of the shunt, elevated CSF pressure could be the cause of her non-responsiveness. The point is clear, yes? We want to know if her current condition is a result of the damage previously done or a new unexplained malfunction of the ventricles. Then let's follow up with an enhanced EEG with electrical stimulation to check for evidence of seizures. This should include continuous monitoring for twenty-four hours. I am doubtful, given her history, that she has seizures. But we want to rule out every possible cause. Of course, the imaging group will need to review all MRIs and CTs, arrange new scans and evaluate."

The Green Team hung on every word and universally took notes on iPads. I was as excited as I had been on my first day in college. Everyone there knew more than me but I was determined to learn quickly and absorb as much information as possible to see my way clearly through hard choices that I knew were sure to come.

For Phyllis, the rest of the day was a flurry of lab tests, blood draws, probing and electronic scans of all types. Phyllis was examined and I was interviewed by neurologists, neurosurgeon trainees, and phlebotomists. This is what we came here for and I couldn't be more pleased. Since it was a weekend, I assumed getting any results would take days. Boy, was I wrong. Diagnosis at Barnes-Jewish Hospital happens with lightning-quick speed. Twelve hours later, the full team showed up a second time that day for rounds on our floor.

Dr. Will and his entourage, which had by then grown to twelve, crowded into Phyllis's room. He spoke in a commanding voice as if he was addressing a student who he doubted had kept up with his assignments.

"Mr. Head, we have the results of yesterday's tests and the ones I ordered this morning, except the EEG, which is scheduled for the next twenty-four hours. *So far*, there's no 'smoking gun' to explain her condition or 'magic bullet' to cure her. The CSF draw from Phyllis's shunt shows that her spinal fluid is totally bacteria-free. The CSF *pressure* in the shunt is normal. This indicates that her current condition is a result of the damage previously done, not a current malfunction of the ventricles. Proper functioning and pressure setting of her shunt was checked. The shunt is regulating the pressure of cerebro-spinal fluid on the brain perfectly. As I said before, we will begin an EEG with electrical stimulation tonight to check for evidence of seizures. I see no symptoms of seizures but it is a possible cause, nonetheless. I will see her tomorrow evening and we will decide how to proceed."

Sunday, May 1, 2011 5:18 a.m. Coma Day 70.

Early this morning, I arrived at Phyllis's room before

daybreak. *Her eyes were open and she turned to me as I entered the door.*

"What's that machine for?" she asked, speaking for the first time in days.

"Now you show up?" I said, grinning. "You're wired up with electric curlers to a twenty-four-hour EEG continuous monitoring test for seizures. See all those video cameras? They're filming every move you make." I asked the nurse for a mirror to show Phyllis the computerized EEG machine connected to her head by fifty wires attached with little swabs of water-soluble adhesive. Her response was to smile but close her eyes and go silent.

By 6 p.m. that afternoon the Green Team was with me in her room.

"The EEG study showed no sign of seizures or other abnormal brain activity," said Dr. Will, again in an emotionless professorial tone. "Phyllis's evaluation is complete. For the record, no condition has been found that warrants further diagnosis. We've ruled out any cause for Phyllis's impaired wakefulness other than extreme insult to the brain cortex from infection and swollen ventricles. There is no known cure other than time and the brain's own ability to reorganize itself. In these cases, complete recovery is *possible* within one year. But it's also equally possible, one might say *probable*, that she will never recover or overcome this incessant entry and exit from consciousness. The insult was *global*, meaning that pressure was applied to her cortex all over and yet her tests show no specific area of damage.

I'm sorry, but science doesn't know enough about the mechanics of a global brain insult to have a cure or even a way of measuring her progress, other than the improvement of symptoms. We will arrange a return flight home for her on Monday."

It was hard to know how I felt. The first emotion was abandonment: *Are they done with us already? Couldn't they keep looking for something?* The speed of the diagnosis had definitely caught me by surprise. I was prepared to be there for up to a month just to get all the tests done, wait for the results and then have an interview with the doctor. Before Barnes-Jewish Hospital, all I've done is complain about the slow pace of medical evaluation. Instead it happened here in a few days. Now, having received the intense evaluation we came for, I realized I was counting on time to think through each evaluation, develop more questions, and devise a plan of treatment. And most of all, of course, I had desperately hoped for an answer and a cure. Some part of me had hoped that the trip here would allow me to surrender Phyllis's fate to wiser and more experienced practitioners. But in the end all Dr. Will could tell me was "wait and see." I felt despair crowding my thoughts like the taste of bile. Dr. Will summed up my despair with a parting admonishment: "Her condition now may be as good as she ever gets."

Clearing my throat, gazing out the window at a clear blue sky, the way ahead was clear. Accept that there is no easy fix, love Phyllis for the warrior she is, believe in the healing power of human interaction, have faith that all is not known by human consciousness, and hit the trail for our Fayetteville home in the Ozark Mountains.

Tuesday, May 3, 2011. Coma Day 72.

With all the tests done and nothing left to do but fly home, the days are spent calmly waiting. Now Phyllis is in a room with no other patients. Today the attending staff moved her to a recliner parallel to the bed, and her eyes were open wide the whole afternoon. I decided to lie next to her in the hospital bed, and adjusted the height to match the recliner so it was just like we were lying in bed together. I slipped my arm around hers, and for a moment it felt like none of this had ever happened, like it was just the two of us taking a rest during a well-deserved vacation to St Louis.

In this still, peaceful moment, I heard her voice say out loud: "Frank." The first time she'd said my name in ten weeks. Joy rose from my loins, through my heart and flooded my brain. Suddenly I remembered what it felt like to be known by her, to be remembered and connected in that way you only can when someone uses your name. My heart soared at this gift from God and Phyllis. I decided it was a good time to read her a text from our son Andrew. As I did, her eyes wrinkled and she said, ever so softly, "He's so sweet."

We continued to hold each other in our parallel universes, in that moment of surreal normalcy, until the nurses returned to put her back in bed. The moment they did, she fell asleep instantly, and I began to think that even if nothing else comes of the visit, a few days of rest may have been just what she needed. And hearing her speak my name, an equally perfect gift to me.

Thursday, May 5, 2011, 5:31 a.m. Coma Day 74.

Yesterday was all about bringing Phyllis home. Abruptly at 2 p.m., the nurse told me "You're going home." By 4 p.m., we were back on the same two-banger prop-plane on a life flight home. The flight crew were the same as the one who had brought us to St Louis a week ago, and when they greeted Phyllis by name, she opened her eyes and said hello. I slept until the pilot pointed out Eureka Springs, then Beaver Lake, signposts to the spot where we live on Mother Earth. Every landmark closer to home felt more exciting. We had gone so far only to be told: *Go home and keep trying.* Landing at Drake Field felt like I was a companion to a returning hero. Family and so many friends would be waiting for her, ready to stay with us as long as the journey might take.

The ambulance team that met us at Drake Field was the same crew that took Phyllis for an MRI the week before. They greeted her too, and were also rewarded with an eyes-open but silent hello. I had hoped to return victorious with a cure in hand. Instead we return with nothing but advice to persevere and Phyllis is nonetheless giving everyone signs of her courage and strength.

The nurses at Regency Hospital were falling all over themselves to greet her and get her set up in her new large room with a new view. The Hospital Director drove over from home to see her and give instructions to the nurses. Family members were texting good wishes; friends who couldn't wait came to the room. After Phyllis was comfortably tucked in her bed, with her leopard blanket and a Care Bear, the nurses finally finished fussing over her. I asked myself, *What does she know that I don't? She's acting like we're on an exciting new journey. It's time I shared her joyful spirit. Sleep is not her enemy. If she has an enemy, it is my misplaced anxiety that she must prove to us as soon as possible that she can function.*

Back at the Regency, I map out our plan as I sit silently in the dark beside her bed. She still has a trach-tube in her throat and a central-line IV, both of which are potential sites of infection, and she needs acute care to nurse her to a state of health where both can be removed. Soon she will need to move to another level of care in Fayetteville, probably a skilled nursing facility. There, with the invaluable assistance of our network of loving *family*, we can support her recovery. Eventually she will need a neurological rehab site, whether in or out of town, to help her recover consciousness and complete use of her limbs. All of this, of course, assuming there is progress and not just an endless loop of returns and departures from an elusive state of wakefulness. Then I remember Dr. Taylor's description of her own experience of impaired consciousness. I remember the strength and love she felt when those around her believed in her and overcame their fear.

"Okay, hon," I spoke out loud to her in the dark. "I'm done with my fear. I know it's peaceful in there but I do need you with me. Our kids need you; we need your company if you can do it. But I can wait as long as you need. We're going to stop the pressure and just go along at the pace you set."

"Go home and sleep," she said to me with her heart.

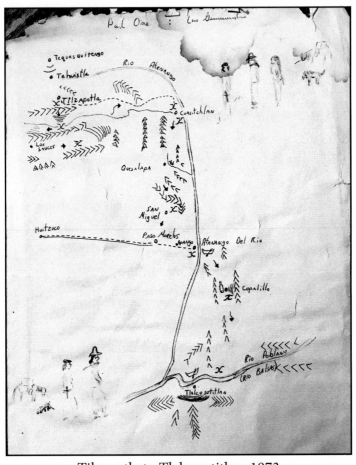

Tilzapotla to Tlalcosotitlan, 1973

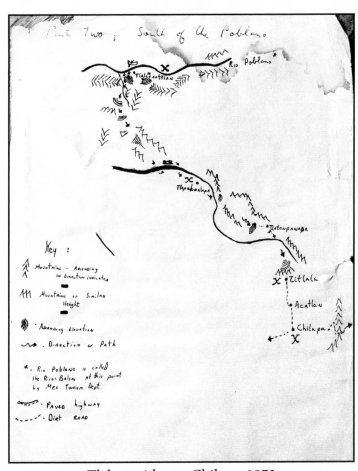

Tlalcosotitlan to Chilapa, 1973

Tilzapotla house of Augustina and Lauro

View from the porch, Tilzapotla

The Muleskinner, 1972

Phyllis at 21, Tilzapotla 1972

Don Lauro, 1972

Phyllis with Augustina, 1972

Gringo and Lather

Phyllis grinding corn
for masa, 1972

Phyllis and Frank, 1973

Crossing the Amacuzac River, 1973

View of Sierra Madre from Tilzapotla

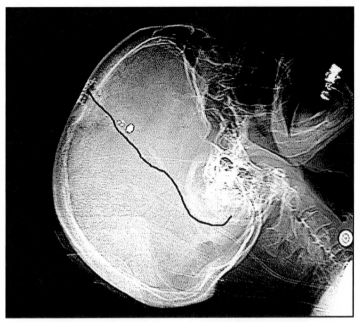

Phyllis's brain shunt, 2011

Our six children with Phyllis, September 2011

Phyllis and Frank, 1974

Phyllis and Frank, 40 years later, 2014

CHAPTER TEN

FINDING PHYLLIS IN NEW YORK CITY

I heard her say over my shoulder
"We'll meet again someday on the avenue"
                    —Bob Dylan, "Tangled Up In Blue"

November 19, 1972

Two months after Phyllis left me in Mexico, I stepped into a phone booth in downtown Elizabeth, New Jersey, in the late afternoon and fished her number out of my wallet. The operator said "Deposit fifty cents, please." The last time I'd seen or talked to her was in the mountains of Guerrero, as she was leaving me. I hesitated before I dropped each dime. I had traveled three thousand miles from southern Mexico, hoping that she would see me. With almost no money, I had hitchhiked to Texas, visited my parents in the Texas Hill Country, hitched on to Lubbock to see Larry, talked him into helping me transport a drive-away motorhome that needed delivery in New Jersey, picked up hitchhikers who helped pay the gas and stood on a crowded, downtown street with my heart pounding.

What if she doesn't want to talk to you? I debated with myself. *I think she will*, I answered. *She never said "goodbye" when she left me in Mexico, just "see you on the bridge or someplace later", throwing back at me a line from Leonard Cohen's "The Stranger Song," the one we had always sung together. Anyway what's the open invitation that comes before that line in the song? "Let's meet tomorrow if you choose, upon the shore, beneath the bridge . . ." If I show up and let her know that it's* our *trip now—instead of her tagging along on* my *adventure, she can't say no.*

I conjured an image of us as an old couple in a photo up on someone's wall. I decided I had to be in that photo. I dropped five dimes in the slot.

"Hello? Is Phyllis there?"

"Frank? Is that you? Where are you?"

"Corner of Broad and Grand in Elizabeth, New Jersey. Wanna come get me? I'd kind of like to see ya. Larry and I just drove here in a Driveaway RV from Lubbock."

"Oh my God! I can't believe it! I just got off work. It'll take me a couple hours in traffic. I gotta cross the Verrazzano Bridge from Brooklyn." There was no hesitation in her voice and my heart soared.

"I'm not going anywhere," I said.

I tied my dog to a lamppost and joined Larry inside a nearby diner. Six lanes of slow, city traffic fought each other outside. Two hours later, Phyllis pulled up to the curb and we all piled into her ten-year-old green Chevy. Gringo, had an excited reunion with Phyllis's dog Lather. We took the Lincoln Tunnel into Manhattan, the night skyline highlighting my first visit to New York City. We drove past the crowds in Times Square and headed uptown to the East Side, Phyllis singing The Drifters' song "On Broadway."

I sat in the front as Phyllis drove. I had come 3,000 miles from Oaxaca, Mexico to find her and I didn't know what to say except "I'm here." She took my hand and brushed her cheek with it as she drove. It seemed like a dream. The New York I knew was from novels: Henry Miller in *Tropic of Capricorn* who claims to hate New York but is obsessed with its lurid underbelly; Thomas Wolfe in *You Can't Go Home Again* who migrates to New York in the 1930s determined to write a novel about the South, and James Baldwin in *Go Tell It On The Mountain* about a black teenager growing up in Harlem. New York was where you went to completely abandon the place you were from and grow wings for a new flight. As a teenager, I had fantasized living in a seedy hotel in Manhattan, walking the streets by day and writing poetry on an old typewriter by night. Driving down Broadway with Phyllis by my side felt surreal—like being an actor in a scene I had imagined when I was fifteen.

"Where are we going?" I asked, touching her arm to be sure this was real.

"My friend Rosemary's apartment. She lives in the nineties on the Upper East Side. We'll stay there tonight."

"Where'd you get this car?" I asked.

"My dad got it for me after I got back from Mexico," she said. "I owe him, though. I got my old job back too, waiting tables at the Milleridge Inn. How did you get here, you tricky devil? I really couldn't tell anyone about you. I never thought I'd see you again."

"Why not?" I said. "Didn't you want to?"

"I came to get you today, didn't I?" she said. "I really thought you'd disappear in Guerrero forever."

"Larry and I walked almost three weeks over the mountains after you left," I said. "We came out of the mountains at a town called Chilapa. Larry bailed out and headed home to Lubbock. I let him drive the Muleskinner back to the border. As agreed, he left it for me in a parking lot in Laredo and hitched to Lubbock. Last week I showed up in Lubbock and talked him into coming with me to New York. I promised to pay his bus fare home."

"Afraid to face me by yourself?" she teased.

"Well, I did think you'd be more likely to come if Larry was along. I wasn't sure you'd even talk to me, after the way you left."

"What did you think was going to happen? Lather delivered her puppies three days after I got home. You were set on walking into the mountains 'til we all starved to death. Sometimes I wasn't sure you even knew I was there."

"I get it; sometimes—maybe most of the time—I live inside my head; it's a place I got comfortable with a long time ago. But after you left, I realized I can't get there by myself anymore. I know you think I'm crazy. I can't say I've figured out where I'm going but, if I do, will you go with me?"

She pulled me closer and gave me a long kiss.

After driving from Lower to Upper Manhattan, we found a rare parking place and walked along Lexington Avenue, the traffic crawling only slightly faster than we walked. Art vendors sold paintings and delivery boys weaved in and out of traffic on bicycles carrying multiple pizzas. People of all sizes, shapes and colors were coming and going. Tall commercial skyscrapers gave way to smaller brownstone apartment buildings. More and more of the blue sky managed to show itself. Our entourage proceeded—Phyllis with long braided hair and blue jean jacket, me with a blond goatee and ponytail, Larry in an Army fatigue shirt from Goodwill with hunting knife strapped to his leg and our two dogs, Lather and Gringo walking without leashes, their heads held high. It felt like we were just another minor act in the street circus and no one stared at us. Walking down a busy street in New York City with my arm around my girl, a cold autumn breeze freezing our breath, I could have died happy then and there.

Soon we turned the corner off of Lexington onto tree-lined East 91st Street and found Rosemary's second-floor, walk-up brownstone apartment. In my head, Phyllis was the woman Bob Dylan was singing about in "Shelter From The Storm."

November 23, 1972. Thanksgiving.

Four days later, we had moved to Phyllis's family home in Bethpage, New York. I woke up before dawn in her arms in a downstairs bedroom next to her parents' room, where she had slipped in to wake me. After a long weekend together, we had dropped Larry at the Greyhound bus station and headed out the Long Island Expressway to Phyllis's parents' house.

Phyllis's brother had given me his room—or been so ordered by her Mom and Dad—to avoid the awkwardness of us sharing a room.

After arriving at Phyllis's home in Bethpage, Gringo had met his own puppies for the first time. Lather had given birth to a litter of eight puppies when Phyllis arrived home two months earlier. By the time Gringo and I came to New York, she had found homes for all but two of them. As soon as I sat on the floor, they assaulted me and Gringo, licking my ears and face and biting Gringo's tail.

"Do they have names?"

"I've been too busy finding people to take them. I haven't had any luck with these two."

"Okay. So let's do it. There's a boy and a girl, right? Let's each pick a name. This little guy looks like his dad, Gringo, kind of a small shepherd mix. I got it—let's name him after his pop. His full name is Gringo Starr but we'll call him Star, for short."

"If we start naming them, we'll get attached. My parents won't let me keep them here at the house."

"Well, that's what I want to talk to you about. But first pick a name for the girl."

The female puppy had installed herself on the bed on top of Phyllis's pillow overlooking us all.

"Alright," she said, with a hesitant, curious smile. "She's black like Lather and she seems to reign over everything. Let's call her Queenie."

"Perfect! Star and Queenie. They'll love living in a tipi!"

"Say what? You've got something going on in that crazy head of yours. Let's hear it."

"After you left me in Mexico . . ." I said.

"After I left to bring Lather home to have her puppies, you mean . . ." she interrupted. I took her hand.

"Yeah, well Larry and I just kept walking through Guerrero. When we got back to civilization, Larry headed north like I said and I kept going to Oaxaca by bus. I got to the city and I'm there, hanging out in a square, I swear, for no more than an hour and this converted school bus pulls up and out comes three tall, beautiful women and this guy named Linn."

"Three women and just one guy? Hmm," she said, teasing. "Convenient, for you."

"No way, filet. I'm a one-horse kind of guy. But we all became friends and I hung with them for a few weeks. They took me down to the Oaxaca coast to a beach village called Zipolite. It's beautiful and really isolated but not really my scene. Everybody smokes pot all day and spends the day naked around the natives. And nobody even bothers to learn Spanish. Anyway I liked Linn and we were tight but they were leaving again and I decided to come find you. But before I left, Linn borrowed my last fifty dollars and told me if I was ever in Woodstock, New York, all I had to do was speak to this lady at the health food store, Nature's Pantry, and we could use his tipi. It's right outside of Woodstock on about twenty acres. I was thinking we could go live there. And we could take the dogs with us."

"A real tipi?"

"Well, I haven't seen it but it must be. Linn said he was in South Dakota for a while with his family and a Lakota guy traded him this tipi for an antique cast iron cook stove they had on the bus."

"And we keep both puppies?" she said with a wide smile.

"Sure, why not?"

Cooking started early at the Petrella home the next morning. It was Thanksgiving Day. All morning, Phyllis and I were either packed into the corner of the family kitchen table or helping her mother and sisters prepare the day's feast. Finally, by 2 p.m. we were seated at the end of their large dining room table, the conversations from her parents, two sisters, one brother, two aunts, two uncles and three cousins drowning out any words I might offer. Suddenly, Phyllis clinked her spoon on a glass to get attention and there was silence.

"Ma!" said Phyllis, "I got a surprise for you."

"No, Phyllis," her mother groaned. "I can't take no more surprises."

"But Ma, this is good. Frank and I are going to Woodstock to live in an authentic Native American tipi. Isn't that fantastic?"

November 24, 1972. Woodstock, New York.

The loud crack of a branch falling from the weight of the overnight snow woke me before dawn. Linn was still on the road with his bus and family but all we had to do was ask at Nature's Pantry and we had directions to the tipi. It was set on the edge of a snow-covered meadow, surrounded by a New

England hardwood forest. The tipi was an authentic Lakota Sioux structure with thirteen long poles covered in canvas with a smoke opening at the top. Inside the tipi flaps, soft rugs and carpets surrounded a central fire pit. We slept on the ground, softened by a luxurious homemade mattress of blankets, quilts and pillows. The outside canvas was pulled up a foot or so from the ground to allow the fire to draw air and send smoke skyward. Inside, another canvas liner went up from the ground three feet for additional warmth. Forests of sugar maples, golden birch and beech trees surrounded us on three sides. A brook down the hill gurgled a constant low melody.

Phyllis ran her fingers through my hair as we tangled together warmly under the multiple covers. "Hey, get up," she said. "It's almost dawn. The fire went out. I wonder if it snowed all night."

I got out of bed and ran naked across the cold tipi floor to peek out the flap at the powder white rolling hills outside. Gringo got up with me out of loyalty but Lather and the puppies stayed warmly huddled together around our quilts. Then I popped back quickly under the covers.

"It's freezing out there," I said as she yelled playfully at the touch of my cold skin. "And there's at least a foot of fresh snow on the ground. Let's just stay in bed all day and I won't have to look for firewood." I snuggled closer, warming my chest with her back and tickling her feet with my toes. "We make a perfect spoon."

"Cool your jets, Romeo. Let's talk about what we're doing next."

I tightened my arms around her and tickled her neck. "It's no fun if we have to talk about it."

"No, you caveman," she giggled, as she skillfully turned back to face me. "I mean let's talk about living here. Let's get the fire going and we can check out Woodstock later. I heard that Bob Dylan used to live above the Café Expresso right in town and there's a vegetarian restaurant where you can get a macrobiotic meal. They have poetry night and chanting once a week and it's happening tonight. I heard from the lady in the store that Joni Mitchell showed up one night. The Band is supposed to have a big place about a half mile from here. They were all coming here years before the '69 concert. Did you know I had a ticket to Woodstock but some people came to visit my family—the people from Mexico City that I went to see last August? So I didn't get to go."

"Bummer. Where was the concert?"

"It wasn't really in Woodstock at all. It was about sixty miles away in Bethel. But everybody in rock music has been coming up here to play and hang out for years. It's been an artist community for a long time. George Harrison came here once to see Bob. There's great food in town, art galleries and lots of political stuff. People are super bummed that Nixon won the election but there's a group here still working to get him impeached."

"Ha, that'll never happen. You got all that out of that woman at the store in fifteen minutes? You would have made a great groupie. Where was I while you got all the gossip?"

"In your own head, where you always are."

"By the way, she said that The Band's property manager is

looking for some day-help to unload equipment and rearrange their recording studio. We could talk to him at the restaurant tonight."

That night I got a temporary job at The Band's farm, working twenty hours a week for good cash wages. I was a huge fan and had the lyrics of several Band songs written in my songbook. "Daniel and the Sacred Harp" was in our top five, especially since it talks about losing your soul for fame and wealth. The Band themselves were out touring though I did meet Robbie Robertson once. He came in while I was unloading boxes from a tour, looking for some tapes. I didn't know who he was until a coworker told me later. After a few weeks, the manager told me the job was done and I wasn't needed—which was fine with me. But the cash was a life-saver and working for a little while in the studio where much of the music that changed my life was exciting.

Days turned into weeks as more snow fell and we created a routine for our new life. Up at dawn to shovel the snow away from the tipi vents. Gather wood and re-start the fire to warm the tipi and heat coffee. Drive to the public library near the village center to get warm, use the bathroom to freshen up, then read *The New York Times* in the library reading room. If I had work, Phyllis would drop me off at The Band's studio barn or if not, we'd go exploring the New England hardwood forests behind the tipi. At night, we'd clean up and check out the scene in town. As Dylan had written—maybe about Woodstock—a few years earlier: "There was music in the cafés at night And revolution in the air."

One morning in mid-December, the weather began to turn even colder. "I heard it might go below zero next week," Phyllis said, hesitantly. "I think we need to make a plan. What about visiting your parents for Christmas?"

"Go to Houston?" I turned silent. Suddenly, I saw myself standing alone in a room with my dad, being grilled on my future plans. "Have you finished what you left here to do?" I knew he would ask. I wasn't ready for that conversation because the answer was no, not yet. I had abandoned all the financial security my father had given me, ignored the employment connections I was afforded, rejected the post-war commercial culture he and his friends had created and set out to find a new world. I couldn't just pop home for a "visit."

"I'd rather jump in the Hudson River in winter," I said. "Seriously, I want you to meet them but don't ask me to go back there right now. Dad's got a whole life planned out for me. A seat on the board at one of his banks, a law firm to join when I finish law school, a house in the 'burbs. Death by a thousand small cuts, I'd call it. I need to figure some things out before I go there."

"I thought you were getting along better now after you ran into him in Santa Fe the day we met. Aren't things better between you two?"

"Well we're not at war with each other anymore but if we go back to Houston, we're stepping into his world. It's going to be the same old story. He'll want to control how I dress, how we live and what we do. He'll be totally obsessed with what everyone thinks of me."

Phyllis was silent for a while, then spoke but in a quiet voice as if she were weighing each word. "Family means everything to me. My parents don't agree with everything I do either but they know I share their values. My dad was one of eight boys and three girls from an Italian immigrant family in Brooklyn, except two of the girls died in childbirth. My mom came over from Italy after World War II. I was born on the second floor of a three-story apartment near Flatbush Avenue in Brooklyn. My aunts and uncles lived on the other two floors. We ended up out on Long Island in Bethpage but our extended family moved with us. Two of my aunts and uncles live in the next block. Mom can call across the backyard fence to my Aunt Eva when both of them are in their gardens. They are who I am."

There was a pause in the conversation and I thought about what she had said before I spoke. "Don't get me wrong. I love my family, too. Mom and Dad took us—my three older sisters and me—traveling together all over the world. We camped out everywhere from the Canadian Rockies to central Mexico. My dad took me on wilderness fishing trips and we floated down the Mississippi River together on a raft. Mom and Dad were great adventurers on the road but when they got home, all that was forgotten. They could never reconcile the joy of the road with the everyday work part of their lives."

"Then why are you afraid to see them?"

"I'm not afraid but I'm not ready either. When I go back to Houston, I feel this giant vacuum sucking me back into the life my parents planned for me. They think it's a BIG plan: law school, business, maybe politics. But somehow their world is too small; there's no room for people who don't look like them. And money is the measuring stick for everything. Even art or music doesn't have any value unless it sells. They don't really hate anyone but they really don't see any color skin that isn't white. It's okay with them if a million Vietnamese people die to keep our capitalist system intact; it's okay if big oil means big pollution; it's just the price you pay for comfort and security. Really, they choose not to think about it. I just can't live that way. And when I go back, I want to know what we're doing instead."

"I know how it feels to be different, even though I love my family," she said. "After high school, I headed upstate to Oswego to college. I was in a sorority and everything was rolling along but I just didn't know who I was. Some friends of mine invited me to a March on Washington. We camped out on the National Mall. Half a million people showed up. I stayed on and finished my second year of college but I felt like everyone was ignoring the truth about Vietnam. And Nixon was making the war bigger."

"I know. Is that why you left home and hitch-hiked to New Mexico?"

"It was more than that. My older sister was on track to get married and have babies. My friends were either doing that or studying for careers. I needed to see the world first and find out what else was out there for me. One day, in the middle of my third year, I just walked away. I quit school, moved home and started making plans to travel. I wanted to see the West, live outdoors and . . ."

"To meet me?" I filled in.

"Hmm. Running into you did complicate things. When I left New York, I wasn't planning on 'anyone pulling the reins in on me,' as Linda Ronstadt says."

"Is that why you keep leaving me?"

"I didn't *leave* you. Both times when we parted ways in Mexico, it was because you weren't listening to what *I* needed. So I just kept on my own path. Are you sure it isn't *me* you're afraid to take to Houston?"

"When you think the time is right, tell me and we'll go to Houston and meet them."

She stayed silent and I rocked her gently in my arms. The snow had begun to fall again outside. The valley holding our tipi was now a sea of white fluff. The forest surrounding the valley was wrapped in white blankets too.

"Hey, I'm getting hungry. I could get up and start a fire and we could heat up yesterday's beans. Or would you rather drive to the public library and warm up? Free coffee!"

She pulled me closer. "I've got a better idea. Let's go back to Mexico."

"This morning?"

"No, dummy, not today. But let's make our way back to Tilzapotla."

I loved that she said *our way*. I'd go anywhere in the world if those were the terms. Truth be told, returning to Mexico was in my plans ever since I went after her in New York. But I wanted her to say it first.

"Okay, here's what we'll do." I said, planning our next road trip in my head. "I'll call the Driveaway company from the phone booth at the library this morning and see if they've got a car that needs to go to South Texas."

"Make it Florida. You know Rosemary, where we stayed in the city when you first came? Last time I talked to her, she offered for us to house-sit her parents' place in Orlando for Christmas. They're coming to New York."

"Florida?" I said, disappointed. Then I realized I was doing it again, imposing my own direction on our plans. I changed my tone. "Wait a minute, did you say Orlando? Lots of guys from Tilzapotla talk about going to Orlando to pick oranges. We could search out some migrant workers and find the best orchards to make some dough which we badly need, by the way."

"Oh you Texans," she said, pretending to be annoyed. "All you ever think about is money."

December was a whirlwind. We got hired to transport Yetta Meisel's new Lincoln Continental from New York to Orlando, found jobs picking oranges, worked at an Italian restaurant, and, after New Year's, left Orlando with $800 in savings. From Florida, we hitchhiked 1,300 miles in three days, arriving at the Mexican border to reclaim the Muleskinner from a long-term parking lot where Larry left it in Laredo.

"There's an Odetta tune we need to add to our songbook," Phyllis said as we approached the international bridge leading to Mexico. "It's called 'Long Time Gone'—like us—leaving home and rambling down the line."

"Odetta sings it fine," I corrected her with my most annoying smile, "but Dylan wrote it, you know. I'll agree to add it if we can also do Dylan's 'Tomorrow Is A Long Time.' Only if my true love was by my side."

Phyllis sang the song from start to finish. "That's one of my favorites. It's so tender. Tomorrow isn't so far away and loneliness don't mean nothing at all—if you're around."

The sun set over the Rio Grande as we looked south from the American side of the international bridge at Laredo, Texas. We slept in the Muleskinner at a nearby city park, saving the border crossing for the next morning.

I pointed out a nearby resort hotel. "That hotel is where my family would always stay before we started out on our annual vacation in Mexico. It's like a marker on a trail my parents laid down for me my whole life."

"My parents have never been to Texas," she said, "much less Mexico. The farthest we ever traveled was to a motel in upstate New York. But they were really gypsies too. My father's father came to New York as an immigrant back at the turn of the century. And my mom came by herself from Italy in 1947. She was following her cousin's footsteps; her sister Emma came later."

Night came on and we went to bed early. We wrapped the long canvas around the bed of the Muleskinner and tucked ourselves into our Army-issue double sleeping bag. I got to thinking of how my dad would judge my last few months, moving back and forth around the continent, barely supporting ourselves. I tightened up and felt alone. A familiar coldness, like a heavy, wet blanket that shut me down but also protected me from an angry voice—my father's?—that made me want to run away.

Phyllis could tell I was going somewhere gloomy.

"Hey!" she said. "I'm here. It's okay. It's just us. It's all we need." She spooned herself around me and magically, the darkness receded. So this is what it means to love someone.

CHAPTER ELEVEN

WHAT'S THE MOST DECREPIT
HOSPITAL IN TOWN?

With your saintlike face and your ghostlike soul
Oh, who among them do you think could destroy you?
   —Bob Dylan, "Sad Eyed Lady of the Lowlands"

Sunday, May 22, 2011, 6:28 a.m. Coma Day 91.

I have to do something! Our time at Regency Hospital is coming to an end; Phyllis no longer qualifies for the particular level of *acute* medical care that Regency specializes in. At the same time, because she is unable to maintain continuous consciousness for a minimum of several hours a day, she doesn't qualify for admission to Neurological Rehab hospitals. I have to move Phyllis to a new hospital—but where?

I feel threatened by the way Phyllis's current condition is viewed by hospital administration and insurance reviewers. She only qualifies to continue the level of care she has been getting if her consciousness is visibly increasing and her physical condition improving. Otherwise, she's just a coma patient without much hope. So she needs a new home, one that offers long-term care to a *partially* conscious patient. But the types of facilities that focus purely on "body maintenance" are not equipped to effect the healing I believe she is capable of.

In preparation for her discharge from Regency, Phyllis will finally have her tracheostomy tube removed from her throat and her IV central line extracted from her chest today. This will leave only one external tube, a line for feeding entering through her stomach; but it will eliminate the two most likely sources of infection and allow her to breathe, swallow and eat on her own, *if all goes as planned.*

This is exciting in terms of restoring Phyllis's control of her own body. At the same time, there is an element of "pulling the plug" here: removing these support systems without any major improvement in consciousness carries no guarantee that she will be able to breathe, eat and survive without them. As exciting as her improvements are, her chance of cognitive recovery is, statistically, still pretty slim. Consequently, our only choice for continuing her care is at a "skilled nursing home." Ironically though, this type of facility specializes in patients with little hope of improvement and thus does not offer Phyllis the stimulation needed to recover her wakefulness.

"City Hospital here in Fayetteville," Dr. Mark told me earlier today, "has the most decrepit, run-down facility in town. I'm on the board and we're always looking for a way to find a new building and close the current one but that won't happen for a year or so. Even so, I'm recommending we transfer Phyllis there."

"Why would you send her there?" I asked. "You don't exactly give it a glowing review."

"Because it also has the best director and the most talented, compassionate staff I've ever known," he said. "Most of the residents have no chance of recovery and yet the staff still gives each patient their personal best and they have quite a few surprise recovery cases. She can stay there for as long as it takes and no one's going to give up on her. They'll be thrilled to have a patient with a real chance to recover." My heart soared at his words, most of all because, like me, he believes in Phyllis. He believes that she is going to find her way out of the darkness. I am so grateful to have someone on the medical side who has hope in her recovery.

By the end of the day, City Hospital faxed over transfer orders. I breathed a sigh of relief; we finally have an exit strategy. Ask and ye shall receive.

Wednesday, May 25, 2011, 2:47 a.m. Coma Day 94.

2011 will be a year to remember. Not only did Phyllis fall into a coma but the weather went crazy and Phyllis slept through it. We live up in the northwestern corner of Arkansas, almost to the Missouri border. In Fayetteville, we are accustomed to being the target for violent thunderstorms, tornadoes, ice storms and all manner of wondrous phenomena slamming in from the west. But not like this: already this year we've set all-time weather records for Fayetteville: biggest snowfall (fifteen inches in one day), lowest temperature (minus eighteen degrees), hardest rain (sixteen inches in a month), biggest hail (one-inch golf balls at our house), and worst tornadoes (four people died in one just west of town). Yikes! And we're only half way through the year.

Tuesday night, the prediction was for more hail, storms and tornadoes to hit right at us again. In Phyllis's room at Regency, we had to remove all her shrine items from the window, as well as her library of poetry and brain books, even her music CDs and boom-box. The windows were cleared, the blinds lowered, and Phyllis's bed rolled to the far end of the room. The windows rattled, hail covered the ground like snow but Phyllis slept.

Phyllis's sister Theresa did manage to fly in between storms on Tuesday. She found our friend Barbara in the midst of a miraculous conversation with Phyllis. Whereas the rest of us have seen Phyllis as either sleeping or drowsily nodding hello since Sunday, Barbara, a professional clinical counselor and longtime friend, found the door to Phyllis's brain unlocked and let herself in without a knock.

Just as Theresa and I walked in, Barbara had told Phyllis "I'm going to wash your hands with this warm washcloth. Can you give me your right hand?"

"Okay," Phyllis said and with no hesitation, raised her arm and hand! It was like she had levitated right off the bed. In ninety-four days, no one had gotten Phyllis to command a muscle to move. Then just to show off, Barbara had Phyllis repeat out loud the names of her children, then her siblings and their children.

"Phyllis, your sister Theresa is here from California to see you," Barbara said.

"Really?" Phyllis answered, without opening her eyes. "She's an angel." This was her first unaided speech since her trach device was removed,

Thursday, May 26, 2011. Coma Day 94.

After yesterday's miracle, Phyllis was, once again, completely *inside herself* today, not waking or even opening her eyes. I wish I could say I am used to this back-and-forth but, in truth, I stop myself from fully embracing these miraculous lucid moments because I'm always thinking "wait 'til tomorrow!"

On the positive side, Phyllis has been breathing totally on her own for the last two days, so the removal of the trach device, an ugly piece of PVC pipe sticking out of her throat, was a complete success. The spot is covered with a bandage but there is almost no wound, the skin having grown around the tube to make a new opening. With the tube removed, the body slowly closes the extra mouth over a few weeks, we are told. The human body is a miracle of adaptability.

Wednesday, June 1, 2011. Coma Day 100.

Another milestone in our journey: today at noon, Phyllis moved from Regency Hospital with its view of the V.A. Park to City Hospital, looking out at the Fayetteville Library. The change was made effortlessly, an ambulance crew transporting her from room to room in less than a half hour. So she begins her hundredth day of *impaired* wakefulness in a new room, a new bed and a new hospital. I'm ready for a miracle.

City Hospital has only one floor, no elevator needed. The doors are open all the time and everything's a little more laid-back than anywhere she's been for two months. Everything that is, except me. The change to a new setting stresses me out. I should be happy with her room's new setting: airy, lots of windows, lots of light, and helpful staff. What distresses me, though, is adjusting to new systems, new people, new schedules. I'll adapt soon but in the meanwhile, I have to re-learn every little nuance of getting Phyllis the attention she needs. I don't know where the extra linen is kept or who to talk to about changing a medication. Every hospital is different and I'm a wreck for the first few days at each new place, a mother hen scurrying around feathering the nest for my only chick.

City Hospital is located just twelve blocks from my home. Her room is a beauty! It must have been somebody's corner office when the hospital was new: it's large and glassed in on two sides, with a panoramic view of Fayetteville's award-winning modern library. Granted, the floor tile is cracked and the bathroom looks like an abandoned closet but the "feel" is that it was once luxurious. According to Jane, the hospital director, the previous room's tenant came to City Hospital with a brain injury from a car accident and left walking on his own, three months later. So we have a good precedent. The staff calls it the "miracle room."

The news about Phyllis's condition is good, though it's hard to celebrate when I'm so focused on making new connections and learning new systems. I measure her progress in two ways: the relative amount of time she is in a wakeful state and the degree of physical and mental functioning she exhibits while awake. Over the last two weeks, there has been a *quantitative* improvement. Her wakefulness varies throughout the day but there is clearly *more of it*: she has more minutes with her eyes open, her ability to respond is more available and her ability to show comprehension is greater, even if her eyes are closed.

There has also been a qualitative change: when she can talk, Phyllis is speaking in whole sentences. Now, she'll say "Tell me about your trip," instead of one-word acknowledgments. She volunteers questions in the context of your conversation such as "Who came to the party?" Each sentence is a huge effort and a few sentences exhaust her, but she can do it. I can see the toll that talking has on her. The more comprehensive her communication is, the longer she sleeps. Phyllis's physical abilities are improving too. Her arms and hands are beginning to show movement. A few times a day she can lift both arms an inch or two. She can squeeze your hand slightly.

Mind you, you might not notice all this if you weren't, like me, watching Phyllis obsessively for signs of life. Otherwise, you might think she's asleep all day. Or you might walk in and think she's in a coma. Well, she is, but we're not accepting that it's a permanent coma and it's vital to me that the new staff understands that we are here to *reawaken* her mind, not just keep her body safe. My team leaders have been busy making new volunteer schedules and training materials to get everybody on the same page. Phyllis responds to something different with each person. I encourage our volunteers to be themselves; Phyllis responds to each person's unique gifts and interests, whether they are musical, intellectual or just good gossip.

I wonder, *how can it be that we have to invent a therapy for her?* There must be many more people who have gone through this pattern of illness. There should be published guidelines and directions. But if there are, we haven't found them so we keep adapting and inventing. Part of the team is up close keeping watch and some are afar, researching diagnosis and treatment or just praying and meditating. We are all walking and traveling with her.

Sunday, June 5, 2011 6:00 a.m. Coma Day 104.

Phyllis's move to City Hospital already seems like a really good choice. It's a hospital run with patients in mind. Physical therapy and speech therapy are given every day by loving, well-trained staff. Since City Hospital does not focus on *acute* medical care, there is no pressure from insurance companies to show progress. Miraculously, this doesn't result in a lazy staff; it lets them give *more* priority to therapy. Phyllis's physical therapist is an angel who sings lullabies to her as she gets her limbs exercised. Beyond her professional expertise, she is a natural-born healer. Phyllis's speech therapist is working on cognition, sight and taste. She is patient, neurologically-trained and interested in comprehending what Phyllis is experiencing. The room is bright and full of sunlight and outside in the hall is an aviary with a dozen live birds.

There was a scene Saturday as I sat outside Phyllis's room that says a lot about City Hospital. Phyllis was sitting up in a recliner outside her room. The staff uses a lift to put her in a specially-cushioned reclining chair on wheels that allows us to move around the grounds. We can sit outside in the sun together. Today, we were sitting in the foyer watching the birds when a white-haired man in a wheelchair nearby started yelling loudly.

"Martha!" he shouted at the nurse in an angry voice. "Where the hell are you? It's time for my trip. You're supposed to be here to transfer me. Martha!"

He seemed kind of abusive or disturbed. He was thrashing from side to side in his wheelchair. The nurse Martha came and talked to him but instead of being upset or controlling she acted like a loving daughter.

"Why are you shouting, John?" she said softly. "I was coming soon. You don't need to shout. Let's get you going; it's time for your drive." But she was smiling the whole time, so John laughed sheepishly and calmed down. Then she helped him into his electric wheelchair and soon I saw him motoring rapidly back and forth on the sidewalk outside as he traveled the hospital compound. Her parting words were "Don't stay out too long and get sunburned, okay, John?" Mutual trust, understanding and affection break all over this place, even with so many people struggling.

Phyllis's rapid change from improved consciousness to

coma-like withdrawal is exhausting and at times I fear it will go on like this forever. My moods tend to vary with her degree of wakefulness. My bedroom at home becomes both refuge and confinement. It is the memory of intimacy, the locus of our lives and the cell of solitary confinement. Much has been written about the importance of grieving and about the barriers to it: one's own denial and society's discomfort with grief. Grieving the long-term incapacity of a loved one, however, is even more complicated. The very process of letting go and accepting what has happened seems counterproductive to the effort needed to support and heal. People advise you to "keep strong," "keep hope," and "keep faith." The reality is that, whatever the future brings, I cannot "keep" the past. There is loss and it is now. It needs to be acknowledged and grieved in order for me to accept change and find the strength to work for a new day.

I do believe in her healing; I have seen her progress. I believe in miracles; the brain can and will adapt but *whatever* comes will also bring a new challenge. I celebrate all that we created and grieve what has changed. So be it. All experience, like all life, is transitory but in the act of remembering, our adventures live in my heart and give me hope. I play old Leonard Cohen songs to remind me that if you give love to and accept love from another human being, this is what you get: *contradictions*. Pain and ecstasy. I give thanks for every day, as dark and as light as they may be.

Sunday, June 5, 2011, noon. Coma Day 104.

This morning I walked to see Phyllis and found her awake. I assumed she would answer questions with a few words as usual. I read her my journal entry and sang Leonard Cohen's "Lady Midnight" to her.

"The stars make you cold," she said, misquoting the song but thrilling me that we still shared the song's message of loss and recovery.

"'The stars eat your body and the wind makes you cold,'" I corrected, "but not bad." I always loved that song, especially because the girl in it admits that the guy has won her over. "Hey, do you remember hitchhiking together from Florida to Mexico?" I asked, trying not to be too obvious that I was testing her memory.

"Of course I do," she said. "Us and the dogs. All the way to the border. By the way, what are those pictures on the wall?" she said. "I can't seem to focus."

"I brought three of Andrew Kilgore's black and white photographic portraits of all our kids from the house," I said, amazed that for the first time in months, she was trying to make sense of where she was. So I started asking more questions and she started paying more attention.

"What are you drinking?" she said.

"Coffee, you want some?" I answered. "Do you miss coffee?"

"No, but I miss drinking *something.*" she said. "I'm thirsty."

"Here, I've got something for you," I said.

I carefully balanced a spoonful of liquid and aimed it into her mouth.

"Grape juice," she said, licking her lips.

"Oh yeah," I said, directing my shaky hand to give her spoonful after spoonful, my heart pounding. "You haven't been able to drink liquid through your mouth for three months," I said.

"Help me get up. I need to go for a walk."

I started to say "You can't—you haven't walked for months," but changed it to "You do need to walk but maybe later!"

A nearby nurse alerted other staff and a bunch of floor nurses came running in who had never heard Phyllis speak and were crying with joy. Soon after she fell back to sleep. But for those two hours she was totally there. Must have been my singing Leonard Cohen songs that did it.

Wednesday, June 8, 2011 5:11 a.m. Coma Day 107.

It is beginning to seem that Phyllis's wakefulness isn't a flash-in-the-pan. She has continued to have wakeful days, conversations and sensations through most of Monday and Tuesday. Everyone who has seen her has a story. She surprised several of us by saying goodbye or answering a question when we thought she was asleep. On Monday, she said she was hungry! Her speech therapist fed her a whole container of pudding. News flash: it wasn't the health food kind! This was her first food taken by mouth since February.

Monday night when my sister Elizabeth arrived, Phyllis

greeted her with a huge smile. Tuesday, she stayed awake all day—through an eight-hour schedule of visitors, physical therapy, speech therapy, Feldenkrais treatment and craniosacral manipulation. My first inclination is to warn *caution: don't celebrate yet*, her pattern is to progress to wakefulness and then slip back into rest. But what the hell, let's celebrate! Bring on the clowns! This is the best she's done in three and a half months and whatever happens next, she and all of us deserve a big "Attagirl!" There will be time enough for me to get back to worrying over feeding her, strengthening her, maintaining her gains, improving her short term memory. In fact, if I get started I could dream all night about the things to worry about. The reality is that today, we got her back! Who of us can guarantee anything about tomorrow? Let's drink a pint and give thanks for today! Here's to all the nurses, techs, aides, cleaners, doctors, surgeons, drivers, pilots, hosts, clergy, Team Phyllis, my men's group, friends, family and most of all to Phyllis for this huge effort to heal with love.

I met with Phyllis's hospital team yesterday; they invite family to their weekly meeting. Everyone's excited about Phyllis's improvement. Ideas were kicked around. If she stays awake every day, could we skip one tube feeding and give her a meal by mouth? How much should volunteers do? Do we keep waking her up or let her rest? She still has almost no short-term memory, no recollection of who was here yesterday or what happened last week. So how can we work on that? Questions, questions. The truth is that none of us knows which therapy is working so we have to keep doing everything.

Friday, June 10, 2011, 4:36 a.m. Coma Day 109.

I'm noticing the strains in my own armor this week. Little things bother me. Phyllis's bed at City Hospital is not the high-tech kind. It has a box that pumps air into a thin air mattress on top of a foam one, instead of the more luxurious low-loss air bed she had previously. I asked the hospital to get her the better kind but it hasn't happened yet. Last night I noticed the black box that pumps the air had accidentally been turned off. It rankled me. Don't they know she needs the air moving under her to prevent skin breakdown? Sixty thousand Americans die of bedsores every year.

I think grief has a way of biding its time so that when you are in crisis mode, it's held in check. Then when things get better, grief says "now I get my due." Something like that was working on me today. I dropped over to the hospital to say goodnight. A friend was with her and Phyllis was doing fine but I just saw a fleeting look of pain on her face and it wrecked me. Sometimes you just have to live with grief until it gets better.

Saturday, June 11, 2011, 6:47 a.m. Coma Day 111.

I read Phyllis five chapters of Maya Angelou's *In My Name* this morning; then I asked her if she'd heard enough. Her eyes were closed. She said: "Read me another chapter." My heart soars when she lets me know she's awake, especially when I assume she's not aware of my existence.

Over the last 111 days of her ordeal, there have been

numerous points reached when Phyllis leapt forward. Some-times it seems they are not improvements at all but rather a loop in which she goes forward and falls back. In those darker days, I wonder if we will forever be marching in the wilderness. Of course I realize how far, in fact, she has come. No longer do we watch every vital sign in fear of a new infection. Her arms and legs have lost their swelling and the muscles are not stiff. *Most days*, she knows where she is and even the month of the year. There's a host of little improvements I'm always noticing. More often now, if you ask her a question for which she has no answer, she can say "I don't know" or "I'm thinking about it" instead of greeting you with a blank look of incomprehension followed by withdrawal. Self-awareness is the key and it's coming back, however fitfully.

So I woke this morning with a surge of hope in the trajectory of Phyllis's recovery. For sixteen weeks, I have worried over her ability to return to consciousness, what inhibited that return and whether the doctors, the hospitals and I were doing enough to keep her safe. While there are no guarantees in life, I now believe that she has begun the return to consciousness and will keep going. However, it turns out that her *return*, over which we have fretted these many weeks, is only a tiny part of the task ahead. Her brain, clearly intact and full of surprises, is still deep in its secret process of re-composing all the attributes of what will be the new Phyllis. Meanwhile, her brain also has to re-learn every muscle movement it has learned over a lifetime, from crawling on the floor to leaping over fences.

Consciousness and wakefulness are concepts that almost

everyone understands intuitively but which science has struggled mightily to define. Experiments and advanced technology
in the last ten years have filled in huge gaps in our understanding
but, as is often the case with science, each new revelation can
cause us to question previous assumptions. It now appears that a
region deep in the brain at the base of the brain's stem called the
central lateral thalamus may hold the key to activating wakefulness. Stimulation of the thalamus in unconscious monkeys has
been shown to revive monkeys from induced comas. And guess
what regions the thalamus surrounds? The same ventricles whose
swelling preceded Phyllis's coma!

My antenna is activated. No wonder her self-reconstruction
is so difficult. Perhaps someday, neurosurgeons will be able to
stimulate the thalamus in human coma patients but for now
it helps me to imagine the physical site in Phyllis's brain where
massive self-healing is happening.

Phyllis has a long, uncharted road ahead in reclaiming the
uniquely human experience of walking, talking and communi-
cating. Her brain must reconnect billions of cells, electrically
and chemically, in order to re-learn *intentional* physical movement as well as coherent speech and communication. Her
new consciousness, moreover, takes place either in the *present*
moment or the *distant* past but still shows little recall of the
recent past. She hasn't been able to recall who was here yesterday
or a month ago. She's not able to show true comprehension of
the process she's involved in (illness, hospitalization, treatment).
She *appears* to wake up each day as if for the first time. Yet she

has an almost perfect recall of long-ago experiences, names, faces and facts. Discovering the borderline between her past and present memory—and where it blurs and goes fuzzy—is one of my new obsessions.

Thursday, June 16, 2011. Coma Day 115.

Waking up every day as a conscious human being is something I no longer take for granted. The experience of watching Phyllis recover all the parts of herself is at times exhilarating and joyously instructive and at other times agonizingly painful and discouraging. And her reality can fluctuate between those two poles as frequently as every few hours. Just this past week, I was with her when she was intact and unscathed, completely aware of herself and her surroundings, even remembering my sister Elizabeth's visit and the impending arrival of our daughter Angela. On several of those wonderful days, she started moving her arms. She proved she could eat, swallow, digest food and drink liquids without the feeding tube that is cut into her abdomen.

Sitting together outside her room by the aviary today, I watched the birds frolic. "Hey, you want to go outside to the garden?" I wasn't sure if I had permission to do that but I didn't care.

Phyllis just looked straight ahead so I wheeled her in her recliner down the dark hallway past all the patients the nurses had rolled out of their rooms but who hardly ever spoke. Phyllis didn't speak at all either. I never know for sure what level of her being I am talking to but today I need a confirmation and I'm ready to break some rules with her, if I can get through.

"How's that for fresh air and sunshine?" I say, as I slip her through a rarely-used back door leading to a garden squeezed between two wings of the single-story building. The outdoor garden is a lovingly designed small getaway with herbs and pine trees tucked between rooms. I pull up a wooden chair to sit beside her as a strong wind blows through the leaves of the trees above us, dappling the sunshine I knew she wanted to feel on her face. It could be the morning breeze as we sat on the porch in Tilzapotla years ago. Really I should be grateful to be right here, right now in Fayetteville, Arkansas, crown jewel of the Ozark Mountains where the hot tongues of the Oklahoma prairie winds rush eastward to be cooled by the hollers, creeks and green hills of our hometown.

"You know," I said, trying to keep the one-way conversation going, "I was writing early this morning—in that journal of mine I told you about—and somehow I remembered the day our dog Gringo died. I know I should just have happy thoughts but that memory just popped up." She didn't answer or show any sign of comprehension. "You and I were sitting in the veterinarian's office as they tried to save him and then all those other dogs started howling and the man came out and said Gringo was dead. And you held me and said 'Do you know how much I love you?' That's how I feel now. This has been rough but this is not where it ends! We're going to get past this. We're going to do it *together*."

Tears ran down her face and her lower lip moved. Shock and grief and joy and tears moved down from my brain and over my body like a cool shower on a hot day. I dried her tears and she touched mine. Then her face went blank. She had been there completely for the moment and then she wasn't.

Back in her room, an aide used the motorized sling to place Phyllis back in bed. She turned inward—not even opening her eyes, over which she has limited control anyway. Her muscles tightened, her knees pulled together stiffly and her arms trembled slightly. Finally, her body was calm.

I want to hope. I want to believe. I *do* believe. And just as I do, hope and belief are wrenched from my grasp, stolen by an invisible thief.

CHAPTER TWELVE

TORTILLAS AND TEQUILA IN TILZAPOTLA

I'll always do my best for her
On that I give my word

                    —Bob Dylan, "Shelter From the Storm"

January 3, 1973

We celebrated the New Year by leaving America behind once more. In the five months since we came together in Santa Fe, we had traveled down the Sierra Madre to central Mexico, adventured into the mountains of Guerrero, separated and then came back together in New York, snuggled together in a snow-packed tipi in Woodstock, and picked fruit in Florida's orchards. In that short time, we had lived what felt like several lifetimes. Now there was no question of our commitment to a course of shared adventure. Heading south into Mexico again, Phyllis and I, together with our four dogs, packed into the front of the Muleskinner as we sang again from our songbook, "Don't try to use me or slyly refuse me, just win me or lose me, it is this that the darkness is for," from Leonard Cohen's "Lady Midnight."

The Muleskinner rolled quietly south out of Ciudad Valles, Mexico. The lyrics were written in a cheap spiral notebook, with others I had started compiling on the road before meeting Phyllis. The power of "Positively 4th Street" is its unapologetic middle-finger salute to anyone who had failed to believe in you. We just sang our hearts out, never mentioning who we were singing it to. But since we sang it together, it also reinforced our belief in each other, an affirmation that we were to each other, unlike the target of the song, the friend that *could* be trusted.

Phyllis and I shared our independently acquired musical influences from the time we met. Our songbook became a manual of mutually agreed-upon songs, a record of our spiritual influences and a contract of our shared beliefs. Neither one of us could carry a tune but we had the notes in our head so it didn't matter. The *spirit* of the lyrics, the message of the song, was everything and we debated whether a given song was worthy of being recorded in the songbook. Phyllis exposed me for the first time to Motown "girl groups," music I would have previously dismissed as pop drivel. Martha and The Vandellas' "Heat Wave" isn't just puppy love radio music; it makes you *move*, it starts in your gut, explodes like a rocket and shouts *heat wave!* and makes you wanna dance.

In return, I turned Phyllis on to Leonard Cohen, a poet often dismissed by critics in the seventies as a dark, depressing folk singer past his prime, the "prophet of gloom." Cohen's self-deprecating, compassionate lyrics achieved the opposite for me, renewing my joy by making it an ally of pain, deepening my faith by joining it with lust and maturing my understanding

of love by offering it as the only way to unite the contradictions of the human illusion of separateness. I sang Cohen's "You
Know Who I Am" to Phyllis, as it was intended, a lover's offer
to surrender to her "a broken man"—along with instructions for
repair.

Was I *broken*? Only where it mattered, in my heart, in the
loss of faith in all that I had been told was sacred. To that, I
imagined Leonard would have said: "Good start. Get over it.
Find someone to love and let some light into the world." Whatever emotion we experienced, there was a tune in the songbook
to fill our hearts.

We continued to wander slowly down the historic Pan-
American Highway, a post-World War II international project
destined to connect the northern and southern continents with
a unitary roadway. The Mexican portion of the Pan-American
opened in 1950 from the U.S. border to Guatemala. As I drove,
Phyllis and I huddled together on the wooden front bench,
our dogs hunched beside and behind us. How was it possible,
I wondered, that I had randomly encountered the one person
on the globe who accepted me for who I was and even seemed
to enjoy the experience? Driving along together at an old-world
pace of twenty-five miles an hour, we watched the passing view
through our open windows like it was a movie in which we
starred but hadn't been given a script. What was there to do but
enjoy each moment?

"Did you know," I said, "that the Pan-American Highway
is the longest continually-paved highway in the world, running
from Alaska to the tip of Chile? In 1950, when I was three,

my family and I navigated it from the Texas border to central
Mexico just after it was finished." Every year until I was ten
we repeated the trip. It was my favorite part of the year; once
our family station wagon crossed the border at Laredo, we were
plunged into the desert on the way to Monterrey. My sisters and
I made up a game trying to be the first to spot the Sierra Madre
mountains looming above Monterrey. From there to Ciudad
Valles, the road goes around to the east of the big mountains,
lingers a few thousand feet above the Gulf Coast, immerses you
in fruit orchards and waterfalls, then tempts you with distant,
out-of-focus mountain peaks in the clouds.

"I love when you talk to me like a travel agent," she said,
with a mischievous smile.

By the time Phyllis and I traveled there, the two-lane,
twisting Pan-American had lost its modern glitter, having been
upstaged by a new divided, four-lane highway a hundred miles
to our west. But I loved the old road all the more, old-world but
still luxuriating in tropical growth, thick jungles with jaguars
and hints of lost empires. Every town of any size had a plaza
with elaborate floral displays and a nearby colonial hotel with
sparkling-clean red tile floors and delicious restaurants set in
outdoor, shaded patios.

After sleeping the night in the jungle outside of town, we
ate breakfast at the distinguished but fading Hotel Valles, an
old colonial-era red-tiled jewel built in the 1930s and set in a
tropical paradise complete with the high-pitched screams of
peacocks that roamed free in the gardens. We had camped the
night before in a fruit orchard near the formerly grand Hotel

Taninul, another of my parents' favorite stops. I half expected to see Graham Greene, master storyteller of decadent expatriates, sipping coffee at a table near us at the Hotel Valles.

Mexico was imprinted in my brain, my family came here so often. After Valles, we'll climb the high road to a Huastec Indian town named Tamazunchale. My dad pronounced it *Thomas-and-Charley*. When it opened, the Pan-American Highway was an engineering marvel, an endless maze of switchbacks snaking its way through a tropical jungle. It's as if they chiseled it out of a mountainside, with waterfalls diving under the highway on two-lane bridges, wild orchids, corn everywhere, avocado trees, agave plants, marigolds, oranges, grapefruits and tangerines so sweet they were like no fruit you ever tasted.

After breakfast in Valles and a trip to the market to buy food supplies, we were back in the Muleskinner, slowly ascending the Pan-American's runway to the heavens. Phyllis rested her head dreamily on my shoulder. "I get mixed up about who is a Spaniard here, who is *campesino*, who is indigenous and who is just plain *Mexican*. When I was an exchange student in Mexico City, it was easy to tell. My host parents were proud of their Spanish ancestry and everyone not in their social class was a peasant to them. But you talk about *Indios* as if they were different from the poor domestic help at their house."

"Ethnic origin is a complicated mess in Mexico because unlike the American colonial genocide against American indigenous people, the Spanish *conquistadores* conquered and then enslaved but also intermarried with the locals. So you have 500 years of mixed families. How *Indian* you are isn't really determined by blood; it's about how isolated in the wilderness you are."

"How'd you learn all this?"

"The last two years when I was living in Cuernavaca, I went to a lot of seminars at CIDOC, this free institute founded by Ivan Illich, an Austrian writer and defrocked Catholic priest. I rented a room in the house of Illich's editor, Greer Taylor, and went to classes at CIDOC. My favorite seminar was one about hidden indigenous communities in Mexico who keep their own languages and cultures and live out of sight in the wilderness. The line between the past and present is all tangled up there."

"What do you mean 'tangled up'?"

"I mean the indigenous people themselves were always fighting and enslaving each other, then the Spaniards came along and enslaved everybody but instead of slaughtering them, they intermarried and formed a new race we call Mexicans."

Understanding Mexico's indigenous history was an obsession for me but it was also personal. Having rejected and abandoned the social contract of my own culture—the shared assumptions, sets of rules, accepted history and national goals that make a civilization cohesive, I hadn't replaced it with anything. I needed to know where I belonged. My parents had been bringing me to Mexico my whole life, somewhere here was a clue to my future.

After a full day of following the curvy highway through the jungle, we arrived in Tamazunchale, a town that in the pre-Aztec 1400s was the capital of the Huastec nation. The Huasteca themselves were a remnant of an earlier Mayan civilization. In the 15th century, the Huasteca were defeated twice, first by the Aztecs as they took control of most of Mexico and then again fifty years later by the Spanish invader Cortez. The Huasteca today still speak a local dialect of Nahuatl, the language imposed by the Aztecs to unify the country, much in the same way as the Romans used Latin to unify the Holy Roman Empire. Nahuatl is the same root language that Indians speak in the Guerrero mountains above Tilzapotla. And like the mountainous regions above Tilza, remote Huasteca villagers live like their ancestors did a thousand years ago.

Feeling strangely very much at home in that ancient land, Phyllis and I drove a few more days to arrive in Tilzapotla. The old Pan-American Highway 85 continues around the high volcanic cones that tower over Mexico City. In a two-day drive, you cross virtually every known climate zone, excepting arctic ones. Finally, in order to enter the state of Morelos, you must pass by the feet of two mystical and still-smoking volcanoes, Iztacchihuatl and Popocatépetl (Izta and Popo, for short), respectively 17,159 and 17,802 feet high. Across the fertile Morelos valley laid out at the feet of Izta and Popo, we could see the cut in the Sierra Madre that leads south to Guerrero and the ocean. At the entrance to the pass lies Tilzapotla.

After a cold night in the highlands, we drove across Morelos in bright sunshine. The climate in Morelos is key to understanding its history. From May to October, Morelos is a rainforest with heavy rain falling daily in the mountains and running down steep barrancas into the "sugar bowl" below. Only one river, the Amacusac, flows out of Morelos, exiting through a cut in the Sierra called Paso Morelos toward Guerrero and the Pacific Ocean.

From November to April, Morelos is arid, almost completely without rainfall. Throughout the 1800s and 1900s, the lowland valley was home to a highly profitable sugarcane industry, for which the labor was provided by indigenous indios living in the highlands. Historically, the indios were allowed to control just enough commercially unproductive highland land to raise their own food in the rainy season and work as agricultural laborers for the sugarcane *hacendados* in the dry season.

Bumpy Mexican roads and the Muleskinner delivered Phyllis and me once again through the fertile breadbasket that was the valley of Morelos, through small foothills carpeted with sugarcane and up the deeply rutted red dirt road to Tilzapotla, Mexico. We brought presents for Augustina, Veronica and Don Lauro, including a $30 used refrigerator we had smuggled past Mexican customs by stocking it with ice and groceries in order to pretend it was our RV fridge used for travel. Augustina welcomed us and our four dogs as if we were her lost children.

Once we were back safely under Augustina's wing, Phyllis suddenly had both purpose and mission. To Augustina, she was a daughter who came home, willing and eager to learn the old ways: when to pick the squash blossom flower for breading and frying and how to gauge the proper amount of wood heat under the comal, the large round clay griddle on which all cooking was performed. Augustina taught Phyllis what every daughter would know in Tilza: how to braid your hair, how to make masa and all the myriad dishes to be produced from that magical corn dough.

We lived with Augustina, who was then seventy years old, and Don Lauro, who was well over eighty. They no longer raised corn but their sons, Abel and Aurelio, did and both gave a tributary portion to their parents. The corn was stored in an adobe and straw egg-shaped granary in the yard. Corn in rural Mexico was both principal food and the coin of the realm, as useful as gold for trading. Augustina saw very few pesos cross her hands but on any given day, she would meter out an eighth liter corn portion as payment for cooking oil at the corner *tienda* or in a pinch, in the middle of the dry season, a quarter liter measure of dried corn in exchange for vegetables.

My role in Tilza was more problematic than Phyllis's. We had returned to Tilza in the winter dry season which meant the men didn't have to tend the corn fields far up the mountainside. Augustina's sons lived two hours away in La Tigra, the high mountain town where previously she and Don Lauro had lived all their adult lives. We lived in Tilzapotla with the old folks.

I spent a lot of time teaching myself to draw. I sometimes hiked alone part-way up the mountain following the steep barranca trail that ascended 3,000 feet to the Guerrero border. A few times I rented a horse from a prominent farmer, Don Felipe, to ride further up the trail. Mostly I daydreamed of returning to the wilderness that Larry and I had crossed and schemed to take Phyllis back there.

Although Augustina didn't really approve of dogs as pets,

she wholeheartedly accepted them as working members of the household, especially as security for her chickens who, since our departure in October, had been relocated to a partially-finished, uncovered adobe room attached to the house. Augustina had her own dog, named Tallarin, who resembled a street-tough, scarred mix of pit bull and collie. Tallarin lived outdoors and split his time between Tilzapotla and La Tigra, two-hours' walking distance away, where Augustina and Don Lauro had lived from 1915 until a few years earlier when Don Lauro's health forced them to move to Tilzapotla. Tallarin was free to come and go and knew he would receive leftover food scraps in either location. Whenever Tallarin entered the compound, all our dogs immediately showed him deference as leader of the pack.

"Augustina," I asked one evening after our light dinner meal of tortillas, rice and beans. "How did you and Don Lauro meet?"

"It was in 1915," she replied. "The revolution began in 1910 when I was ten years old. I lived in Huazulco, not far from the *revolucionario* Emiliano Zapata's hometown of Anenecuilco. By the time I was fifteen, our town had been burned twice and bombed more times than I can count. The war was still going on. All the men from our town had either gone to the mountains to fight with Zapata or had been arrested by the government and sent to jails in Quintana Roo. There was nothing to eat and nowhere to live. My parents were dead. A group of us girls heard about a place across Morelos in the mountains where there were young men hiding out and planting corn who needed wives. We walked across Morelos to La Tigra. I worked for a while for an old lady who didn't treat me very well. I was up before dawn, drawing water from the town well. That's where I met *mi pareja*, Lauro—at the well."

"Did he ask you to marry him, just like that?"

"No, his sisters hated me and tried to run me off. The way it was supposed to be done back in those days, once a man was sure you wanted him, he would ride in one day on his horse, grab you up and you would go live in the Sierra for a few days. Then, you would come back to town and that was it; you were together."

"Ay yay yay!" I said. "Is that what Don Lauro did?"

"No, he was too shy. I had to tell him he better hurry up and catch me."

Tilzapotla had a population of almost 10,000 but it felt much smaller.

Electricity had recently arrived but most houses used it sparingly, perhaps for a light bulb or two. If there was a TV in town, I didn't know of it. Having returned in January, we were in the beginning of *las secas*, the dry season. Typically no rain would fall for five months. Water levels in wells would slowly fall as the water table evaporated. By late February, we were helping Augentina carry buckets of water from the only still-functioning well five blocks away. Many fruits matured in the spring: ciruela plums in our yard and papayas in the neighbor's orchard. After chores were done, we often hiked with Augustina to gather *nananches*, a small yellow fruit the size of a cherry, that grew wild in the fields.

Living in Tilzapotla with Phyllis had an other-worldly feel. For all my travels in Mexico, I had always been a foreigner—either a tourist's kid or a tourist myself. Under Augustina's wing, we were somehow accepted as residents of Tilzapotla and were being taught the ways of living in a village. And I was divinely happy, most of the time anyway, to be just living a simple domestic life with Phyllis. Since Tilzapotla was only a few decades past being an indigenous village itself, there was plenty for me to learn. When Augustina arrived in the valley in 1915, most inhabitants spoke only Nahuatl. Now sixty years later, most observers would call Tilzapotlans *Mexican*. No doubt almost all had mixed indigenous and Spanish genetic roots, the correct term for which is *Mestizo* (literally *mixed*). But to a middle upper-class resident of Mexico City, they were all *Indios*.

Families in Tilzapotla almost universally planted corn. *Maiz* grew in every possible spot and in a few that seemed impossible. Every family had their own heirloom variety, saved and carefully selected at every harvest for centuries. Corn itself evolved from the teosinte plant whose origin is in the nearby Sierra Madre Del Sur of Guerrero. With the help of humans, corn has adapted with miraculous accuracy to the climate of the humans nurturing it. Winter squash and climbing beans were planted shortly after the corn stalk emerged. The work of planting, tending and harvesting lasted from May to November; the rest of the year was free for the rest of the tasks of self-subsistence and celebration.

Domesticated life in Tilzapotla was easy and dreamlike. Our American savings seemed to last forever since there was so little to spend money on. Augustina introduced us to family and friends around town and in the country. We helped her sons, who still lived two hours away in La Tigra, to make adobe bricks from mud by the lake. Sometimes we borrowed horses to ride together up the mountain trail to a swimming hole by a waterfall. We waited in line at the neighbor's *molino*, a mill recently adapted to electricity, with eight-year-old Veronica, while Don Serapio ground her bucket of lime-soaked corn into pliable white masa, the basic foodstuff of the culture.

While my high school and college classmates from Texas were pursuing careers in business and getting married, I was getting a master's degree in village life. Phyllis and I walked daily through this ancient village—Tilza—as it buzzed with activity: men baking bread in outdoor brick ovens, neighbors replacing adobes and whitewashing the walls with *cal*, and farmers milking cows and making *queso fresco*—a quick white cheese made from warm fresh milk, vinegar and salt. On the central plaza, vegetable and fruit stands lined the square, in the center of which were fondas selling tacos and tortas, and carts selling fresh fruit cups with chile powder and a new phenomena made possible by electricity—the licuado stand, offering delicious smoothie blends with the fresh fruit of the day.

Domesticated life in this setting came easy for us, the weather suited our clothes. But it was still *domesticated* life. Standing in the square, carrying the produce Phyllis had bought for Augustina, I only had to look up to see the tropical mountains of Guerrero towering above us and calling my name. I felt the pull stronger every day—the convergence of all the trails of my life. From the time I was an infant riding in the back of my parents' station wagon traveling this same route south on the backbone of the Sierra Madre up to my most recent hike up the mountain over Tilza, each trip brought me slightly closer to an understanding of why that path was destined for me.

Now I had a *mujer*, a woman who not only loved me but who gave me credibility as an adult in village life. As wonderful as that was, it also reminded me I had not finished the journey I'd set out on to find out *who I really was*. Somewhere up the trail that led up the mountain from Tilzapotla to Guerrero lay the answers to where my life should lead. I had refused to join my country's army and fight to defend it against enemies my government claimed to be a threat to all I loved. I knew the government was lying but what kind of life was I proposing instead?

It was the siren call I had heard all my life, calling from just up the mountain, just around the next bend, just beyond what everyone knew as home. I had been, I realized, on this path all my life but now I realized I didn't have to do it alone. I had found the *secret ring*, the magical amulet that let me keep going: it was Phyllis, the one human being who did not try to protect me or defend me or depend on me or change me but who just wanted to be my friend—forever. Could I risk that treasure on a crazy walkabout in the wilderness?

September 25, 1973

I had barely been able to sleep the night before. After eight months in Tilzapotla, I was ready to tell Phyllis I wanted us once again to say goodbye to Augustina and Don Lauro and head *up* the mountain path south into the wilderness of Guerrero. I had planned and schemed for this moment from the time we arrived in Tilza. During every visit to a neighbor and every errand run, I was taking mental notes and learning how life was lived on the land, what clues I could pick up on how to survive moving through the mountains. The song I chose frequently from our songbook was Cohen's "Winter Lady" with its sad question from a lover which I translated to: *Why would you leave me now? You chose me before you knew me.* It was the question I imagined having to ask Phyllis when she turned cold at my call to adventure.

"Are you awake?" I nudged Phyllis as the first light of dawn snuck through the roof tiles. "I have to tell you something."

"You think I can't read your mind?" she said sharply but softened her tone by snuggling close.

"No, you don't understand. I'm talking about leaving everything here and going over the mountain. I mean I want *us* to go. I *need* you to go with me. But I have to do it." I clenched my teeth waiting for her reply.

"Of course we're going," she said smiling. "We both knew you had to do this. I've just been waiting for you to prepare yourself. And this time, we're ready for it. I want to go as much as you."

CHAPTER THIRTEEN

PEEKING OUT FROM THE UNCONSCIOUS BRAIN

You must have seen a miracle time and time again
If I can leave a number and the next one you see . . .
— Jesse Winchester, "I'm Looking for a Miracle"

Sunday, June 19, 2011. Coma Day 118.

Our six children rearranged their lives and gathered this morning at City Hospital in Fayetteville to celebrate Father's Day with Phyllis and me. Seeing them together is like a review of the decades of our history. Travis, Julia and Joey were born in the 1970s; Preston, Angela and Andrew in the 1980s. All were born at home—wherever *home* was at the time—the older three, respectively, in Vermont, Mexico and Houston and the younger three all in our house in Fayetteville, Arkansas with the help of the same midwife, Kate. Today two of them— Joey and Preston—live near us in Fayetteville. Two others —Travis and Andrew—are in Austin, Texas. Our two daughters live the farthest away, Julia in San Diego and Angela in Chicago. For the last sixteen weeks, all our children have been coming and going in a round-robin schedule to be with their mom.

Phyllis is dressed today in a blue hospital gown, seated in her portable brown-leather recliner. Her eyes are closed; she doesn't look like she's going to make a "conscious" appearance today. Staff lets us borrow the hospital boardroom and with our son Travis on guitar, the whole family belts out rounds of old-time family songbook favorites: "You Are My Sunshine," The Band's "Daniel and The Sacred Harp," the Beatles' "Rocky Raccoon," and Traveling Wilburys' "Tweeter and the Monkey Man." This is the family singing tradition that began with the songbook Phyllis and I carried through Mexico and evolved into our family's at-times-obscure, never-in-tune but passionately well-practiced repertoire.

Phyllis's eyes stay closed but I imagine them to be smiling. The more we sing, the more Phyllis looks like, well, *herself.* Our friend Ginny arrives and suggests we sing one of Phyllis's favorite songs, a Dylan ballad called "Boots of Spanish Leather," an old standby from our songbook. Travis knows the song and plays it but falters a bit on the lyrics. Remembering to always include Phyllis *as if* she was conscious, I say "Phyllis, help us out with the song." To everyone's amazement, she proceeds to sing the remaining three verses out loud without ever opening her eyes. Lines like: "I'm sure your mind is a-roamin', I'm sure your thoughts are not with me, But with the country to where you're goin'" bring tears of pain and joy as we sing, especially when her voice wavers a bit on the line: "I might be gone a long old time." The song itself isn't clear whether the wandering lover will ever return, but it offers solace that those left behind are not forgotten.

Everyone is crying with joy at this exhibition of Phyllis's presence. No one knows whether to call it consciousness; her eyes are not open, after all, and she does not otherwise speak to us. But our tears now are universally ones of joy; we don't need the distinction between awake and asleep. We needed Phyllis today and we got her.

Today all the kids walk with me in a procession as I wheel Phyllis's chair back to the sunny room at the end of the hall, past the blank-stares of patients neatly wrapped with blankets in wheelchairs, for whom no visitors arrive. The movement of her chair causes Phyllis to open her eyes but she doesn't speak. The strong arms of Joe, her Oklahoma Cherokee orderly, lift her into bed. Love and loss, tenderness and loneliness whirl around my head as I fall asleep.

Monday, June 20, 2011. Coma Day 119.

Early in the morning I walk the five blocks from home to City Hospital, the sky already awake. Phyllis is sleeping. As I touch her head and massage her feet, I play another songbook entry, "So Far Away", on a CD from Carole King and James Taylor. She opens her eyes and we share a bowl of oatmeal.

She speaks. "You have a bite," she says, as I feed her. The nurse enters with her rolling sling lift that looks like a giant version of the baby-slings we once used to take our babies hiking. With Phyllis up out of bed and tucked into her brown movable recliner, we wheel around the single-story hospital, past the cafeteria to the physical therapy room.

As I watch the therapist move her limbs, I blot out of my mind any reminders that Phyllis has no short-term memory and may not even truly recognize me. I fantasize running away together. We could just roll down the sidewalk and keep going. I could buy a handicap-accessible van and we could live on the road, singing memories from our songbook.

Tuesday, June 22, 2011. Coma Day 121.

Phyllis *does* remember that she has an appetite. She has made a huge transition to *eating* three meals a day. She still has a feeding "Peg Tube" inserted through her belly into her stomach, hidden under the sheets and her gown but it's gradually becoming obsolete like all the other tubes, wires, sensors, pathways, intravenous highways and electric monitors that once covered her body.

What comes now is the task of preparing food for her. How funny life is; Phyllis always encouraged me to learn to cook. I have been a faithful cooking *assistant* for forty years but never was I in charge of choosing the menu or even deciding the main dishes. Of course, the hospital cooks food and they do make a lot of their own dishes from scratch. But Phyllis has been enmeshed from birth in the Italian tradition of the importance of home-cooked food and all of her adult life has taught and practiced the art of healing through whole food. Now it's my turn to learn what I've lazily benefited from all these years and return the favor of freshly prepared meals.

Phyllis is very happy today, smiling with her whole face, enjoying her food and making funny one-liners. Some samples: When someone asked when I would be back, she said "Frank has a *weird* schedule," raising her eyebrows. While sitting out in the garden, she sent me off to get her ice water to drink. "I'll just wait here," she said, as if there was another choice.

I know that whether Phyllis could open her eyes and say hello to them or not, our children's visit last weekend has fed her soul, strengthened her will and given her six more reasons to carry on.

Sunday, June 26, 2011, 5:03 a.m. Coma Day 125.

The art of watching Phyllis this week has turned back into the slow meditation of watching a tree grow. There were so many giant leaps early in the week climaxed with Phyllis leading us all in song—that it was expected that some consolidation/sleep was inevitable. Sure enough, she hasn't spoken or opened her eyes for four days. But just as I began to despair, Phyllis sang again with me this morning as we harmonized on (granted I'm stretching the meaning of *harmony*) Cohen's "A Bunch of Lonesome Heroes," Leonard's song of young soldiers talking out along the open road, one of them desperate to tell his story. Maybe it's why I want to tell *her* story, so she can feel *known*.

I was with Phyllis at all her three meals today. She lifts her arm to hold a cup as I move to steady it with my own arm. She waves me away. One-hundred-and-twenty-five days have passed since she could hold a cup by herself! I'm struggling to come up with home-cooked meals, although she eats really small portions. Eating makes her sleepy, so sometimes I have to keep waking her up during the meal. Sleep is still the thing she does most of the time but she can wake up from it in the funniest ways.

One day, she was sleeping in her chair. The nurse came in behind her, out of her sight, and said hello in a quiet voice. Phyllis immediately responded "Hello Tonya." She calls the hospital staff her "nurse friends"—when she's talking, that is, which isn't that often. As always, the hard part is balancing these incredible gains with the hours of lethargy that follow them. Also, with her being awake more often, it's harder to leave her as I keep my "weird work schedule" as she calls it. She has this way of asking "Where are you off to?" that makes me not want to leave. But as soon as she sees me staying, she goes to sleep! By the afternoon, she won't remember that I left. It's a confusing mess because she has no short-term memory; every day is groundhog day; every day I tell her all over again where she is and why. And yet she knows the names of all our children and all their stories. Round and round we go as the carousel turns.

Wednesday, June 29, 2011, 5:45 a.m. Coma Day 128.

The last three days for Phyllis, like so many before, were taken up with interior journeys. For me, as both reporter and anxious suitor, the sleepy days don't sit easy. Sunday, she slept. Monday, she woke and ate light meals but was groggy. Tuesday, she slept. After eating with gusto and serenading her family, she returns to mostly sleeping and being non-responsive. I know the pattern well but I haven't learned to like it. I turn back in my journal for clues and I hear my own advice. *Let go and accept what is. Breathe through frustration into patience. Wait for the carousel to finish turning.* I know it's all good advice but the turning of time's wheel wears me down. She's come such a long, long way from the days three months ago when all her body functions were monitored and controlled, with wires and tubes attached to a screen with wavy lines that made us fear every breath could be her last. But then we've got such a very long, long way to go. She must begin to move her body consciously or she may be permanently half-awake, while her body continues to deteriorate. Her only chance at recovery is to get up out of bed and begin to move.

Monday, July 4, 2011. Coma Day 133.

Dr. Mark decided today that Phyllis needs to push the envelope. He has ordered a full daily schedule of physical (leg), occupational (arm) and speech therapy. How, I wonder, is this going to work if she can't stay conscious? Nevertheless, at 8 a.m., her nurse uses the mechanical lift with a sling to position Phyllis in a rolling chair. She is wheeled off to therapy and I am left behind like a parent watching his child leave for the first day of school.

Friday, July 8, 2011. Coma Day 137.

Dr. Mark's decision to move ahead with therapy quickly proved to be a very good one. Previously impossible movements are starting to happen. Phyllis lifted both arms (though slowly and with great effort) and almost touched her nose with her left hand. Just yesterday, after massaging her legs, I asked her to move her leg and she picked up her right leg several inches! That is the first controlled leg movement she's had since the bacterial infection blew up her brain 137 days ago. Please, God, don't let me get attached to anything as permanent; just let me be grateful for today.

During the limited hours Phyllis was awake outside of therapy, she was more clear-headed. I put on a boisterous Eric Clapton CD and she repeated the refrain of the song "Hoochie Coochie Man." The line goes "Everybody knows I'm . . ." and she asked what the last word was. I had to Google it but appropriately the line was "Everybody knows I'm *here*." Indeed we do, Phyllis! Even more exciting, she has shown a few glimmers of short-term memory improvement. She remembered all week that our daughter Julia was in town. She remembered that our friend Barbara's daughter-in-law and son were expecting a baby and cried tears of joy when she heard that a healthy baby girl was born.

So, her progress is steady (although even in saying so, I question for how long), her hair beautiful, her skin rosy, her mind clearing and her limbs stirring. All this awakening happens, of course, against the background of a *very* slow pace of change, many more hours asleep than awake and many more impaired hours than clear ones. She has no comments on the last four months or, so far, any memory of them.

"Hey Phyl," I ask her in the afternoon after therapy, "where are we?"

"In the hospital," she says wearily, as if she's bored by tedious questions.

"How long have we been here?" I press.

"A damn long time!" she says, as if to tell me *enough with the interrogation.* "Frank, you know how Chris signs off of the emails you read to me with *baci e abbracci*? Does that mean hugs and kisses?"

I am smiling and my heart is racing now at the clarity of her presence. "It does! Maybe we should get some Italian language training CDs from the library. We could practice together."

I get two raised eyebrows and then closed eyelids for an answer.

Saturday, July 9, 2011. Coma Day 138.

Early morning in Phyllis's room and she is asleep. I close my eyes and put one palm on her forehead and the other on her belly. We pass electrons back and forth for a while until the nurse arrives. Just as she does, Phyllis begins to twitch her face and roll her eyes. It's another electrical brain-storm; her eyes close and she doesn't respond to me. This has been happening more lately and it unnerves me, though the doctors are not alarmed.

Early in her diagnosis, doctors feared the swelling in her

brain had caused seizures and the seizures led to her coma. But our life-flight plane ride to Barnes-Jewish Hospital in St. Louis in April ruled that diagnosis out. Even so, something abnormal is happening in her brain! When electrical pathways in the brain are blocked by an injury and the signals are short-circuited, the disconnects can be generalized all over the brain, or more localized, causing a myriad of symptoms from twitching to anxiety and great fear. Although medical diagnosis ruled out seizures in her case, she continues to have these localized electrical short circuits in parts of her brain, small thunderstorms coursing through her brain as she journeys through the unconscious darkness.

Because of these continuing symptoms, I made a hard decision for Phyllis a week ago which was implemented this week, one that gives me pause and leads me to second-guess myself: namely, we increased her dose of Ritalin. She's been receiving Ritalin for three weeks now. Commonly known for its use in children with Attention Deficit Disorder, Ritalin is supposed to have a stimulating effect in cases of impaired wakefulness. It is a psycho-stimulant thought to work by altering the brain's supply of dopamine and increasing oxygen supply. We started her on a pediatric dose and have slowly increased her from five milligrams to twenty twice a day, still a relatively small dosage for this application. Now the dose will be doubled to forty milligrams, twice a day.

My reservations about Ritalin are, first, that Phyllis doesn't like psycho-stimulants and has refused to take them in the past. If it wasn't a "natural substance" occurring in nature, she didn't want it. Over the years, she felt depressed at times, given the stresses of raising six children and recurring financial difficulties. But even when all those pressures weighed her down, she always felt it was her own responsibility to evaluate and control her behavior. She refused the pharmaceutical remedy. So I feel guilty just deciding on my own to give her mood-altering medication.

But this is not about mood, is it? It's about jarring the brain into wakefulness. But it's also hard for me to know the side effects she might experience. She doesn't appear to suffer from the listed side-effects but so little is known about someone in her condition. My experience as a caretaker is that you have to assume these responsibilities; doctors are simply not going to do it for you. Or if they do, you will be stuck with their choices. So you make the best decision you can and you live with it. Ritalin *seems* to be helping but it might be that her recovery would have progressed the same without it. It's even possible that Ritalin causes some of her cycling from wake to sleep or is causing her mental confusion and eye-twitching. You don't know but you have to try. You hope that love and time will prove you right.

Sunday, July 10, 2011. Coma Day 139.

Phyllis's family in California is celebrating her mother Julia's ninetieth birthday with a big-tent celebration. She has been in poor health and so Phyllis's father hasn't told Julia of Phyllis's coma. Nor have I mentioned her mother's ill health to Phyllis. The fear is that the emotional strain would be too much for both of them. Somehow it feels wrong.

It is hard to really know Phyllis without experiencing her family. Her mother, Julia Petrella, was born Giulia D'Auria in 1921on the Amalfi Coast of southern Italy. The year she was born in Italy was a time of political upheaval and unrest in Rome. Her town, Maiori, more than 2,000 years old, was a Roman beach resort for centuries. Maiori was also a beachhead for the American invasion of Italy in 1943, when Giulia was twenty-two years old. After the end of World War II, she bravely set out on an ocean voyage to New York City. Connected by centuries of traditions to Amalfi, the lady we now lovingly call Grandma Julia, started a new American story when she married Frank Louis Petrella and started a family in Brooklyn, New York. Several brothers from the Petrella family married D'Auria family sisters and cousins, so the bonds were infinitely strong. Whenever there were family events in Brooklyn or later in Queens, and Long Island, there were aunts, uncles and cousins by the dozens. Phyllis was born into a giant extended family with her mother at the center.

Sunday, July 17, 2011, 6:04 a.m. Coma Day 146.

Phyllis's consciousness hasn't flowed this week. In fact, nothing has flowed this week. It's been too hot for me to even get out and walk. If I don't move my legs, I don't move my lungs. Without enough oxygen in the blood, my brain imagines the hospital walls are caving in. I know the pattern; I know the alternatives. I just didn't do it this week. As I make my way back and forth from home to hospital, I become obsessed with the multitude of decisions to be made in the future, all the unanswerable questions. Phyllis is on this path slowly climbing a mountain but I get tired and it's hard to keep the long-range view.

In an effort to escape the fearful slowness of Phyllis's progress, I am looking hard to regain perspective. I found a fascinating book called *Enigma: The Secret Lives of the Brain* by David Eagleman. He makes a compelling argument that "consciousness" is just the tip of the iceberg in the explanation of how our brain works and that consciousness, therefore, is extremely overrated as the driver of human achievement.

Eagleman implies that the drive to self-awareness reveals the infinite wonder of our mental structure and ability. Our brain only trusts a small percentage of our actions to our conscious mind at any given point because conscious thought is so slow that the brain can't be bothered with it most of the time. If a professional tennis player were to think *consciously* during a match about how she moves her body to strike the ball and what her strategy should be to outwit her opponent, even I could beat her. Instead the subconscious brain spends a lifetime *memorizing patterns* and then hiding them from your conscious mind.

Eagleman's explanation makes sense to me. Phyllis is *re-learning* and passing along to her more powerful unconscious mind, physical movements of many kinds. If I had a freeze-motion video of her feeding herself with a spoon, you would see the experimentation of the mind and how it adapts and experiments until it finds a way to balance the utensil, hold it tight and memorize the movement. If there is some soup on her lip, her tongue explores the feeling of viscous liquid and how to remove it at the same time as her hand slowly rises to aid the tongue and finish the job of cleaning the lip while gripping a napkin. All this happens in slow motion which, with repetition, becomes automatic. And so do a thousand other processes she's relearning: eating, chewing and swallowing different textured food; smiling, frowning, speaking and joking, to name a few.

Imagine what it took her this week in therapy to sit up erect on a yoga mat for fifteen minutes, yes with props to support her, but needing to fire 10,000 brain synapses to keep her skeletal muscles taut to avoid collapsing. Or what it took her to stand on her own two feet, again with human support on both sides, but bearing her own weight, relearning the evolution of the human species in standing erect.

If consciousness is this endlessly complex process of connecting neurons to one another, each with some tiny thread of experience attached, replicated over and over almost endlessly, then small wonder that Phyllis has little space in her brain at the moment for short-term memory. She is relearning the entire process of relating to and moving in the outside world, photographing it in her neurons and memorizing thousands of processes that enable a child to move, feel and speak.

Modern brain scientists like Eagleman are literally re-writing the scientific understanding of the brain's plasticity—the ability to change and adapt how the brain creates consciousness for us. The brain is constantly storing sensations and experiences—first in the prefrontal cortex and then the hippocampus. If the experience is repeated, the hippocampus compares it to previous input and eventually stores it permanently in the cerebral cortex. Single short-term memories, on the other hand, are stored very briefly in the hippocampus. Doesn't it make sense that the brain would have to give all its resources to reconnecting long-term memories before short-term ones? Why can't I be patient?

The increase in Phyllis's Ritalin to forty milligrams twice a day seems to have helped in a big way. It takes an hour or so to kick in after she takes her pill and the brain machinery begins to show its stuff. The effects last about six hours; then she sleeps four hours, gets more Ritalin and is awake another six hours. It appears to have the effect of three cups of espresso coffee.

It seems like half the staff at the hospital has either taken Ritalin as a child or has a child who takes it. Most of their experiences with Ritalin are negative; at best they see it as a necessary evil. No one I've talked to loves it; some hate it and describe their experience as torture. Needless to say I am ambivalent in using it with Phyllis. It is one means by which she is relearning functionality in the physical world, and I am deeply grateful, but I also know her mind seeks a kind of self-control in its drive for self-awareness that a drug, especially this one, cannot give. Once last week, she told our friend Carole, "I'm confused." It's great that she's self-aware enough to express confusion, but disconcerting; I fear Ritalin may add to the confusion.

Wednesday, July 20, 2011, 5:24 a.m. Coma Day 149.

Phyllis kept her eyes open all day today, from six in the morning until eight at night. For most of us, that doesn't sound like such a feat but for her, after five months, it was a total surprise. She skipped her afternoon nap; she was awake for all three meals and she stayed up through Ralph's Hebrew healing prayer at night. It was anything but a clear, peaceful day for her; in fact, she was stormy and confused much of the time. At times, her eyes were glassy, then roving, and then suddenly focused, as if she had just awoken from a bad dream. Other times, her eyes were wide and looked terribly frightened. At one point, lying in bed, she saw me and said, clearly:

"Frank! Can you help me get in bed?"

"You're already there. Where do you think you are?" I asked her quietly.

"On a boat off the coast near Anchorage, Alaska," she said, after some consideration.

"Actually, we're in Fayetteville, Arkansas, and you're already *in* bed," I said.

"Oh," she said." You're right." looking down like a child who was told she forgot to wear shoes to school.

Scary as the process was to watch, my intuition was that something good was happening and that she was okay. I was just there to be the captain and let her know the ship was on course. In between several electrical brain storms, she focused on the room as if seeing it for the first time. I queried her and for the first time, she could clearly see the photographic portraits of our children by Andrew Kilgore hung on the far wall. She stared intently at the shelf directly on the wall in front of her bed that we have turned into a colorful shrine. She smiled and appeared fascinated, recognizing and naming out-loud: Jesus and Mary, a

Padre Pio statuette, an "El Nino the Doctor" figure supported by a framed Jewish prayer, a Buddha statue, some Arkansas crystals and other relics made holy by the prayers of dear friends.

As evening arrives, I manage to lie down on the bed beside Phyllis, no mean feat on a hospital air bed with railings and support props. I feel a bit self-conscious, as if the nurses are her parents and might walk in and catch me in bed with their daughter, though I could assure them that in this position nothing untoward was humanly possible. We touched our heads and lie quietly for a long time.

I said, "I'd better go home and get some sleep."

She said, "Stay a little more." I would have stayed a lifetime.

I lay beside her in the dark thinking of the progress she has made, silently begging forgiveness for not more frequently thanking all her angels. From the first week in February when Phyllis fell unconscious, friends, family and perfect strangers have reached out with prayers and offers of unconventional therapies. At first, I was overwhelmed and at times even put off by aggressive assurances of who and what could heal her. Over time I learned to accept and embrace every offer that did not require traveling to a far away land, swallowing dangerous substances or abandoning conventional medical treatment.

I sensed from the beginning of Phyllis's coma that we, her family and friends, were not helpless bystanders in her effort to regain consciousness. In fact, I am convinced that without massive stimulation from outside, repeated input and stimulation from those that loved her, her effort to rebuild consciousness would fail. Consequently we continue to have ongoing convocations of multi-faith prayers, visits by Catholic priests and lay ministers, Tibetan prayer chants, homeopathic remedies, regular Jewish prayers, Jin Shin Jyutsu, on-site choir performances, daily Feldenkrais treatments, cranio-sacral therapy, palm healing, shamanic journeys, and love wished by those with no religious belief whatsoever. This on top of physical therapy, somewhat unconventional use of ADHD drug therapy, brain shunt surgery and a feeding and breathing tube. In addition to all the above, more than fifty volunteers, organized by angels Ginny and Barbara, continue to sit with Phyllis from morning until night (each volunteer averaging two hours a week), speaking to her, playing music, reading newspapers and above all, attempting to engage her mind and lure her back to consciousness. If and when Phyllis recovers fully, I will never be able to distinguish what made the difference; everything and everyone will have their part.

As I fall asleep I sing to Phyllis our No. 4 songbook listing, The Grateful Dead's "Ripple." With glowing words, the song speaks to us of forty years together, of the need to sing in spite of the silence, and points to the path that only you can follow and to the way home that only you can find.

CHAPTER FOURTEEN

TAKING ON THE SIERRA MADRE TOGETHER

Now when I see myself, I'm a stranger by my birth
Yankee Lady's memory reminds me of my worth
— Jesse Winchester, "Yankee Lady"

October 5, 1973

"Okay, Marco Polo, so what's the plan?" Phyllis asked eagerly. It was the end of the first day out of Tilzapotla on our return to the Guerrero wilderness. By late afternoon, we had climbed the peak overlooking town, made camp and bathed under a waterfall. Phyllis had agreed to go and was excited about going back with me to the Sierra Madre.

"No plan, really," I said, immediately unhappy with my response. "Just to climb over the wall."

Why *was* I here? Eight months of scheming to get to this mountainside and the only image that came to my mind was pushing a giant cinematic *freeze* button on all of *human* civilization—holding it still so I could answer the question that had been gnawing at me my whole life: Why are *we* here? A hundred years before, 500 years before, 3,000 years before, our ancestors walked these same trails, kicked the same rocks, drank from the same springs and all we had learned was how to *amplify* our mistakes. We made bigger and more lethal weapons; we made *hatred of others* global instead of local; we invented technology capable of killing the *enemy* halfway around the globe but were unable to recognize our own brothers. It was still tribe against tribe, race against race, religion against religion. Jesus had pointed out the futility of hate and the power of love 2,000 years ago. Now a third of all living beings claimed to follow him and what had changed? We just got better organized at hating.

"I don't want to scare you again, hon, but I still really just want to get *lost* here," I continued, breathing deeply, hoping I could make her understand and share my dilemma. "If I know the destination, how will I discover anything?"

"When he talks like this, you don't know what he's after," she sang with a laugh, quoting from Leonard Cohen's "The Stranger Song." "Let me weaken your will and offer you shelter. Why don't you set up the bed?" I melted into her arms.

In Tilzapotla, I had been transported back a hundred years in time to a world where horses were still the primary transportation and telephones were almost unknown. Now, one day's walk away from Tilza, we had traveled a thousand years further back, leaving behind most of the "improvements" brought to the Earth by mankind in recorded history, whether in communications, transportation, agriculture or medicine—and yet humans were still living here and thriving. I just wanted to be led by their tracks to the place where it all started.

The final week in Tilzapotla had been filled with goodbyes, more admonitions about the *mala gente* we would encounter and last-minute preparations. We had no modern camping gear and I didn't want any. We hadn't brought anything that wasn't readily available to a campesino: no cameras, no pop-up tents, no freeze-dried foods and only utensils we could use on a wood fire. All week Augustina and Phyllis had cooked traditional food for traveling: corn cakes cooked with mashed beans and queso fresco cheese or just masa and oil. I had been obsessed with getting every detail figured out, remembering which tool had helped on the previous trip and what provisions had been lacking.

A few days before leaving, Augustina's son Abel had delivered the three burros we bought. Our logic was that burros were more suited to carrying heavy loads than horses. Everywhere in Mexico, you would see burros with impossibly large packs. Surely, we thought, they could carry Phyllis and my gear with ease. We were certain about the burros' capacity but not so sure about their famous stubbornness.

Phyllis took my jaw in her hand. "Look, I know how much this means to you. I'm here, aren't I? But you think too much. Just let it happen. I know you better than you think. All this year in Tilza, you've been observing people, seeing what makes them tick. At night you tell me everything you've learned. But the thing you don't do is *talk to them*. You keep it all inside and people don't really know who you are. You need to open up more. For now, let's just keep going over the mountain and let it happen. Okay?"

I smiled, stirred the coals in the fire and thumbed through the songbook to sing Kris Kristofferson's "Why Me Lord?" What had I ever done to deserve the one person in the world who could see through my masks?

On the second day, we camped beside a brook in the mountains above Coaxitlan, back in the ancient world as if no time had passed since we stumbled up here with Larry a year earlier. The brook ran west, away from Tilza, telling me that we were in Guerrero again. This high in the Sierra, there were no grazing animals to foul the water and springs dripped out of rock faces, so we had ample fresh water. Corn season had reached harvest time, which meant fresh corn for the eating, anywhere on our path for the next month. And oh, the corn.

Walking through a narrow pass, we looked up at corn plants ten feet high, clinging to patches of earth between rock faces. Phyllis threw both arms up toward the corn. "How in the world did they learn to raise corn in these wild places?"

In fact, corn can grow just about anywhere you put it; it just needs humans willing to spread the seed. The land where we walked has been the epicenter of the marriage between corn and the human species for millennia. A thousand years before the Aztecs, the Olmecs coaxed corn out of *teosinte*—an ancient wild grain—then planted, cross-bred and selected the best ears, year after year, generation after generation until they had something like these ears of corn we see. Somewhere near us on the Guerrero-Morelos border, scientists found a cave with 4,000-year-old toasted seeds of teosinte, which, with the help of human endeavor, evolved into modern corn. This incredibly versatile plant can grow in virtually any climate or soil. What corn can't do is propagate itself; it can only spread its seed if humans lend a hand. And for 4,000 years in Morelos and Guerrero and around the world, corn has helped humans to prosper.

"Maybe that's why they call corn *mother*?" Phyllis said.

October 6, 1973

Following the trails familiar to us from the previous year's trip, we returned to our former hosts in Coaxitlan, a village compound of conical huts, adobe rooms and fruit trees: plums, lemons and bananas. We greeted our hosts, Tizoc and his wife Izel, with the few Nahuatl words we knew: *Tlaquilte* ("good day," pronounced klakeeltay) and tlazocamatli ("thank you," pronounced klatsokamatlee, more or less). We were treated like old friends, reunited after many travels. A place on the porch was again cleared for us to sleep, the corn having been shucked and stored carefully in the always-present *coscomate*, the egg-shaped granary built of adobe mud plastered on woven branches. No one asked about our destination but seemed to accept our unusual expedition rather matter-of-factly.

In the early morning, Izel toasted blue corn masa on the comal, ground it on a stone petate to flour, added it to a pot of water and boiled it with cinnamon to make a delicious drink of blue corn atole, and served it to us with gorditas, plum-flavored fat tortillas hot off the comal. After breakfast, she loaded our bags with extra corn cakes and hugged us both. Her husband Tizoc walked with us as we trekked with our four dogs and three burros, up the trail toward Quetzalapa. Izel was headed for his corn *milpa*, a few hours along the trail.

An hour later, the path divided, our way going up the mountain pass and Izel's along a creek. I repeated orders to the burros to get them to hurry up the trail, then Phyllis tried pulling their ropes but they were in full rebellion and refused to budge. They wouldn't even start the ascent—a steep rock channel with steps etched out of a granite mountain. Izel noticed our dilemma, doubled back and with a few guttural commands, sent the burros packing up the trail. Another language to learn: *burro!*

As we hiked, Phyllis and I sang to no one's chagrin from our songbook. We chose The Band's "Daniel and the Sacred Harp," feeling very much like Daniel spiriting away the sacred harp with no idea what price we would pay. As we sang, we climbed into a highland world as old and unchanged as any on the planet, a self-sufficient universe whose resources, so far at least, had remained unnoticed to the wider, modern Mexican civilization around it and so, had been left alone all these centuries.

Somewhere below us, the Amacusac River was cutting a deep canyon on its way south to join the Balsas. Emiliano Zapata and his peasant revolutionaries, like Don Lauro, used this path to disappear from federal soldiers sixty years before us; Tlahuica Indians used it 500 years before Zapata to escape the Aztecs collecting tribute for the empire they were building in Mexico City, and Olmecs or some tribe whose origins are long lost, cut the original trails here 2,000 or 3,000 years before the Tlahuica.

Is there some master plan, I wondered, *for all the ghosts, living and dead, that travel so lightly on these same trails?*

October 7, 1973

We camped that night near Quetzalapa in the *milpa*, a corn field using an ancient sustainable food system known as the Three Sisters: corn, beans and squash planted together as a mutual aid society. The moon rose full and golden through the tall corn stalks. We found a small squash left behind from a recent harvest and ate it with no guilt. After watching the moon rise in the milpa, we decided to forgo our tent and sleep on top of the sleeping bag on a tarp, the night too warm to use a tent.

The dogs, Lather and Gringo, set up like sentries around our fire. The puppies Queenie and Star, now almost a year old, cuddled under the edge of our sleeping bag, barking lowly in their sleep—lost in sweet dreams of ancient harmonies. Dogs in the city adapt to varying degrees to domestication but take a few dogs into the wilderness and they immediately return to their ancient origins, acting as a pack in which their humans were definitely included. By day, they tracked our path running ahead and lagging behind and then at night watched our camp diligently. No animal could reach our campfire without being announced by loud barking. The puppies were constantly in training, reined in by their mother Lather or nipped on the ear by their father Gringo when they strayed, learning to respect the order in which things are done. At night, camping in the country, the dogs set up a perimeter of protection. Gringo would roam away from camp but always within earshot of Lather's bark.

When Larry and I walked through Guerrero the year before,

we had advanced relentlessly and, for the most part, avoided villages. When we did cross through towns, however, I had benefited from Larry's strong, silent military bearing. The long knife strapped to his leg made a strong statement to anyone with bad intentions, the *mala gente* Augustina had worried over so. Now I asked myself, *Are we ready to defend ourselves without Larry's protection? Am I leading her into danger? Remember, she chose this journey as much as I did. She is right; I think too much.*

Several hours before dawn, Phyllis woke me with a shout as the moonlight pierced the shadows. Before I was awake enough to process her shout, I was yelling too. Swarms of invisible insects, buzzing tiny black flies with vicious bites were attacking. We tried to cover ourselves but to no avail. Finally we surrendered our peaceful bed in the milpa and raced to pack up the burros, who were quite disgusted with the sudden hurry and the trip in general. The swarming, biting flies gave us no chance to whine about our predicament. Finally even the reluctant burros seemed to respond to my urgency and we moved out briskly.

Back on the trail, bright moonbeams struck like lightning through a pitch-black forest, highlighting the interminably-upward path, the surreal sight suddenly too beautiful for us to be scared or resentful at our uprooting. Nonetheless, we were exhausted and were compelled up a trail in the moonlight toward an unknown destination. The flies stayed behind in the field. We didn't speak, we just kept moving. I had the distinct feeling that other beings were moving with us, maybe jaguars tracking us in the night? No, some kind of more ethereal beings, spirits of other travelers who had moved like us, under compulsion, up this trail in the moonlight of early mornings centuries before, unwilling wanderers equally exhilarated and enthralled but also against their will, enchanted by the undeniable beauty of this sensual dance between the light and the dark, the forest and the heavens, the path and the wilderness. Foot soldiers ran these same trails from Oaxaca to central Mexico a thousand years ago, carrying messages to the ruling elite. Slaves captured by warring factions before the birth of Christ were driven along these paths and somewhere, sometimes one of them had the same experience as ours, their fear overwhelmed by the sheer beautiful timelessness of the act of moving over the earth at night by the light of the moon.

By dawn's gleam, the trail had peaked and we started downhill. Unable to stop our exhausted forward motion, we stumbled down to a fork in the trail.

"I hear something," Phyllis said.

"Running water!" I said. "We're back to the Amacusac!"

Actually we were another half hour's walk but we could hear and smell the fresh water in motion. Laid out before us was a backwash from the main river, lapping up over a bare field. Clear, clean water a few feet deep with a sandy bottom. We tied the burros so they could graze. We unashamedly removed our dirty clothes and soaked naked in the cool water and welcome sunshine. Not even the fear of the return of the black flies, who seemed *not* to have followed us, could spoil the moment. We splashed, rested, washed, then collapsed on the tarp—clothes and bodies stretched out to dry in the sun. Blessedly, we had several hours of solitude and were dressed when we heard voices.

"Tlaquilte," said a young man, one of a party of six men, women and children. Following behind them were more women and children. The children giggled shyly at the sight of such strangers and the adults showed cheerful smiles. They passed by us and continued toward the main body of the river.

We began to organize our camp, gathering wood, starting a fire, cooking oatmeal. Soon one of the men returned. Speaking in Nahuatl, he was quietly gesturing in the direction he came from. We followed and over the rise, saw an amazing sight: beds of every kind of vegetable and fruit, growing alongside the river. He offered us several small green-yellow melons on the vine from his patch. Beyond the melons were beds of green beans, sunflowers, marigolds and amaranth.

After a delicious meal of oatmeal and honeydew melon, we walked along the river. More families had come to work in the beds. There was an elaborate web of small irrigation channels watering the garden. Mothers were bathing babies in the river. A teenager seemed to be flirting with a young girl. Men and women worked side-by-side, weeding, watering and shielding small plants from the hot sun with sticks and leaves. The Rio Amacusac was swollen and brown with mud washed out of the mountains, lapping at the shore just a few feet away, but no one showed any concern.

In the afternoon with our energy high, we headed back out on the trail. From the peak of the Sierra above Coaxitlan, we were now slowly descending into a semi-tropical valley along the river. Phyllis, as always, engaged fellow travelers on the trail, even though we could only speak a few words of Nahuatl. She usually managed to get their estimates of time to reach the next village—if only by gestures and finger-counting. The dogs scouted far ahead as well as behind us but could be summoned with a loud call.

I walked, lost in my thoughts, taking in the scenery. We were slowly descending a river trail out of the mountains into Atenango Del Rio, a river town that briefly broke the spell of trekking in ancient lands since Atenango was the endpoint of a paved highway coming up the mountain from the coast, a two-lane ribbon of highway connecting this outpost town with modern Mexico.

The year before I had been warned the government was setting up a checkpoint at the entrance to town that would be guarded by federal soldiers. Banks in Acapulco, the capital of Guerrero, had been blown up recently by violent revolutionary groups and the government was nervous about political revolt, not to mention drug trafficking, which was an enterprise over which the Mexican government preferred to exercise its own monopoly. All traffic into and out of the town was stopped and searched. We could see the road from the mountains as we descended, a dark line snaking through the bottomland toward the town. In three hours of descent, we hadn't seen a single vehicle on the road. We had been told to expect to pay a bribe to the soldiers, which we couldn't afford. Our destination route lay across the Amacuzac River over which there was no bridge and where, on the opposite bank, lay an even more remote wilderness.

We could see the town itself for a long time from our vantage point on the trail above town. Unlike the *Mehica* Indian villages we had been encountering, Atenango Del Rio was a white-washed adobe town with a long history. Because of its strategic placement on Rio Amacusac, a major tributary of the Rio Balsas which itself slices across central Mexico and rushes from Guerrero through Michoacan to the Pacific Ocean, Atenago Del Rio was, in the 1400s, the capital of a tribal kingdom paying tribute to the Aztecs when Columbus arrived. Two millennia before that, more than a thousand years before the birth of Christ, this city was the farthest outreach of the Olmec, currently thought to be the earliest civilization of the Americas. But Atenango Del Rio was also about ten centuries beyond its prime, now a river town with no marine navigation, other than two ancient dugout boats that bravely sliced their way back and forth across the churning, brown waters to an isolated peninsula between two rivers.

As Phyllis and I approached Atenango Del Rio, I watched from the mountain-top outside of town. I noticed that locals came and went across the highway on footpaths, avoiding the government guard station. Why not just follow the locals and find our own way into town without confronting the guards?

Feeling more at peace in my own skin than any time I could remember, our little gypsy tribe—Phyllis, me, the dogs and the burros—began our descent into town, limping along the highway leading to the soldiers' outpost. Phyllis, with her long, black, braided hair, her olive sun-tanned Italian skin and native skirt could easily pass as Mexican. I, on the other hand, with my long blond hair and blue eyes and native blancos—white cotton pajamas—looked anything but local. Our food and water supplies were depleted but we had enough pesos for a room, a cold *cerveza* and a hot meal. The rest of the plan would have to take care of itself.

Following a woman with a heavy basket balanced on her head as she skirted off the road and down a narrow path between two Adobe walls, we made our move and followed her. I was convinced we could *blend* into the scene and pass unnoticed.

The strategy seemed to have worked at first; we circumvented the guard gate and after some maneuvering and confusion ended up in an open plaza in front of an adobe church with two bell towers. It was mid-day, the sun was hot and not much was happening. I tied the burros to a tree and we sat on a bench to take in the scene. Then I began to hear horses' hooves clicking rapidly on cobblestone streets. Before we knew it, we were surrounded by four horsemen. They weren't wearing soldiers' uniforms but they did carry pistols and I assumed the Guardia had figured us out.

"*Bajense sus cosas. Donde estan sus armas? De donde vienen?*" The leader barked questions rapid-fire. Open your bags, Where are your guns? Where are you coming from?

The leader dismounted but the other three sat astride their nervous and snorting horses, cutting off any escape route. If they were *banditos*, we had no one to protect us. Our burros were nervous. The dogs were beside themselves; it was all I could do to keep control of them.

"Just keep calm," I told Phyllis.

"Who do you think *you* are?" Phyllis barked back at the men. "What gives you the right to molest us?"

"He's wearing a gun, Phyl, do what he says," I whispered to her.

She made a snorting sound but agreed to the search. So we opened our bags and laid everything out on the ground. It was quite a spread. Bags of leftover vegetables, oatmeal, corn cakes, a comal, a clay pot, wooden utensils, a sleeping bag and tarp, an extra pair of my *blancas*, as well as Phyllis's extra bra and panties. Other than the leader, the men seemed embarrassed at how normal our possessions were and at having a woman's undergarments displayed on the cobblestones.

"Where's the money?" the leader sneered, picking up a pair of her panties with a stick. "The money you stole from the widow in San Miguel?"

"We know nothing of this widow, sir," I answered. "We are from Tilzapotla, over the mountains. We are just traveling for pleasure. May God protect that poor grandmother," I answered calmly, my heart racing.

We were at a standoff. The dogs stood ready but weren't barking or biting. The three men on horseback were smirking. The leader was flustered and Phyllis was pissed.

"You aren't soldiers, are you?" Phyllis said. "In fact, you have no authority at all to assault us like this."

"Phyllis, calm down, they aren't soldiers but they represent the town authority," I said, for the leader's benefit. "They are looking for a scoundrel who robbed an old lady, someone's grandmother."

"They were foreigners and young people like you," said the leader, on the defensive.

"Well, we aren't foreigners, we are from Tilzapotla. We have a house there," Phyllis said. "We didn't hurt or rob anyone."

Phyllis started packing up our things as the leader scowled but seemed confused about his next move, tapping his fingers on his pistol. The other mounted men looked away from us. I looked down but Phyllis glared back directly at the leader. Something shifted and it seemed we had the upper hand.

"Do you know where we might get a meal and a room?" I inquired, testing the mood and trying to deflect the tension. The leader frowned and pointed to a cantina across the way. As quickly as they had come, they mounted and raced away. Phyllis had stood her ground and shown no fear.

We both took a long breath. I realized how scared I had been. The dogs must have sensed my fear; for some reason, they made no attempt to defend us.

"Welcome to Atenango Del Rio, Bonnie and Clyde," I said to Phyllis, after they were gone.

"I can't stand injustice," she replied. "We did nothing wrong and meant no harm. Who are they to push us around?"

"What do you say we check out this cantina?"

The cantina was an adobe house that served as a hotel and restaurant. We were welcomed into the yard by a white-haired man and our weary burros were led away as if they were respectable horses instead of lowly work animals. The yard was entirely covered with a canopy of vines and bougainvillea.

"Welcome!" A broad-shouldered, smiling woman greeted us from a patio covered with clay tiles and flowering vines. "I saw that you ran into *El Diablo* out in the plaza, that *matón* who thinks he's a bull but really is a poor *vaca castrada*. I am Pilar. How about a shot of mescal on the house?"

"*Si! Como no!* I'm Phyllis, this is Pancho and that's the best offer we've had all day!"

Pilar offered us two leather-covered *equipale* chairs and poured a round of Mescal shots. The Mescal was followed by a meal of hot beans *de la olla* with cream, tortillas, breaded squash flowers and chicken in mole sauce.

After the meal, Phyllis waved at Pilar.

"Thanks so much, Pilar. We could use a bath and a good rest. Do you have a room to rent?"

Pilar replied with a knowing wink and a smile. "Follow me."

A cleanly swept hall led from the bar to an outdoor white-washed set of steps and up to a second-floor room, spotlessly clean with one bed, one chair and one water basin. Leonard Cohen could have lived there, writing "Tonight Will Be Fine" and listening all night for steps on the stairs.

"We'll take it," I said.

After our encounter with the four horsemen of Atenango, Phyllis and I settled into our new accommodations. The place was less hotel and more house with a covered courtyard. There were four rooms looking down on the small cobblestones quadrangle. Electricity had made it to Atenango but just barely. The room had one unadorned bulb, as did the courtyard, but the power was turned off by nine at night, anyway.

"Shall I carry you across the threshold? I have brought my wild-eyed gypsy lover to town and intend to exact my price."

"You better watch yourself or you'll sleep in the courtyard," she said, as she led me up the stairs.

We realized from our confrontation in the plaza that the authorities knew we were there and were suspicious. Even so, I wasn't in a hurry to leave. Phyllis hung out with Pilar and learned her story. She and her husband moved here from another state, hoping to make a new life. But locals had made them feel unwelcome and murdered her husband. She refused to leave when he died and kept running the bar. She had persevered. Phyllis recognized a kindred spirit.

When we weren't exploring the town or drinking cervezas at various cantinas, we were in bed, watching the Amacusac River, roiling with brown froth where it widened to several hundred yards and making rapids where it narrowed and hit hidden rocks. Mountains rose high on the horizon across the river. Time stood still and vibrated silently with the rhythms of several thousands of years of being home to travelers, lovers and *conquistadores.*

October 15, 1973

Phyllis and I stood looking at the bottom of a steep bank on the southern end of town. Two longboats, canoes twenty feet long, dug out of old-growth tree trunks, waited to take those who wanted to go beyond what was known, across the Amacusac.

Three thousand years ago, the Olmecs, the first advanced civilization in North America, used boats to go up and down this river. Their capital city, which is lost now, was somewhere on the other side. I could hear it calling.

"So! Are you ready to find the lost passage to India?" I said with a laugh.

"Your imagination gets ahead of you. Let's just cross the river and see what we find."

CHAPTER FIFTEEN

KNOWING WHEN TO MOVE ON

Well I've been waitin', I was sure
We'd meet between the trains we're waitin' for,
I think it's time to board another.

—Leonard Cohen, "The Stranger Song"

Saturday, July 23, 2011, 9:18 p.m. Coma Day 154.

With no warning, Phyllis's mother, Julia, died today. My daughter called me at 3:30 a.m. to say that her namesake, Grandma Julia D'Auria Petrella, Phyllis's mother, had passed over into the embrace of God. Only two weeks before, all the clan except Phyllis had gathered to celebrate the ninety years of life and love of this incredible woman who such a short time ago was laughing and playing with her great-grandchildren. Grandma Julia had suffered from heart disease but had been able to live at home and only felt severe pain in her last few days.

I have not told Phyllis about her mother dying. I fear she isn't ready yet to process what has happened. As much as she would want to know and want to be there for her family, it will have to happen on a delayed time schedule. I need to wait until I know the time is right. I take that decision with a heavy heart. Phyllis values honesty above all and in normal times it would be *her* strength that others would draw upon. But now is not the time.

Phyllis continues her deliberate climb up the mountain of consciousness and recovery. So much to learn, so many moves to make, so much repetition. Every morning at 8 a.m., I take her to "therapy class," leaving her in the excellent care of Trudy, Candace and Leah, her physical and occupational therapists. They are devoted professionals and have accepted all the help they get from Team Phyllis, friends like Anita who treats Phyllis with Feldenkrais and John who performs cranio-sacral adjustments. For Phyllis, each step, each movement, each thought process has to be repeated hundreds, maybe thousands of times for the brain to make it automatic. I keep thinking: this is how *children* learn to move and speak. Like a child, Phyllis is repeating all her steps, moving limbs, standing up, holding objects, building muscles, learning concepts, over and over and over.

As one would expect from Phyllis, social interaction is her strength. When friends and family come to call, she reaches deep inside and finds the strength to communicate. She remembers that cousin Francine and Tom have retired; she asks our friend Albert about his daughter Marina. She cries with joy when she hears that Barbara's grandchild was born or at the announcement that a friend's daughter-in-law is pregnant. At the same time, she suffered a lot of confusion this week, uncertainty about where she is, who has been around and what activities she has been involved in. As the carousel of her memory turns on any given day, she can be clear and perceptive and then turn confused and silent. With Sandy on Saturday, she recalled a visit by someone from our parish two months ago when we thought she wasn't even awake! Then she goes for days without recognizing anyone.

Joy and fear, joy and fear. I feel elated at Phyllis's return and in the next moment fear that her condition is progressing into an endlessly repeating cycle of memory retrieval and loss. How do I process the deep sadness and dark grief of Grandma Julia's departure without sharing it with Phyllis? Her mother has left on a journey we all must face and none can know, the eternal enigma that love gives birth to life which leads to death as more life and love are made. But later will be the time to understand and even celebrate Julia's journey; for now I mourn and cry at the cruelty of life's loss and the loss of Phyllis's companionship to help me grieve.

Her mom, this Italian baker, New York seamstress, family comedian, intrepid adventurer, dad's lover, Keeper of the Hearth, Magician of the Kitchen, mother to us all, how to go on without you? We all send you our love and tears baked in pizzas drawn hot from the stove and wrapped for your trip as you did for us for so long. Ma, you are the salt in our tears and the yeast in our dough. You live on in us all. Life is so sweet to live, so hard to part, our only strength is the life of love you gave us. Dear God, hold her well, she was everything.

Wednesday, July 27, 2011, 5:31 a.m. Coma Day 158.

My time with Phyllis this week has been dreamlike but bitter-sweet. Her wakefulness and short-term memory has slipped and she has been having some confusion about where she is. At the same time, when she is awake, she is very affectionate and wants me to be present. After four months of her hardly being awake or being able to express any feelings whatsoever, the intimacy of our simple conversation is, as the old hymn "Balm of Gilead" says, a comfort that makes the wounded whole and heals the sin-sick soul.

"How are you?" I ask upon arrival.

"Much better, now that you are here," she says.

On Sunday, several friends gave up their afternoon to stay with Phyllis and convinced me I should get away for an afternoon sailing at the lake with my friend Ralph. Within a half hour of leaving her, my cell phone rang just as I happened to get a connection on a dirt road leading to Beaver Lake.

"Frank?" she asked.

"Hi, Phyl, is that you?" I said, in great surprise. I had disconnected phone service on her cell phone months before when her coma had no end in sight. She was calling from the hospital phone. My wife, my beloved gypsy girl, who a scant few weeks before was not speaking at all was now calling me on my cell phone.

"What are you doing?"

"I'm almost out to the lake to go sailing."

"Oh, I didn't know," she said, in a disappointed tone (even though I had told her an hour before). "I'm glad. Have a good time."

"I can't believe you're calling. I'm beside myself. I'm so happy. You're amazing."

"Well, hurry up whatever you're doing. Somebody just came by; I gotta go."

When I returned from the lake that evening, I was ready to tell her how excited I was to talk to her on the phone but she no longer remembered our conversation. The probable cause is a UTI (urinary tract infection) diagnosed last week. For some strange reason, according to the nurses, contracting a UTI causes mental confusion in neurologically-compromised patients. So the good news is that treating the UTI with antibiotics should help her to be clearer and more present. The bad news is that, once again, any chance to celebrate an advance—a shared phone call—is quickly overcome by the limitations of her condition.

In spite of the UTI setback, Phyllis goes to physical therapy every weekday and works for hours on sitting, standing, pushing, lifting and coordinating her limbs. It is exhausting and when I praise her for her progress, she says "I don't think I'm getting very far." I showed her a picture of herself in intensive care four months earlier with her face and body covered with tape and tubes and wires and monitors. She was shocked but impressed.

"I look terrible. Is that really me? Why did I have all that stuff?"

"Just to scare you, I guess," I said, laughing.

I had suddenly seen in my mind an image of Phyllis facing down four horseback riders with guns in Mexico decades ago. When will I learn to trust her bravery and determination?

I'm proud of my kids and grateful they have taken up the role that Phyllis and I would normally play in our family's grieving process for the loss of Phyllis's mother, if we were able. My daughter Julia—who lives in Encinitas, California near Phyllis's family, the Petrellas—has been visiting her aunts and uncles and Grandpa Louis to bring love and help make the hard decisions. I know Phyllis will grieve not being able to say goodbye to her mother. Not a day goes by in Phyllis's life, even now, that she doesn't remember the joys of extended family life in her New York childhood. Every aunt and uncle, friend and grandparent had a special place in the pantheon of her remembered introduction to life on earth and her mother sat at the center of that clan.

A lesson I have learned from Phyllis who learned it from her parents and extended family: bravery doesn't mean you can't cry. It's healing to admit all that you have lost when life changes. It honors our love to admit our own suffering and cry for ourselves. There is a time for everything and now is the time of loss. What will follow will be a great joy, a healing river of togetherness and appreciation for the ties of love and human struggle. We will rise and go on; we will heal and rejoice in Phyllis's recovery as she carries on her mother's bravery. For now, we wave in forlorn sadness as we watch Grandma Julia's boat sail toward the horizon.

Saturday, July 30, 2011, 10:38 p.m. Coma Day 161.

So we finally made it to the real dog days of Summer, early August, the time when *it's supposed to be* hot, muggy, and bone dry. In Phyllis's room at City Hospital, we close the curtains at noon and get all the fans and A.C. going full blast so we can coast into dusk, hoping to stay relatively cool. It's annoying but when we came to City Hospital, we knew it was the oldest hospital in town, a dilapidated structure with the least to offer in modern amenities.

What a great move it was, though; the place is a hidden jewel where, even though most of the residents will be here for the duration of their lives, they are cared for with love, devotion and humility. The nurses and techs treat each other like equals and treat their patients like favorite aunts and uncles. The staff takes great pride in Phyllis's improvements, perhaps more so because most of their other patients have so little chance of significant improvement.

Phyllis is re-acquiring skills none could have imagined even a few weeks ago. And as usual, she is the last one to see her strength. Friday, as we wheeled along to her physical therapy class, Phyllis told me: "I don't really want to go. I'm not getting anywhere."

"Stay with it," I said. "You're too close to it to see how far you've come."

In class, the PT asked me if I could stay a while, so I did. Eventually, she wheeled Phyllis out to the middle of the room.

"Phyllis?" she said. "Can you pick up your right leg?"

With no hesitation, while sitting in the wheelchair, she picked up her right leg a foot off the floor.

"That's great," she said. "Now extend your leg."

Again with no hesitation, Phyllis extended her leg straight out and held it. Then, on request she proceeded to do the same with the left. I was astounded, ecstatic and flushed with joy. Her brain has laid down yet one more track and allowed her muscles to respond to a consciously-directed command. For the first time in four months, I can really imagine her walking again. I remember the chief neurologist at Barnes-Jewish Hospital three months ago saying, as she lay paraplegic and unconscious: "She may never get any better; this may be as good as it gets."

Of course, these moments come all mixed up in a package of fading, then increasing wakefulness; clarity which deepens then slips away. Some friends who drop by, never see her in any way but sleeping. But the point is that these moments *do* come and they build on each other. Her brain is buzzing like an army of secret spies reconnoitering enemy territory, building intelligence for the next move. More and more, she wants to hold the fork or the glass, however long it takes to reach the lip.

This weekend I'm doing a sleepover at the hospital. Phyllis has been asking me to stay every night this week; how could I say no? We listen to music on the radio or watch movies on the laptop. When I am holding her, now, she never forgets who or where she is. Late in the evening, armed with my air mattress to augment the Army-issue hard mattress of the extra hospital bed, my pajamas and some melatonin, I'm trying to get a night's sleep. Last night I didn't do so well. I awoke for every two-hour shift when they came in to reposition Phyllis. If they did that to me every two hours for six months I'd be a basket case. What a milestone it will be when Phyllis can turn her own body in bed and get a real night's sleep.

Sunday, August 7, 2011, 5:31 a.m. Coma Day 168.

Late in the afternoon, Phyllis and I are just talking quietly. I tell her again about how I found her unconscious six months ago and how family and friends had rallied to care for her. That inspired her to want to make some phone calls, especially her father. I couldn't let her call him without telling her that her mother had died. So I trusted my intuition and just told her about her mother's ninetieth birthday party in July where all the clan had gathered to celebrate Grandma's life and about how, just two weeks later, they had returned to mourn her death and wish her goodbye and Godspeed.

Phyllis cried and I cried. I told her how sorry I was that life and her loyalty to me had kept her so far from family all these years. We called her father Louis and shared more tears. After the call, she fell asleep, exhausted.

How strange this life that we should always be welcoming newborns and then ourselves parting from it so soon. We become these incredibly, uniquely conscious human beings with insatiable curiosity about life on Earth, busily making connections to life in all its forms, only to lose it all to another journey, the details of which we can only know in faith and imagination. But in having known a spirit as sweet, brave and beautiful as Julia D'Auria Petrella, we knew our connection to Infinity. Her recipe was so simple. You take what you are given and you make pizza. You invite the world to sit at your table. You serve love until they are full and then make them take more.

Wednesday, August 13, 2011, 10 p.m. Coma Day 171.

Sometimes life is so clear and the path ahead so straight; other days, you can't even remember where you thought you were going. Today, it's not too clear. Soon—I'm guessing maybe two more months at City Hospital but that's sheer speculation— Phyllis will need to move on to another level of care, probably a neurological rehabilitation hospital. But where to go and how to choose the best one and how much will insurance cover and what's really best for her anyway?

While the term "neurological rehabilitation" *sounds* like just what she needs, each provider has its own definition. Some hospitals treat neuro-rehab with "tough-love" as if it were drug rehab (family visits on Sunday only; no phone calls; the patient must learn to feed herself or not eat). Others are more holistic and include the patient's family in therapy. Local choices are limited and offer a mix of every kind of treatment for conditions from strokes to eating disorders; Little Rock has a neurological center four hours away that I don't know much about. The best-known and highly-publicized programs are in major population centers: Chicago, New York, Houston.

No physician I've met knows exactly what kind of therapy

is perfect for Phyllis because nobody knows exactly how "global insult," her generic brain diagnosis, damages the brain. Once again, I find myself becoming *the great decider*. Shouldn't neurological experts be making these decisions? Then out of the blue today, Phyllis's physical rehab team told me that Phyllis had gotten all the help they could give her. The therapy she needs is beyond their capacity. Knowing they feel inadequate increases my anxiety.

Sunday, August 14, 2011, 5:30 a.m. Coma Day 176.

I arrive at Phyllis's room at City; the staff has moved her to one side of the bed so I can sneak onto the air mattress beside her. It's a precarious balance. This last week was a good lesson in not being able to see the forest for the trees. I assumed we had two months to sort things out. Suddenly, I am catapulted into deciding about a quick move to a new location and I can't see my way out of the woods. It all started Thursday, with Phyllis's physical therapist informing me that Phyllis really wasn't responding like she had been, in fact that she suddenly wasn't really participating in therapy at all. Like finding out that your kid who you thought was getting As is now failing and cutting class. I was taken off-guard, especially coming from a therapist who had already achieved a greater response from Phyllis than I ever expected.

The therapist suggested strongly that it might be time for Phyllis to move to a neurological rehab facility. The social worker suggested several locations. I made a flurry of calls on Thursday to rehabilitation programs locally and regionally to explore options. One hospital even sent an evaluator to assess Phyllis as a potential patient for their hospital. By the weekend the rumor was around City Hospital that we were moving *Monday*—which was news to me. Nurses and techs started telling me "we hate to lose her" and "we are proud of how far she's come." They seem to want to keep treating her. So why is this there this groundswell to push us out?

I'm afraid of change but also easily seduced by the hope that another facility has a magic bullet to heal her quickly. I get caught up in the frenzy and call everywhere from Little Rock to Chicago to compare treatment options. I am trying to keep in mind what I know about her condition, namely that the only truly successful remedy prescribed by any medical professional to date has been *time and loving attention.*

Physical therapy, occupational therapy, speech therapy, Ritalin therapy, even the pantheon of deep healing we're doing behind the scenes (Christian prayer, Feldenkrais, cranio-sacral, Jin Shin Jyutsu, Shamanic healing, Palm healing, Homeopathy, the list goes on . . .). It's all about creating a time and place for her brain to make itself whole. Can't we just stay in one place for a while longer?

In spite of what I want, change *is coming soon.* The staff is assuming she is being moved to the next level of treatment.

Tuesday, August 16, 2011, 11:20 p.m. Coma Day 178.

"Mr. Head? This is City Hospital. I wanted to let you know

that your insurance case manager is telling us to transfer Phyllis to HealthSouth Rehab *today*."

Phyllis woke up in a visibly more conscious state today. Right away, I could tell a change. When I asked her if she wanted breakfast or if she was ready for therapy class, there was none of the usual hesitation or confusion. When I took her to physical therapy, they transferred her to a platform made up like a bed. They told her they wanted her to experience what it felt like to turn over by herself in bed, a very important step to independence.

Once they got her in position on her back, they asked her if she could raise her hips. She immediately arched her back and picked her hips four inches off the table in a bow! We were all gasping; this was major progress. Then they talked her through a rotation to the right and the left. She needed prompting and it was slow and painful but she did it. This was the most miraculous moment ever. I could sense her "unconscious" brain watching very carefully so it could start memorizing these steps.

Maybe we have this whole conscious/unconscious idea backwards. We are so proud of what we do *consciously*, yet almost every process, whether it is physical, intellectual or even sight-based is only part of our conscious process for a very short time, just long enough for the unconscious brain to learn the steps and then *zing*, it is taken over by this internal supercomputer that can move at lightning speed.

As I watched Phyllis learn the roll technique (remember the stage when a baby first rolls over in her crib?), the speech therapist asked her a distracting question to judge her mental state, "What's your most memorable vacation?" Phyllis couldn't answer the question. She was totally focused on all the muscle commands involved in turning and the pain signals from joints not used for months. Then she looked up at an elderly lady across the room seated in a reclining exercise machine and said "Lena, why do *you* look so comfortable?"

It was classic Phyllis strategy: when the focus is on you and you're stressed by it, change the subject, make a joke and shift the focus. Everybody cracked up. She doesn't usually speak to anyone in therapy, much less remember their names. Phyllis laughed along with the rest of us.

When I asked Phyllis tonight if she thought the move to HealthSouth was a good idea, she said "I'm ready." Finally, I don't have to make all these decisions by myself. This feels more like *our* life all the time. I have struggled and agonized over *every* hospital change, trying to divine whether I was making the best choice and every time the change has been what she needed. May it be again. Dear God, help me give up the illusion that I am in charge and that I can control the future of my or anyone else's life.

CHAPTER SIXTEEN

THE HARD ROAD TO COPALILLO

"The adventure is always and everywhere a passage beyond the veil of the known into the unknown; the powers that watch at the boundary are dangerous; to deal with them is risky; yet for anyone with competence and courage the danger fades."

—Joseph Campbell, *The Hero's Journey*

October 15, 1973

By daybreak, I retrieved the burros from a nearby stable. Phyllis loaded their packs as I settled up affairs with Pilar, who was seated on a chair in the sunny courtyard as a young girl brushed and braided her long hair.

"Pancho, I am happy to know you and your *mujer*, Feliza, but you should know, there were police—federales—here last night asking about *gringos*. They are not good people. I told them nothing but I fear they will return."

"Gracias, Pilar. We plan to be far away by the end of the day. You have been very kind. But why do they care about us? We aren't a threat to anyone. We're not revolutionaries and we're not drug dealers."

She lowered her voice to a whisper and looked around before she spoke. "No, the *federales* aren't worried about *drogas*; they have a deal with the *traficantes*— 'stay across the river, grow your stuff over there and we'll leave you alone'. No, the soldiers don't want outsiders around Atenago because the government has a secret: they plan to build a dam on the river that would flood us all. And they don't like strangers asking questions. Now *andale*, get going; I've said too much."

We hugged Pilar and led the burros down a path to the river. The Amacuzac River ran along the western side of Atenango Del Rio and could be seen from our room above the cantina. By the end of the rainy season in mid-October, the river was a mighty force, roaring its way down through the canyons of the Sierra Madre, past the plain at Atenango and plunging southward to mate with the Rio Balsas and on to the Pacific. In the mountains above, far upstream from Atenango, summer and early-fall rain causes the river to swell and froth and since Olmec times has provided year-round irrigation to nearby fields. Large traditional dugout boats—some fifteen feet in length and carved by hand from one giant tree—are the only way to cross the river in Atenango Del Rio. Fashioned from huge trees washed downriver from the Sierra by floods, the boats were wide enough to hold two side-by-side passengers with the rear of the boat reserved for cargo and animals.

We arrived at the boat landing without any contact with the soldiers. We watched as the boat was tied to two mules downstream from us and pulled upriver along a riverside trail to where we waited. I paid one of the two oarsmen who helped us load our burros along with one other traveler and his horse into the boat which was shifting side to side in the fast current. Our fellow traveler had a hard face with a scar which was half covered by a crumpled straw cowboy hat. The river at that point was about a quarter mile across. When the loading was done and everyone seated, the ropes were released and the two oarsmen rowed like hell, directing the boat toward an exact point on the other side, as the rushing water propelled the boat like a wavering rocket toward our apparent certain death on the rapids visible just below the landing. The oarsmen made great sport of our anxiety but our fellow passenger didn't look much more confident than we did.

For fifteen rollicking, life-in-your-throat minutes, the boat bobbed in and out of the waves, the animals shifted and snorted their fear and then, suddenly, the wild ride was over and we landed precisely at the point the boatmen had reached hundreds of times before. We unloaded the burros who looked as if they preferred jumping into the river rather than continuing with these crazy gringos. Nevertheless, with our newly gained trail experience, we were able to coax them up the steep bank. Behind us the boat was being pulled back up-river by more mules.

We were on our own. The only other passenger on the boat headed down a path along the river, ignoring Phyllis's goodbye greeting with a blank stare. We followed the main trail up the bank toward the high Sierra, crossing into a peninsula never accessed by wheeled vehicles, a land occupied by humans for

3,000 years but without the ravages of modern technology, a culture unaltered by machine-made parts or process, a place where all the needs of life were supplied by what was immediately available from the Earth.

Somehow I had been waiting to walk in this land since childhood—a land out of time where perhaps the earliest humans on this continent had lived. I had *sensed* this world from the time I rode horses in the woods of the Texas Hill Country as a four-year- old. Fueled by a subscription to *National Geographic* magazine as a child, I had traveled in my imagination on excursions to every continent on Earth. Born with this irresistible urge to step outside of the banal world of my parents, I imagined a living universe where everything was alive, conscious and aware—plants, animals, and sometimes humans. In lectures at CIDOC Institute in Cuernavaca, I heard theories that this part of Guerrero was the center of a pre-Olmec, undiscovered civilization dating back to 2500 BC, which would make it the oldest in the Americas.

Phyllis shared my excitement, but needed to keep me solidly grounded on Earth.

"What time do you think we'll get to a town?" she asked.

"Tomorrow, maybe," I said, in a forced whisper, intent on remembering every detail of this walk. "Copalillo is several days' walk, according to Pilar, but I want to feel our way there, not just barge into town."

We had reached the top of the bank and saw ahead of us the backdrop of the Sierras, vaguely purple in the clouds. In the valley spread out before us were large round mounds covered in vegetation.

Phyllis touched my arm. "Wow. You're right; it's magical here. I don't see anybody but I feel like I'm being watched. This must be like what Columbus would have seen, exploring the New World."

"You got it. Only you're off by a few thousand years. We're seeing what lost Siberian sailors saw in 2500 BC. The new thinking is that the whole Bering Strait theory—about cavemen crossing on foot and gradually moving south for millennia—had it all wrong, well not all wrong, just incomplete. There's evidence that humans came down the West Coast by boat thousands of years before getting here overland. There was an entire civilization built here that disappeared into the background a thousand years before Columbus—into little isolated sanctuaries like this one."

"So, what *do* you want to find here, my insane, blond-haired stranger? Are we looking for ancient temples, the first civilization in the New World?"

"No, it's crazier than that—and simpler. I don't want to *find* anything—I just want to walk back in time into a little corner of that world that never disappeared. And it wasn't the *New* World, from their point of view. It was the *Old* World—one that's been forgotten now."

I looked at her to see if she thought this was a game or if maybe I was psycho. She didn't. She understood me. Desire and gratitude filled my being.

"Okay, so it's 2500 BC," she said. "How is life different?"

"I don't know. We have to find out. I'm thinking every one of those bumps out there in the valley was a village or something."

The topography of the land across the Rio Amacuzac had changed subtly from the other side. It was still semi-tropical and green from the rainy season, but the soil was red-orange splotched with vibrant green shrubbery. In the background were huge mountains, even a volcano or two perhaps, but in the foreground were twenty or thirty elevated mounds shrouded in greenery and topped with copper and blue hues, shining in the sun. The effect was stunning, as if the roofs of temples were reflecting sunlight. The trail wound in and around them in endless curves.

We walked along the widest trail we could find for half the day. In mid-afternoon, we picked one of the mounds and looked for a path going up. There were no signs of habitation and no paths leading up to the flat top, fifty feet or so above the valley floor. We circled almost the entire mound before I found a break in the shrubbery, an almost hidden opening between two rock faces that contained a path to the top. We pulled the reluctant burros up the trail to a secluded spot by a spring for camp.

Once we were up in the clearing, we were surrounded by a forest of tall trees with bright copper-colored trunks and bluish-green leaves. Accentuating the copper and blue trees were even taller pale green cactus trees, hanging off of which were some kind of orchids. The combined effect was of shining gold.

"Look," Phyllis said. "There's a spring and a pool over there.

Let's make camp." The dogs who had been strangely quiet and on guard, began to run and play. Having re-provisioned in Atenango Del Rio, we made dinner: beans cooked slowly on a fire and reheated rice, strips of nopal cactus, hand-made tortillas from Pilar's cantina and fried sweetbread. After the meal, we shared a cerveza stashed in my pack. By early evening, a waning moon gave the valley an eerie blue light. We lay by the fire and studied the coals as we dreamed of spirits hovering nearby.

"Ready to retire?" I asked.

"So early? Don't you want to talk about ancient history?" she said with a smile.

We talked a while as the moon rose higher, then undressed in our makeshift tent, embracing as we tumbled into our sleeping bag, invoking the improbable balance, counterbalance and supernatural flight of human lovemaking, feeling the pull of shared body heat and the burning desire to trust another human being to enjoy your body as it were her own and to be rewarded in return by the yielding of her body to you as your spirit briefly escapes the artificial confines of your own skin. The hard ground yielded, undulated, supported, surrounded and then comforted us. Later, in the dark, as Phyllis slept, I recalled all the white-knuckled nights I had spent alone. How unimaginable to finally find this place of my desiring and to discover that trusting someone else with my dream was part of the path.

The next day, we lingered at camp, not tired, just happy and playful. Watching from our canvas lean-to as the sun revealed the morning, listening to birds announce our presence, we eventually bathed by the spring, lay naked in the warm sun, made black coffee, and imagined ourselves travelers in Tolkien's Middle Earth.

Around mid-day, we got it together, found the way down to the valley and fell back into the cadence of walking on the path. As Phyllis and I and our menagerie of dogs and burros moved away from camp, the path led up and out of the valley and southward across a mountain range. We walked all day, not talking much and re-immersing ourselves in the Sierra. We reached the summit and had a pleasant camp in the evening. The dogs seemed excited to be in charge again, leading the pilgrimage in the day and guarding the campground at night.

The next morning, we started the descent. The trail split into so many ways down and the view became so obscured that, by the end of the day, we really had no idea where we were. We hadn't seen any settlements or any travelers all day. To make things worse, my stomach started to feel queasy and then Phyllis's did too. Thinking back, we realized we'd made a terrible mistake. Just before making camp the night before, we had passed a spring dripping into a small pool under exposed tree roots. Breaking our rule of drinking only from known sources, we had both drunk deeply of the cool water.

Losing all attempts to follow the right path, we looked desperately for a place to camp. At the height of the sun the next day and unsure of our bearings, we came upon a clearing by a stream and quickly laid out a place to lie down. We were convulsed with stomach cramps and dizziness, alternating between vomiting and diarrhea. We had both lost a lot of fluids and were too weak to move.

We slept in fits through the night, groaning and turning on the hard ground. I dreamed of slaves pulling large loads of rocks up a mountain, falling and then feeling the lash of the overseer whipping them back to labor. I saw the faces of jaguars sneering at me through ferocious teeth.

By day's dawning, at least the cycles of cramps were taking longer to hit Phyllis but I was still just lying on the ground in pain. By noon Phyllis was able to hold down some water. I knew we had to get some of our fluids replaced. I considered the options and they weren't great. Neither one of us could walk nor were there any emergency services for one of us to seek. I could ride on a burro but then we couldn't carry all our gear and Phyllis couldn't walk far anyway. We passed the day just lying on the ground feeling very far from home.

That night, the dogs were restless. It was a moonless night and several times the dogs woke us with low growl and occasionally loud barking. I heard noises in the brush which I imagined to be hostile animals. Distant drum beats throbbed in my head. I dreamed of eyes shining just outside the circle of our fire and human sacrifices. By the next morning, Phyllis was feeling better. She was able to cook some rice but we couldn't eat more than a few spoonfuls. The cramps were gone and we began to be able to hold down some solid food but were very weak.

"Are we going to make it out of here?" Phyllis asked.

"Of course, we are." I answered, with no conviction.

"I think we're completely lost."

"Pilar said any way you went downhill, you reached

Copalillo. I'm going to climb up above us and see if I can pick out a route down."

"You're leaving me here alone?"

"I won't lose sight of you."

Gringo accompanied me, leaving the other dogs behind with Phyllis. After slowly climbing up an animal trail above our camp, I scaled a large rock outcropping. On the horizon I thought I observed what looked like a village on the horizon, highlighted by the sun. Was it delirium? Blocking out the clear sky on the horizon were rain clouds, high in the peaks to the west.

Encouraged by the view, I returned to Phyllis and talked about what to do. Although we were camped by a stream, we were dehydrated and dangerously low on safe water. We had no choice but to start walking if we were going to survive. I had watched the sun's path and made my best guess about the direction to Copalillo. With no swagger and heads down, we managed to put one foot in front of the other.

The crossing was shallow, a foot deep and thirty feet across. We wore huaraches, made-in-Tilzapotla sandals which are a marvel of form and function. With a sole cut from a discarded tire tread and the top a single piece of leather laced through four metal staples, huaraches are comfortably cushioned and molded to the foot. They fit my feet so well I almost didn't need the strap. One pair of huaraches was the only footwear either of us carried.

"Does the creek look deeper to you now that we've crossed it?" Phyllis asked, after we found the path on the other side.

"Yeah, I think it's rising," I said. "Look at the rain clouds up at the peak."

An hour later, we came to another intersection with the same creek. This time the crossing was deeper and wider, but it still looked passable. The dogs were good swimmers and usually the first ones in the water but this time they held back. The burros held back from *everything* by instinct and this was no exception. Halfway across the creek, coaxing the dogs to follow and pulling the burros through every step, we realized we were in trouble. First, we underestimated the depth of the water in the middle of the creek; it was over my waist. Secondly, the water was rising rapidly and moving faster. Too late to turn back, we held hands and pushed and pulled from rock to rock. The burros were swimming, having partially submerged our packs in water but, at least, they were moving in the right direction. The dogs were swimming but had to fight the current to stay with us.

Phyllis, who normally could drive me crazy asking inappropriate questions to strangers or just making idle conversation while I was "in the zone," was uncharacteristically quiet and didn't panic. We fought our way to more shallow water with the burros and three of the dogs.

"We can't rest here," I shouted. "The water's still rising. Let's push on."

"Star can't make it across. Oh my God, he's trying to reach us instead of going for the closest shore," Phyllis shouted, looking behind us. "The current's carrying him downstream."

"We have to move now! Let's hurry for the shore so he'll follow," I said.

By the time we made it to dry land, Star was out of sight around the bend. We headed for higher ground followed by the other dogs, who were close behind us. The creek was turning into a flash flood. All the dogs made it to shore except Star, who was carried downstream. I was calming the burros. Phyllis ran to find Star, but returned soon in tears.

"The banks are too steep down there and there's no access. I can't see him; I can't even see the water. He's gone," she said.

"I never should have let us cross," I said. "It looks like the trail follows the creek. And I lost one of my sandals in the river. It's really going to slow me down. But we have to keep going and keep calling Star. He'll come."

We moved slowly along the trail for an hour, Phyllis yelling "Star, here boy, Star, where are you?" while I limped along with one bare foot, trying to keep the other dogs close. Without shoes I was completely incapacitated, my right foot already sore and painful from rocks on the trail. We came to a partially fallen adobe wall with a gate, so we entered, yelling out "*Bueno?*"

Suddenly a man appeared in the path with a machete in his belt and his hand on the machete. He did not look *indio*; he was heavier and had a round face and the look of a *mestizo*, the mixed race of indigenous people and Spanish conquistador that is the quintessential Mexican look. As I was about to speak to him, our lost dog Star came panting and running up the trail and collapsed into Phyllis's arms. There was pandemonium as we all greeted Star: the dogs barking, the burros braying, Phyllis crying and me trying to be calm.

As I looked around us, I realized we had stumbled into a

courtyard of sorts, the ground paved with flat stones, surrounded on three sides by flat-cut rock walls partially covered by tropical growth and dissolved by time and rain into a matrix of carved stone and jungle overgrowth. The man who had met us at the entrance had a curled lip that projected something between contempt and cruelty.

"What are you doing here?"

"We had a hard time crossing the creek. I lost my sandal. And we almost lost this puppy."

The man did not speak but spit on the ground.

"Could we buy some tortillas?"

"Got none."

"By any chance do you have a spare sandal? I lost mine in the creek."

"Got none. Stop asking questions."

As he spoke, the man took an aggressive step forward, and my dog Gringo curled his teeth and growled. All the dogs took the cue and stood as a pack. The man pulled out the machete but stepped back.

"Wait here," he said, and disappeared behind another crumbling stone wall. One of the top stones was eroded but resembled some kind of animal.

"I get the feeling he's protecting something," Phyllis said.

"Should we split?" I said, feeling we had a better chance with flight than fight.

"We'd be in the open out there, if he followed us. Let's just stand our ground for a while."

The man returned, with his machete in his right hand.

"Here, take this sandal and get the hell out of here!"

"What did we just stumble into?" Phyllis asked, as we hurried down the trail.

"*Los Sinverguenzas*, I think." I said. "The Shameless Ones. Guess that's who Augustina and Pilar were warning us about. This side of the Sierra is where they grow poppies for heroin."

We gathered our wits and kept moving along the main trail, finally encountering a few travelers who gave us directions. Not speaking but compelled by some unexplainable strength, Phyllis kept pushing when I wanted to rest. It still took the remaining daylight hours until we got a glimpse of Copalillo. Built on the largest of the strangely rounded hills, Copalillo was an island in the plain, an eroded rock feature rising like a medieval castle built by Nature. There was no imposing architecture but rather a compelling circularity. The trail leading into town circled around the hill instead of charging in; the path up to the town rose in concentric circles, even the cactus fences between residences were not laid out in straight lines.

It was dark when we arrived and the path into town kept winding up and around without bringing us to an inviting gate. Finally we came to a clear spot where, just over the cactus fence, an oil lamp lit a compound of numerous conical woven-reed houses. With the stars shining and the moon not yet risen, the mystical mounds loomed dark in the valley below like islands in a sea. As a kid, I had seen *National Geographic* pictures of conical structures like this before in other parts of the world: Harran, Syria, Italy, the coastline of Wales. It was the oldest known way humans built homes.

We shook the gate and shouted *"Bueno?"* The greeting was soon answered by an elderly man and we were welcomed in, strangers deemed by tradition to be potential bearers of good fortune.

"Tlaquilte. Could I buy tortillas?" I asked.

Asking to "buy tortillas" always seemed ridiculous because no one would take money for hospitality but that's what Augustina had taught us to say (instead of "Hey we're tired and hungry, would you take us in and give us food and drink and a place to stay?"). We were welcomed in without a question and practically collapsed on a wooden bench. The burros were led away to be fed, our packs lowered off them. The dogs were fed old tortillas soaked in bean broth.

We were obviously too late for dinner but an older *abuelita* gave orders to several young women who went scurrying off to a separate kitchen house to prepare food for us. Our hands were taken by small children to lead us into the kitchen hut and seat us in small chairs to eat thick hand-made tortillas, *nopales* (peeled cactus), rice, and a bowl of ground chile salsa that was *muy picante*—very spicy. Water was poured from a large clay vessel. To my sensitive palate, the chile was liquid fire; Phyllis had no problem with fiery foods. I survived the burn and felt surprisingly satisfied with such a simple meal. After eating, we were served a hot beverage which had a strong bitter herbal taste mixed with a soothing sweetness. The numbness in my feet and hands melted away only to reveal the weakness and physical pain of multiple days of exertion and illness. Phyllis must have felt the same.

Outside by a small fire, the extended family sat in a semi-circle. Their ages ranged from young children to the very old. The whole family carried on a lively discussion in Nahuatl of which we didn't understand a word. Phyllis and I spoke to them in Spanish. The elders and one young couple close to our age, introduced as David and Marta, were the only ones who spoke any Spanish and they spoke it at about the same level as we did. The elders smiled a lot and the children looked at us and laughed and we all smiled some more.

We motioned an offer to help clean our plates, but the girls just giggled and took our hands to lead us back to our accommodations.

Room was made for us to sleep in the elders' house, a round structure twenty feet across resembling a tipi made of woven reeds with walls four feet high topped by a conical structure of posts covered with thatch. We were given a bed consisting of four posts driven in the ground with poles across to make a frame. The mattress itself was made of straight sticks woven together and covered by a straw mat. It was quite comfortable; a blanket was hung for privacy. No resort hotel could have felt more exotic than this room and our own parents couldn't have made us feel more at home. How we had survived the ordeal, how we had found this family; it all seemed dreamlike. We fell asleep holding on to each other as the sounds of insects, birds, animals—domestic and wild—cried out a welcome.

CHAPTER SEVENTEEN

REHAB AND THE REBIRTH OF MEMORY

"These circuits remain throughout life as the agency that generates the feeling of our being. It is the anchor of our loving. It is the quiet voice inside of us. It is our innocence. It is the source of our creativity, our conscience, our free will. It is the fountain of our aliveness. None of this is mystical or magical. It is just the way the Authentic Being is organized in the brain."

—Robert A. Berezin, MD
"On Consciousness: Explaining the Brain's Beautiful Illusion"

Saturday, August 20, 2011, 10:08 p.m. Coma Day 182.

Three days ago, we moved to HealthSouth Rehabilitation Hospital. At least that's what my diary says. For me, it's been mostly a blur of activity. For Phyllis, this is hospital number five in six months. I'm practicing my now familiar medical routine for getting acclimated to a new hospital.

1. Meet the medical nurses and doctors and establish yourself as a partner.

2. Meet the staff, the ones who really do the work.
3. Stake out your claim to the space. It shouldn't feel like a prison.
4. Cultivate your champions among the elite (doctors and administrators).
5. Look for angels among the downtrodden. Other patients are sometimes warriors.
6. Hope for miracles; no, *expect* miracles.
7. Keep up the familiar pace; routine is a lifesaver.
8. Never panic (good luck!)
9. Keep dancing in the moonlight, even if the dance floor is in your dreams.

Moving from City Hospital to HealthSouth is a bit like leaving a tiny garage apartment and moving into a brand-new hotel suite. Everything's clean and roomy at HealthSouth; City Hospital was old and crumbling. But when you leave your garage apartment for the hotel, you also leave behind the metaphorical kind landlady who always made you chicken soup and fretted over you constantly; instead you get professionals trained in efficiency. The tradeoff isn't a bad one but you realize how much you owe to the place you left.

When Phyllis left City Hospital on Wednesday, the whole on-duty staff, from cleaning lady to director, lined up to give her a hug goodbye. Tears were shed on both sides. At Health-South, we have daily doctor visits and an individualized, printed therapy schedule delivered daily at 6 a.m. with a free newspaper. The schedule includes a shower at 7 a.m. and breakfast in the cafeteria at 7:30. Then Craig, Phyllis's young physical therapist (think physical trainer) comes to get her to go to the gym.

Unlike City Hospital, there's *nobody* here for long who doesn't have a good shot at getting better. If you're not improving here, they move you out quickly. On the other hand, most patients, like Phyllis, look like they've landed on a planet with five times the force of gravity as that of Earth. Steps are tortured; leg lifts are slower than a slow-motion video, the patients are in one universe and all the rest of us in another parallel one where we walk around without thinking about it.

Sitting in the brightly-lit and colorfully-painted hospital cafeteria at dinner, Phyllis and I are assigned to sit with three other female patients, Beverly, Jimmy and Sara. They all appear older than Phyllis. Beverly and Sara are not as handicapped as her, but Jimmy is worse, her eyesight affected by a stroke. They all chat: talking about their dinner, talking about the techs, talking about their condos and talking about the little dog with tuna breath they left behind. They all have a determination to persevere, Sara most of all. At dinner, she dictates a crash course to the table on how to "disturb" a doctor.

"The first thing you have to figure out about a doctor," Sara says, her silver hair well-combed and coiffed, "is whether he chats *about* you or talks *to you*. If he's gonna go on and on, looking professional and telling the nurse, '*She* has this condition and *she* needs to do this therapy,' you gotta look him in the eye and say 'Hey Buster, you need to talk to *me!*' I call it disturbin' the doctor. Otherwise, they don't know you're alive."

Male patients are rare in the cafeteria. They tend to take meals in their room and if they do eat in the cafeteria, they almost always sit alone in silence. There are no families joining their loved ones, no other spouses other than me, and no children: where are they? Are they afraid of this place, afraid they might catch something and be condemned to stay here themselves?

Meanwhile, every day here feels like a miracle is unfolding. Phyllis has responded well to the increased stimulation. She doesn't complain about the work or about anything. She's awake from morning to night to some degree, in and out of her wheelchair and bed. She's started learning to roll her own wheelchair. She stood unsteadily on her own legs today, holding herself with two rails. Her eyesight has sharpened; she can read the nurse's notes on the white-board across the room. In a hundred ways, I see her body begin to twitch and move and start to coordinate, her unconscious brain secretly watching it all carefully, recording, memorizing, and helping her do better the next day.

Her wakefulness, however, varies throughout the day from alert to drowsy. At any given moment, she might not know she was in Fayetteville or where her room was. A little gentle grounding reminds her that she is in our home town. I list all the hospitals she's lived in for six months and it brings her back. There's a tune stuck in my head but I can't remember the lyrics, so I make up my own words, imagining Bob Dylan and Leonard Cohen in a duet, singing alternate lines:

> *Wish the news could be all good*
> *Don't you know I dream that it could?*
> *None of it really makes sense, how we go round*
> *But I'd jump off a cliff just to hold you going down.*
> *I love to watch you, baby, fighting hard just for me*

I see you lost in the storm, how hard it must be.
It's so hard to get back, when you're lost in the woods
I'd steal from heaven, baby, just to get you the goods.
I'd walk by your side; I'd crawl in the mud
But I got nothing to save you, darlin', nothing but love.
Wish the news could be all good
Don't you know I dream that it could?
None of it really makes sense, how we go round
But I'd jump off a cliff just to hold you going down.

Tuesday, August 23, 2011, 10:50 p.m. Coma Day 185.

Our first week at HealthSouth Hospital has flown by. I'm *almost* relaxed after seven days of stress adjusting to a new hospital. At first, the nurses all have their routines, the techs are busy. You feel you are either in the way or being actively ignored. Doctors come and go, mostly during the day when I'm away at work. Orders are given and carried out without any notice; tests are performed and prescriptions administered. They don't know me here yet. At first, I feel strongly that I have to assert myself as the primary gatekeeper between Phyllis and the medical staff; but that's hard to do when you arrive without any credentials.

The second day here, a nurse came with an antibiotic I knew nothing about. When I asked why, I was told Phyllis had a UTI. I told the nurse that I felt strongly that the doctor should have notified me. I asked her to *please* have the doctor let me know, in person or by phone, any time a new condition is diagnosed or a prescription given. *"No new meds without my permission—please add it to the notes."* You usually have to repeat it to the next shift nurse for the word to get around. Most nurses respect that attitude if it's stated without rancor and pretty soon, they explain to me every pill they're giving her. They pass the word to the doctors who start making sure they tell any medical news about Phyllis to whichever Team Phyllis volunteer member is here at the time. Yes the Team has moved with me, slipping into the room in two-hour shifts as before, recording everything in a little spiral notebook.

I try to balance my tough-guy act with listening skills—the ones Phyllis taught me. I ask every tech and nurse their name and try to find out something about their life: are they married, how many shifts do they work a week, where they're from. The nurses are great sources of practical medical experience; they usually know more than the doctors about the daily realities of different medicines and illnesses. Everybody has a life and most of us like to talk about it and medical staff is no different. While I'm listening and learning, I chat about Phyllis's health, what she's been through, and what the idiosyncrasies of her condition are. By now, the hard edges of the fast-moving efficient ones are softened and the lax discipline of the spacey ones are sharpened. Everybody's on the team and cheering her on.

Phyllis's doctor is on the ball. From the first day, he suggested something I wanted to do months ago: schedule her second daily dose of Ritalin at noon instead of 4 p.m. That way, she's most awake when she's doing therapy, instead of when she's trying to sleep. He also has had experience with a patient like her—albeit years ago—the first doctor to make that claim! He suggested a second medication, Amantadine, an experimental drug (in this application) which releases dopamine and norepinephrine from nerve endings. It's used together with Ritalin and so far, it seems to be working miracles. Phyllis is doing four hours a day (spread out over seven hours) of therapy; one more than required by insurance (as proof of progress) and she still says "I'm not doing that much." She wants to get up out of her wheelchair and walk. By God, I think she will!

I've been sleeping in the room with her. At first, the staff pointed out that, technically, the other half of the two-bed room was for another patient. I noticed, though, that most patients here don't have a roommate, since the hospital is only about half occupied. So, by now, I've managed to occupy the whole room. I just started staying over. No one said I couldn't and the nurses act like they're collaborators in a conspiracy. I make my bed neatly in the morning. I've been trained by a tech and cleared by staff to do a "transfer," that is, to safely help Phyllis into or out of bed. I don't shy away from doing anything that the staff does, so they accept that I live here and I can help make their job easier. I've even changed her nighttime diaper. With my help, Phyllis can shower and use the attached bathroom and she is brushing her own teeth! The nurses try hard to be quiet when they come in at night to turn Phyllis on her side but I always wake up. Even so, I'm sleeping better here than at home. Like Dylan sings, I've thrown away my ticket 'cause "Tonight I'll Be Staying Here With You."

Sunday, August 28, 2011, 7:15 a.m. Coma Day 190.

It's not easy to get away with much at HealthSouth Rehab. I know because Saturday night, I slipped out with my daughter Angela to a concert by master songwriter Guy Clark ("Desperados Waiting for a Train," "L.A. Freeway," etc.), who was the headliner at our local Roots Concert. Although Guy looked a little worse for the wear from all the years, he sang his heart out, picking the guitar and telling stories until almost midnight, way late for me. I rang the buzzer at 1 a.m. to get into the hospital and barely managed to convince the skeptical night nurse that I lived here with my girl. A few hours later, at 5:45 a.m., they came to the room to wake Phyllis and get her up in her chair for breakfast. Even on Sunday, there's a schedule: eat, bathe and be social. I'd really rather sleep in but no one's asking.

Our daughter Angela leaves today after a wonderful two-week visit, in between leading student tours to China and returning to teach in Chicago. She's a girl to make a dad proud: smart and opinionated, humble and easy-going, able to chat with a president (Bill Clinton at her graduation), bum around China on her own and maintain a website describing her travels for her elementary students in Chicago. She's a total believer in her mom's recovery and has been with her every day for the last two weeks.

This coming weekend is our celebration of Phyllis's sixtieth birthday. I ran into a roadblock with the case manager at HealthSouth who was adamant that Phyllis couldn't leave the facility for a celebration or my insurance would cut her off. I fretted over that but a call to my insurance manager, Brett, assured me that nothing could be better for her than a birthday celebration so we're back on track. I could tell that the HealthSouth case manager didn't like me going over her head.

Just to get in practice, I sneaked Phyllis away for a long walk in her wheelchair this afternoon on a nearby walking trail. It was easy. Patients are frequently wheeling around the halls for exercise; I just took a quick turn out the double doors that lead outside and there we were in the Great Outdoors. We were gone for an hour and she did fine, sitting upright, staying awake and taking in the sunshine. Leaving the premises is definitely against hospital policy and a nurse coming in to work spotted me but she just smiled in complicity.

After ten days at HealthSouth, Phyllis is much stronger although a bit sore from all the stretching and standing. She's suffered swollen legs and feet, some tiny capillaries breaking in her ankle and a really sore tendon in her right foot. Getting all the joints and muscles to work together is a huge effort and is a painful struggle that takes all her brain and body's concentration and will continue to do so for some undetermined time. But she labors on and she smiles a lot and doesn't really see what all the fuss is about. She is just a kid with a dream.

Tuesday, August 30, 2011, 10:45 p.m. Coma Day 192.

Six months of watching Phyllis progress from comatose to eyes-wide-open and back around the carousel to unconscious again has made me afraid to celebrate her progress, followed as it has inevitably been by regression and back-sliding. Even so, I *have* learned to celebrate each present moment with her, even the tense fearful ones. By loving the journey, not the destination, I cheat despair and stay ready for the good fight. With Phyllis's direction, I've turned the hospital room into our home—declaring it our sacred space. I remember, day by day, how Phyllis and I started our lives together and how we learned to make life magical. Remembering the magic keeps me from the fear that time will leave us behind.

So today, sitting in the hospital cafeteria with Phyllis and several visiting friends eating dinner, I experienced her being fully back with us—eating, laughing, turning up her mouth on the right as she raises her eyebrows (as if to say in her unique way "I get you, I know you, I like you, I think you're funny, I see your shortcomings, I like you anyway"). Everybody there was blown away. They didn't know how they knew but they *knew* this was Phyllis undergoing a new advance, a new re-discovery of self and we were all grinning giddily.

Phyllis doesn't get why we are smiling. No matter how many times we tell her how miraculous every step is, she just waves her hand in the air (and we gasp that she is able to wave her hand!). She seems to have returned from her journeys in the mysterious inner-world that we experienced as the passage of time without any such idea of linear experience. She is awake in the present and yet remembers no hospital stays or Life Flight rides or nights of prayer and chanting. She does remember some individual nurses or events or visitors during her coma but they exist for her in suspended reality, without the context of time or what part they played in her healing. Who's to say which under-standing of time is reality? To misquote John Lennon: "Phyllis and me, that's reality."

While in this euphoric state eating cafeteria food with gusto, the hospital case manager came up and told me that all difficul-ties had been resolved with her "issues" over Phyllis going to her sixtieth birthday party on Saturday. I had been chewing steel screws for days over her intransigence against letting us leave and be normal for two hours. All the frustration with months of medical bureaucracy melted away and she wished us well ("Just this one time, though," she says). Memories flood over me of all the bureaucrats in all my life who said I couldn't and I felt pure love and gratitude to my dad who always taught me I *could*. Our journey isn't even close to being finished but for today, I'll shout a very happy but uncertain *Hallelujah*.

Friday, September 3, 2011, 9:50 p.m. Coma Day 193.

Phyllis finished the week with a flourish of physical feats, staying upright in the "standing frame" for forty-five minutes, holding herself upright on the parallel bars several times. She's heard it a thousand times, if she's heard it once, how well she's doing, but it's all very strange to her. She doesn't have any perspective on how far she's come. She just knows when she wakes up that she's ready to get up and get on with *stuff*.

Not that the waking up part is total or finished. The more physical exertion she manages, the more it seems to borrow energy from her short-term memory. So by Friday, the day before her birthday party, the whole thing is very confusing to her. When I run home to feed the dog, she wants to go with me. I have to keep re-orienting her. She just wants to land here on Earth again and be part of the scene. Instead everybody keeps asking her to *relive* the coma, to tell them what she remembers, did she see a light or have a visit with God. I think she feels, as James Taylor sings it in "Country Road," that she'd have to be a fool to want to go back that way again.

As much ground as she has gained, there is that much further to go. The days come, like last Tuesday, when I wrote about her being "back with us," when it all clicked and she could grasp her vision, past, present, and future the same. But then, don't we all have those moments when we see it all so clearly? And which one of us can make them last forever?

As she prepared for her birthday party on Saturday, Phyllis was struggling to keep it all together but she did. She wanted me to take her to our house (as if we could just jump in the car together), to cook for her father and sisters who came for the celebration, "just to make them comfortable." Our friends Rich and Sharmon came to the hospital to cut and style her hair. Our son Preston shuttled the arriving family from the airport to our house. Our son Andrew came early on Saturday and wheeled Phyllis outside for some fresh air. Finally, the time came. Daughter Julia adorned her mother in a colorful dress and scarf. We strapped Phyllis down in a wheelchair which was bolted to the floor inside an ambulance and the parade began. Julia and I followed closely behind in my car. Phyllis arrived ceremoniously at my son Joey's house. A waiting crowd of more than 100 friends and family were there for her entrance as guests lined up for an hour to greet her sitting in her wheelchair like a celebrity.

Images of happiness: a giant birthday cake, her Dad singing her a French love song (co-dedicated to our late Grandma Julia), a gift of a shirt printed with her proclamation as an eight-year-old: "I'm from Brooklyn and I'm tough, too!", Travis and baby Iris singing their anthem song about "living in the woods and the trees," Joey and Nikki's new house in its first grand soiree, grandkids Iris, Maddie and Hayden welcoming everyone to their party, so many dear friends!

I hovered and fretted, of course, worried that it would all be too much but she took it in grand style. I panicked when Phyllis insisted Nikki serve her a glass of wine and proceeded to drink it down but there was no stopping her. Never has been.

Tuesday, September 6, 2011, 10:53 p.m. Coma Day 196.

Today (Phyllis's sixtieth birthday) completed three weeks at HealthSouth. I began our stay here with great trepidation and uncertainty about the choice of this facility. Looking back, it's been like a volcano erupting with flows of new energy and possibilities. Brett, my insurance company case manager, pushed me to come here and now I think he had the right intuition about the place. HealthSouth is modern and up-to-date but there's something more than the physical therapy happening: the combination of all our experiences with hospitals for the last six months together with just the right timing for Phyllis to wake up and be herself. Every day that she wakes up more, it's a little frightening to her but it seems to happen with just the right amount of incentive to get moving and return to living.

I've completely moved into HealthSouth with Phyllis. The room is comfortable, the food is tolerable with some supplementation and the staff is single-minded in their goal to get you up and out of here. Most people stay for a few weeks at most; we're going on four weeks, making us already old-timers (and the only resident couple!). I'm sure there are facilities somewhere that are more specifically trained in neurological disorders and treatment but I can't imagine a place as flexible given our support network or one that would be a bigger inspiration to her.

There's no resting on your laurels here. Insurance only pays if you're progressing. Hit a plateau for very long and the support goes away. At the same time, everyone here, including Phyllis, has to face the discouragement of their handicap. We who live in the *physically functioning* world cheer her on for her stamina and progress but for anyone who has once known how to walk, articulate their limbs, think, and tie their shoes, only to have it taken from them, then the tiny incremental changes that come with one session's exertion are an insult rather than a boost to your self-esteem. The universal praise the patient receives for each tiny step only reinforces the gigantic task ahead. If each small change in the use of her fingers, for example, is such a huge accomplishment, how many thousands of attempts will it take to be back to "normal" functioning for every part of her body and mind—something that the rest of us do every day without conscious thought or gratitude?

Phyllis's battle is fully engaged now but it is perhaps only just beginning. The more she can do physically and think clearly, the more she must struggle with all the "second thoughts" of her life, doubts we all have but manage to console with a back seat in our psyche, unable to derail our forward progress. Find yourself in Phyllis's condition and you will have to battle all those mental challenges as well. The battle is about summoning the will to be fully functional again and not letting the demons in your personality tell you to give up. It's a battle worth fighting and I see it in all our dinner mates at the cafeteria as well. It is a long way home from here but Phyllis has a good chance of making that journey, especially with a devoted family and tireless friends to back her up.

Sunday, September 11, 2011, 7:25 a.m. Coma Day 201.

Three weeks of family reunion is almost over. We've had all six of our children here at some point in the last three weeks. We've also had Phyllis's dad, her sisters Ro and Theresa, and first cousin Rita. Our dog Bernie, now fifteen years old, got extra attention all week. The family repopulated our house on Ila Street with great gusto and much cleaning. Theresa organizes; Rita is the voice of calm; Ro cooks (or rather, everyone cooks but Ro *loves* to cook); Dad tells stories and meets people. They bring life wherever they go. If houses have feelings (and I'm sure they do), then the heart of 402 Ila Street is bursting with joy to be filled once again with the sounds of laughter and the aroma of garlic being peeled for pasta fagioli (pronounced *fazool* in

Neapolitan dialect). Ah, Grandma Giulia, your spirit was there at the hearth, laughing and telling us how to cook.

Unfortunately, I wasn't a very good host to my visiting family. Most of the week, I was too busy to be at the house and when I was there, it felt eerie. Given that Phyllis was unable to be there, I had a ghostly feeling of invisibility, as if I was watching a play but not acting in it. Back in our hospital room, I had a leading role to play and a leading actress to inspire me even if there was no script to follow. Phyllis's dad, Louis, spent most of the days with Phyllis in her room. Wherever he is, there is fellowship. It might take *me* a week to remember a tech's name and know something about them. Dad somehow can meet someone in the hallway and by the time he reaches Phyllis's room have learned the essential details of their background and make them smile. Louis gives off this vibe that he's always known you. Everyone he meets is interesting to him; no one leaves the room without feeling celebrated by Phyllis's dad. His memory is populated with people and stories from the streets of Brooklyn of the 1930s to the changes in Fayetteville today. He always leaves you better than you were.

This last week at HealthSouth was Phyllis's most intense therapy to date. Typically, she has six forty-five-minute physical, occupational or speech therapy sessions during the day. After finishing three weeks here, her progress is not as dramatic as at the beginning. Now it's repetitive, the hard work of using the muscles over and over. Her upper body, shoulders and arms show the most recovery in both strength and coordination. Her legs have gained in strength and will hold her up but they are still unstable and steps are torturous.

Most patients here stay two to three weeks in preparation for a return to independent living of some degree. That makes me second-guess the wisdom of having Phyllis here at all, even though her progress in a month is phenomenal. The facility's orientation is on quick recovery of basic functioning and Phyllis's case is so much more complicated than most because her neurological damage was so unusual. Speech therapy, for example, is intended to rehabilitate her neurological condition but it is the weakest of their treatments. Exercises are supposedly aimed at memory and concentration but are so trite and mundane, they bore the patient beyond interest: counting buttons and threading a block with three holes.

What is needed is a way to pique her interest and give her a motivation to learn, Some engagement of reason that will help her brain slow down the carousel that revolves between engaged consciousness and random storms of electricity firing from one part of the brain to another. "Speech therapy," in this context, is a misnomer. The goal for her is not improved speaking capacity; it's improved mental functioning. Many exercises focus on numerical acuity. Numbers are as hard for Phyllis to remember as is her physical location. I sit in on classes with her and the enormity of the task before us is depressing. Fortunately, I am the one preoccupied with dark thoughts, not her.

Phyllis fell twice this week when I wasn't looking. No harm was done but both falls happened because her impulse to move is waking up faster than her coordination and strength, and definitely faster than her self-awareness of any limitations. The human brain is an incredibly evolved miracle—recognizing and coordinating all the information coming at you from outside, meshing and comparing it with all your memorized, unconscious experiences and potential responses and making sense of it all while you drive the car, talk on the phone and eat French fries.

So why isn't *my brain* processing all this more clearly? Questions I can't answer: how long will it take for Phyllis to make sense of it all, how long will we stay here, where will we live after and how will we make it all work?

When I'm falling like this through a hole in the floor of my otherwise solid universe, I ask myself: *What do I know?* I know that whatever path life chooses for us, Phyllis and I will walk it together. I know that to be alive, no matter the circumstances, is a gift and an adventure. So what if I don't know how we're going to put all the pieces together? We never did. As Leonard Cohen says in "The Stranger Song," none of us has a secret chart to get us to the heart of the past or the future. But we do have the miracle of the present.

CHAPTER EIGHTEEN

ANCIENT WORLD, NEW DISCOVERIES

"Archeologists digging here in the remote mountains southwest of Copalillo, Mexico where villagers speak an ancient Indian tongue, have unearthed the earliest stone buildings found so far on the North American continent, along with a monumental carved stone head. Confirmed dates for the site, built by the ancient Olmec civilization, are 1200 B.C."

—Mimi Crossley, *The Washington Post*

November 1, 1973

"Are you awake? Something's going on outside."

"It's still dark. I think the family is starting their day."

Outside our thatched roof hut, we heard the sounds of people talking and animals responding to commands. We got up wearing the clothes we had fallen asleep in the night before, having arrived in Copalillo exhausted and recovering from a near-disaster on the trail. We joined the hub-bub outside.

Marta explained that her family was preparing to go to the well to bathe and draw drinking water. We dressed and joined

them in the dark outside the elders' house. Two horses were
saddled with large clay vessels nestled in a wooden frame. We
followed the processional out the gate in the dark and down the
path. Families were stirring throughout the village, smoke was
rising from cooking huts and animals were being fed. Donkeys
brayed, dogs barked and roosters crowed. As we made our way
down the hill, I noted there were no stores, restaurants, or
businesses, although the town was big enough to hold several
thousand people. By the time we descended the town hill to
the valley below, there was a hint of light on the horizon. Time
was hard to judge as our procession joined others in a parade of
families slowly dispersing in various directions.

Sometime after the sun rose, we arrived at a large opening
in the brush, surrounded by tall trees giving shade. There were
several wells nearby, apparently belonging to our host family;
other families had taken separate paths to their own water
source. We were a group of fourteen people, spanning three
generations. The men and the women separated, the men to fill
the vessels at a designated drinking well, the women to bathe in
a private area with its own well. After the women had finished
bathing and the young girls had helped Phyllis to brush and
braid her long hair, we changed places and the men bathed by
pouring buckets of water over our heads while standing on flat
rocks as the sun beat down. After lots of conversation in Nahuatl
with chuckling and jostling, we dressed again and re-joined the
women. Then we processed back up the hill. Unlike the early
morning trek down to the wells, which was done in the dark
and in an almost silent, Biblical pilgrimage, the return trip was

full of laughing banter and chatter with neighbors on the trail. The burros, heavily laden with earthenware jugs, delivered the compound's water for the day.

Back at the family compound, we were seated with the elders in small chairs in the yard. Everyone else had chores to do. It took two men to unload the water pots and heft them onto stands in the kitchen house. The compound consisted of five conical thatched houses, one for the grandparents which we shared, the kitchen house, one for David and his family, and one for each of his sisters and spouses. The houses were spaced over several acres belonging to the family.

We were treated with the attention and care accorded to the young and infirm, both because we were exotic foreigners and because we obviously knew so little about how to take care of ourselves in this ancient world. We were served breakfast and after eating, joined the children who patiently shared their work with us, braiding strips of plant fibers into tiny ropes which would be woven into hats and straw bowls. All the adults worked on various stages of the family business—weaving hammocks. The sun warmed and soothed us as we watched the compound buzzing with activity. We were fully awake but extremely weak from sick days in the mountains. An elderly woman brought us small cups of a bitter drink and insisted we drink it down, pointing to her stomach to explain it was to treat our intestinal disorder (which was probably dysentery).

Patience wasn't something a child was *taught* in village life in Copalillo; it was, quite literally, woven into the fabric of everyday life. Phyllis and I settled into life with David and

Marta's family as if we had always been there and would never leave. We were treated not only as honored guests but in fact more like young family relations, *children* in spite of our age, because of our obvious lack of practical training in the ways of survival, but lovingly and with complete acceptance. We slowly recovered from our ordeal on the trail. I felt as if I had been wrapped in a warm blanket and I could tell Phyllis felt it too: the experience of coming *home*, the prodigal children returning and being lovingly healed and welcomed.

After a few days, Marta showed Phyllis how to wind cotton thread around both arms to feed the warp threads of the loom used to make hammocks; David asked me to help him bring weaving supplies from the storage hut. Hammock-weaving was the family occupation and had been as long as anyone could remember. Copalillo hammocks are renowned all over Mexico for their fine weave. Balsas River area hammocks are mentioned as items of tribute in records of Aztec emperors from 1,000 years ago.

"How do you sell the hammocks, David?" I asked.

"I cross the river and take them to Atenango Del Rio but I get very little," David said. "Atenago is where we always sold them. I want to go farther, *quizas* al norte, maybe as far as your homeland."

Two looms were set up under a thatched canopy to weave the family's hammocks. Posts were set up six feet apart, connected by horizontal posts. Hammocks are woven in a continuous loop, not tied, with the warp passed through the thread hundreds of times. Everyone in the family takes part: men, women and children, old and young. Children practice on two sticks stuck firmly in the ground to make small basket hammocks.

Starlit nights ran into busy days. David's family was always making and stockpiling hammocks and there were also chores to be done in the *milpa*, the family corn fields. Though the dry corn had been harvested, the fields were still filled with stalks which needed to be chopped, tied in bundles and transported to the family compound for use as animal feed. Trips were made to the winter gardens near the Rio Balsas to begin preparation for planting in the dry season.

"*Porque no queden aqui?*" David asked me one day in the milpa. Why don't you and Phyllis stay here?

"How would we live?"

"Plant corn and build a house on our land. You're part of our family now."

I thought about a life here, living as part of an ancient network, learning how to truly be at one with a place. But I also thought of all those we had left behind and how impossible it would be to explain all this to our families at home.

"Thanks David. I'm not sure. It's complicated."

"You have to keep going, don't you?"

"I think probably so."

"I understand. I too have things that no one wants me to do. I want to take our hammocks out into the world of the others—your world. My father doesn't want me to. We have always sold them in Atenango but no farther. Why should we be afraid of the other world?"

"I don't know David, your father might be right. The world I come from has a way of offering you more stuff than you need and making you believe it's the only way to be happy."

David's wife Marta was pregnant with their second child. It didn't slow her down; her first child Moisés was two years old and already had been taught to weave grasses into hat-making material. Phyllis did her best to help her with the weaving, child care and cooking.

"David invited us to stay here and live, you know," I said, one night in bed.

"I know. They talked about it. Marta wants us to stay too," said Phyllis.

"What do you think?" I asked.

"Part of me says absolutely yes. But it's a long way from home," she said. "If we stayed with the family for a while, it would only get harder to leave them. Just like Augustina and Don Lauro. I already miss them terribly. But we can't just abandon our own families."

One night we sat with the elders in a ring of small chairs and looked out at the world. David's father, Don Pablo, had a small battery-powered transistor radio David had bought in Atenango. That night Don Pablo tuned it to his favorite channel, a fundamentalist Christian broadcasting from Brownsville, Texas. It was in English and the preacher was excitedly proclaiming the evils of modern culture and the approach of the *end times*. Don Pablo didn't understand a word but the cadence of the speaker fascinated him. He asked us for a translation of the preacher's words.

"*Dice que terminara el mundo,*" Phyllis said. He says the world is coming to an end.

Don Pablo's smile twinkled through his thick black mustache. "It's always ending and it's always reborn. Every morning." Then he raised his eyebrows as if he had remembered something and his expression darkened. "The ancient ones told us this change would come."

Phyllis's expression was so intense I thought she might cry. "Your family lives here together and you make room for everyone. Your town has many people but there are no police and no guns. Where I'm from, there is so much war-making but here I see only peace. Can't we all live this way?"

Don Pablo smiled. "Nothing goes on forever. Until now, the world forgot us. Our ancestors acted the same as yours are now: very powerful, very warlike but they forgot their place in the circle and they lost it all. That's how it is. Our tradition says all the world must encounter each other's ways before the current era—we call it the Fourth World—can end and the Fifth World begin. But even so, I am afraid for my son to travel out there. We have everything we need here. Why leave?"

November 25, 1973

We had lived with the family for almost a month. We helped with the weaving but so clumsily, we were like two-year-olds "helping" in the kitchen. When we weren't getting in everyone's way, learning to weave or cook, I suggested to Phyllis we go exploring.

"Let's check out some of those raised hills in the valley."

"After the sandal incident with the drug people, I'm not so sure we should."

"That was up in the Sierra. I don't think we have to worry here. Nobody's going to grow poppies in this valley, exposed as these islands are."

"They aren't islands. They're just bumps in the basin. Anyway, why are you so restless?"

"Look at this stone Don Pablo gave me. It has a spiral carved in it."

"Wow. It could have been carved or maybe it's just a fossil. Alright, let's take a day trip and see what we find."

To go exploring, the family packed us food in a woven bag, a petate mat and a water gourd. The round hills rose several hundred feet above the terrain, covered with trees. None of them was occupied or cultivated, so they were great for adventuring. They were just large enough to be totally isolated but not so big as to get lost. We wandered for an hour through the valley until we came upon one of the hills with a flat clearing surrounded by trees. We could not see the valley below or be seen because of the tall trees. We set out our picnic on the petate and lingered for hours.

"Have you noticed how this hill is terraced? Like to get up the hill from the field, there's big rectangular chunks of earth or maybe stone underneath. Maybe they were built by the ancient Olmecs."

"It's getting late; we better get going," Phyllis said. "We'll be walking in the dark."

"We just got here! Look around."

Towering in the distance around us was a dramatic panorama. The sun was setting full blood-red over the distant Pacific Ocean to the west and directly opposite was a snow-tipped volcano high in the Sierra, highlighted by the rays of the setting sun. I stretched my legs out, lying down on the clover-covered field. I could almost hear the sounds of the ceremonial ball game being played by the ancients and the roar of the crowd with each shot.

"I feel some strange vibe here," she said.

"Now who's restless?" I asked. "It's just 3,000-year-old spirits. They don't mean any harm."

"Yeah, like *you* know what they are!"

"Listen, we need to talk. I love it here but maybe we need to think of going home."

"I can't believe I'm hearing this from Marco Polo. Seriously, this was your dream to come here. Why go home now?"

"I don't know. It was something Don Pablo said about everyone learning each other's ways. I think this magical feeling of being part of something bigger that we feel here is something we can take with us. It's the same magical planet we live on whether it's Central Park in New York or the piney woods behind my parent's house in Houston. I want to go home."

She touched my hair and kissed me. I closed my eyes and

felt the Earth under my feet carrying us along in a merry-go-round ride at a thousand miles an hour through space. So what if the ride doesn't last forever? What intoxication to join with another for the journey.

November 30, 1973

The dogs were excited the day we finally left Copalillo, happy to return to a dog's life on the trail. We exchanged gifts: from Phyllis, earrings and a scarf for Marta; from me, a pocket knife for David. They gave us traveling food and a hammock; we gave the family women our five-pound bag of rice. I paid my respects to Don Pablo. Phyllis hugged Marta and with tears in her eyes, patted Marta's now-ample belly.

"*Cuidate*, Marta," said Phyllis. Take care of yourself.

"*Vaya con Dios*," they all said. Go with God.

So we left, continuing our search for something we couldn't articulate. We certainly hadn't landed yet in the land of *los sinverguenzas*, the bad people Augustina had warned us against. There were the poppy-growers we now knew had hidden plantations in the Sierra. But there was something else, an intangible presence of ancient wisdom with hope for the aspirations of humans to live at peace on the Earth.

After a few days of travel, we reached the shore of the Rio Balsas. There was no organized town on the north side of the river but local inhabitants gifted us with fish, tortillas, vegetables, and fruit. Unlike Copalillo's mountain austerity, discipline, and other-worldliness, the river people were sensual, permissive and playful. Children ran naked and swam in muddy pools beside the river. We drank pulque and ate fried *mojarra*, a river fish chock full of tiny bones but sweet with flavor. We washed and dried our clothes and swam in clear-water pools with the children.

The Rio Balsas itself was another matter. Chocolate brown and three times as wide as the Rio Amacuzac (the first river we crossed to enter this "land before time"), it stood beside us as a reminder that life was fierce and unforgiving. The crossing at Atenango had been swift but exhilarating, funneled as it was between bluffs, with rocky rapids below threatening us like schools of piranhas. The Rio Balsas felt like a huge snake slithering fast through the grass; the last thing on earth you wanted to do was touch it. But on the third day, touch it we did, torturing the reluctant burros on board an even longer, wider dugout than before, passing on board each dog and our gear, sharing the wooden benches with four Mexica Indians, all dressed, like me, in worn, white pajamas and brown, sun-weathered skin.

Ropes were thrown from the shore into the boat and we were off. Moving silently like a rhino swimming in a tsunami, our boat moved by the grace of two oarsmen's very strong shoulders. Two men rowed an impossibly heavy wooden boat loaded close to the water line with all we had precious in the world through and across this giant, moving reptile of liquid earth carrying our fears, hopes and ecstasy. Phyllis sat on the floor of the boat in front of me, my legs and arms wrapped around her in a tight embrace. Although I realized this was a dangerous boat trip, I couldn't help but wonder, *can life get any better than this?* Adventure and adrenaline fueled my love for this beautiful, innocent creature, this black-haired Italian beauty who had come with me to the spot that had called to me my whole life.

To my consternation, Phyllis distracted the focused oarsmen with a question:

Shouting over the roar, she asked: "Is it far to where the rivers join?"

One of the oarsmen stopped rowing and the boat turned sideways. "Half an hour. But nobody ever lives to see it. First comes the falls," he answered.

The other oarsman stopped rowing, held his hand level, pointed downriver and said, "The falls!" Then, dropping his hand rapidly, drew his finger across his throat. We looked downriver at the horizon where the mist rising from the impending falls clouded the sky. Then both oarsmen roared in laughter and returned to rowing.

"I think he means we'll get to shore *before* the falls," I said. I wasn't sure if I was trying to convince Phyllis or myself.

The dogs clung to the floor in a pile. The burros shifted their skinny legs and locked their knees against each lurch forward of the boat. Behind us the view of our launching point was lost forever. The opposite shore slowly came into focus but the river had narrowed slightly and the water moved dangerously fast. There was no obvious way we could land on shore. But with renewed effort and a series of elegant, practiced moves, the oarsmen directed us into a back eddy, steered our wooden dugout into a small cove and voila!—solid earth. Above the bank was the ancient river village of Tlalcosotitlan. We would live to travel another day.

Holding hands as we entered the town, Phyllis and I shakily but proudly made our way up a cobble-stoned street into the Tlalcosotitlan plaza on the Rio Balsas. We walked into a town whose origins lie in Olmec history centuries before the birth of Christ. Spanish monks recording the Conquistadores' defeat of the Aztecs made note of Tlalcosotitlan in 1527 as the thriving center of a river-based region that paid tribute to the Aztec King Moctezuma. But you won't find the town listed on any tourist brochures now nor do any motorboats ply the river, only the ancient dugout-ferry route we had just survived. The town is part of the forgotten past and we reveled in its obscurity. The plaza was graced with a few adobe houses; the rest were thatched-roofed temples, giving the town a look of a patchwork-quilt with the orange adobe tiles at the center, surrounded by cones of thatch spreading up the hillside.

Burros tied to a rail in front of one of the adobe houses pointed us to an exciting novelty: a café and bakery! No Starbucks logo here but by entering through a wooden door in a two-foot thick adobe wall, we found wooden tables and a half-wall in the rear, open to a flower-filled courtyard behind. We could see trays of *bolillos*—small wheat rolls—being removed from a wood-fired adobe oven. *Atole*, a sweet rice porridge, was being served in hot steaming clay cups. Some ancestral memory of travelers passing through medieval Germany on a burro and stopping at an inn for a cold ale slipped into my mind as we

walked into this earth-cooled garden room with a shaded courtyard view serving hot bread and atole.

Completing our rapture, we discovered that the inn had a
few rooms for wayfaring pilgrims. We needed no urging. Again,
as in Atenago, we were led through the courtyard, up a set of
almost-hidden whitewashed steps in the garden to an upstairs
room overlooking the empty plaza. The windows had no frames
or glass, just thick white-walled openings with a view of the river
and the green mountains we had descended. The dogs stayed
with us in the room, no questions asked. We spent the night in
each other's arms and the next day hiking the winding streets
to explore the town. At night, we smelled the Balsas River in
the breeze and saw the moon rise over Copalillo somewhere
in the distant mountains.

In the morning we were shown the bath house in the
garden, an outdoor private room with four adobe walls and no
roof, where buckets of sun-warmed water were set out. We took
turns pouring the healing, cleansing water over each other. Over
breakfast, my relentless need to move away from myself returned
and I was anxious to get going.

"We need to get moving; we don't even know the way out
of here," I said.

"Why don't you ask them here?"

"Nah, we'll figure it out as we go."

"Have it your way; just don't get that *dark* look."

"I don't know what you mean."

"Do you remember what that old man in the square in
Santa Fe said?"

"The panhandler that had a line about needing money to get home?"

"He wasn't a panhandler; he was an angel. But yeah, him, what did he sing when you turned away and said no?"

"Only believe, all things are possible, only believe," I said, smiling.

Following the trail along the river away from Tlalcosotitlan with Phyllis by my side, we had no clear direction. Having left Augustina's house in Tilzapotla, to climb the Mother Mountain, we had stumbled into worlds unknown and unimaginable. What now? We had crossed two impenetrable rivers. Was it time to head home? And where *was* our home? Tilzapotla? Texas? New York? America was 2,000 miles away.

The Vietnam War was ending, but nothing was resolved. There was no national reckoning or reconciliation. Like the end of the 19th century when America had finished the Indian wars and sent all the tribes to their graves or to Oklahoma, the country was ready to move on. I knew my home was wherever Phyllis was but I had no other answers for our future. The trail we followed arrived at a fork, the left path heading up the mountain, the right lazily following the river. We sat and waited until a traveler approached.

"Disculpe, senor, sabe donde esta el camino por Oaxaca?" I asked, returning to my old ploy of asking directions to an impossibly far point. Excuse me, sir, do you know the way to Oaxaca?

"No se, joven," he said, drawing out the sound of the "se" into a *saaaaay* sound. Who knows . . . young man?

"Well, where does this trail go?" asked Phyllis, gesturing uphill with a smile, knowing my preference.

"Tlapehualapa. Two days walk but you shouldn't go there. There's bad people there."

Say no more, I thought. *Must be our kind of town.* From an airplane's view 10,000 feet above, we would have been seen crossing numerous subtropical zones and slowly making our way to the sea. But as it was, we were glad just to find a wider trail. After a night camping at the peak above Tlalcosotitlan, we continued down the mountain toward Tlapehualapa. The trail skirted a creek which drained to the south. We had left the drainage basin of the western-flowing Rio Balsas; from that point, all rivers ran south to the Pacific Ocean. But the first time our trail crossed the creek, we were confused.

"I think we're lost," Phyllis said.

"You always think we're lost," I said. "We're not lost; this was the only trail." For once, I was right.

Soon we reached the edge of Tlapehualapa. At the first house where we asked for hospitality we were greeted by a hunched-over woman wrapped in a long skirt and rebozo. She showed us into her single-roomed, thatched house and motioned to a corner of the room for us to sit. The house was barely lit by a candle. Something about hospitality on this side of the mountain was different.

"I don't think she likes us being here," Phyllis said. "Maybe she's a *bruja* and she's casting spells against us."

"More likely, she's *afraid of us*," I said.

The woman made no offer to feed us. Perhaps she didn't

have enough to share. I thought of a way to free her of the obligation to house us.

"Excuse me, Ma'am. Is there someone in town who sells tortillas?"

She didn't answer but got up and left the house. Soon, a man our age came in and beckoned us to follow him. Outside, he lit a torch of tightly braided cactus fibers and waved us on. He ran out of the gate carrying the torch as we tried to keep up. The night was pitch dark and clouds covered the stars. Running blindly at a fast pace down the dark paths with a fiery torch throwing off sparks demanded a suspension of caution and produced an exhilarating release of adrenaline just to keep up.

"What's the rush? How come nobody talks in this town?" Phyllis asked. "And where's he taking us?"

"Just keep up," I said. I wasn't going to mention it but it occurred to me that we left the burros, the dogs and all our stuff behind.

Finally, we stopped at a gate. The man led us inside the fence and, extinguishing the torch, into a thatched-roof house with a tall ceiling. Inside was a more familiar scene: several generations of women, seated on the floor around a charcoal fire. No one acted surprised at our intrusion; all greeted us with smiles. The eldest woman, maybe sixty years old, sat with her legs tucked underneath her, grinding corn on a stone metate, each stroke creating a few tablespoons-full of masa. The next woman, a generation younger, took the masa and patted it and whirled it into tortilla rounds and dropped them on the comal, a clay griddle straddling the charcoal fire. Around the comal were two more younger women who turned the tortillas at just the right moment, letting them brown ever so slightly, then puff and be turned. Lit by the glow of the charcoal, these women enacted the complete, miraculous transformation of corn from soaked hard seed to human sustenance in front of our eyes. This ritual has been repeated on this same land for 4,000 years, a corn morality play performed in a private audience just for the two of us.

The young girls surrounded us and motioned to sit and be served *frijoles de la olla* and fresh tortillas. No one ever looked up at us or started a conversation. We ate greedily and gratefully; the family strain of sweet, blue corn did not disappoint.

"Thanks so much for the meal. We want to pay you; please let us," Phyllis said to the oldest woman, offering pesos. The woman looked down, never speaking but shook her head no. Phyllis took out a bag of rice from her bolsa and left it on the table.

"Excuse me, Señora, could you tell me something? Have we done something wrong? Why is everyone afraid of us?" Phyllis asked the woman.

The young man who led us to this hut, now sitting in the corner, spoke up.

"You're not with them? You really don't know what they do?"

A stern look from the woman made him sit back down, eyes averted.

"We know nothing," she said, her only words of the evening.

Soon, we were racing back across the town in another Olympian sprint, led by the torch and delivered to the house. Our hostess did not speak but sat in a chair lighting a candle to

La Virgen. Apparently we were not the first travelers who did not belong in Tlapehualapa. We had crossed the river closer to the modern world and even though old-world values persisted, there was more to fear.

Phyllis clung tightly to me that night in our sleeping bag, waking occasionally to the sound of horses hooves thundering by. Dawn could not have come early enough for Phyllis and me. I dreamed of the edgy man in the hacienda protecting a pride of wild jaguars with flaming torches for breath and needles dripping heroin. The next morning, the trail away from town took us through the creek twice more but without incident. We were descending in elevation rapidly, following the creek but occasionally veering away into steep ascents and switchbacks, only to repeat the process back down again. The view at each peak was stupendous: a shimmering turquoise ribbon of water was clearly distinguishable on the horizon a hundred miles away, sandwiched between baby blue sky and dark green tropical underbrush—the Pacific Ocean! Each sighting was like a shot of espresso that gave us the adrenaline to stretch muscles to meet the ups and downs of the trail. We passed the village of Tlatenpenapa at the second crossing without stopping. We camped outside of town and dined on leftover tortillas and fresh-cooked beans.

December 2, 1973

The terrain changed to tropical, as the descent became less steep and in a few hours we came into Zitlala. Somehow on the trail that morning, we crossed into another era of history, from the 2,000-year-old Nahua villages of the mountains to colonial Mexico of the 1800s. Zitlala had no electricity or paved roads. But instead of the thatched roofs and paths of mountain towns, it had classic Mexican adobe houses, a plaza and a whitewashed church framed by a pair of three-tiered bell towers. White is the ubiquitous color in colonial-era Mexican towns. The dirt streets are made of white caliche clay. The adobe walls and houses are bathed in whitewash made from crushed limestone. Offsetting the universal white are terracotta tile roofs and green bushes and vibrant red flowers.

In Zitlala, clothing came in a rich palette of colors as well. As we entered the edge of town, the men we saw had the same white pajama blouses that I wore but adorned with colorful red, yellow and purple bandanas with print patterns. The women wore dark-blue tube skirts with bands of red and purple flower patterns with white embroidered huipil blouses.

We walked the last few miles into the valley of Chilapa in Guerrero's foothills with Mexico's Sierra Madre for a backdrop. It was a return to modern civilization for us and we walked with some trepidation about what we left behind but also a new swagger from what we had survived. Not that Chilapa had anything most Americans would call *modern* but it did have a highway carrying diesel trucks, buses and old pickup trucks. It also had a dusty bus terminal with five or ten buses imported from the U.S. that probably had once carried American school-kids in the 1950s.

Chilapa was a valley center, a crossroads of numerous dirt and gravel roads leading down from the mountains. On every corner, there were cantinas, pulquerias and other establishments to purvey alcohol. Although Chilapa had recently received electric power, a newly paved road and motorized transportation, the change that was coming only appeared as a dark cloud in the early morning sky. The proud tradition of 2,000 years of self-sufficiency based on the miracle of corn still reigned. *Maiz*, the most prolific grain on Earth, *harnesses human labor* to distribute itself in unbelievable abundance to impossible terrain. Corn also has allowed the people of the valley and the Sierra to be self-sufficient and thereby to resist the domination of outside cultures since before the Babylonian empire.

Chilapa was the hub of an invisible abundance, invisible because it produced just enough to sustain itself and no more. Indios came and went on foot and on horseback as they had for millennia but now there was an ominous roar from the highway as diesel trucks churned through the hills delivering the poison pill of progress.

As Phyllis and I walked through town to the central plaza, we passed several liveries to stable our burros overnight. There were two options for horses and burros: self-service stables where you only paid for the stall, or full-service where your animal was fed and groomed. We decided to reward our by-now-beloved burros with the very best. They had come a long way with us and deserved a rest. So did we.

It was mid-afternoon and we took a room for ourselves at the second hotel we found, a centrally-located *casa de huespedes* with hand-carved wooden front doors opening onto a stone-paved courtyard, with rails to tie your horse. Above us were rooms arrayed along tiled corridors. We asked for a room facing the plaza. Out the windows of our room were giant trees forming a canopy over the street, shading and cooling our room as the ceiling fan beat a sleepy seduction.

We spent the warm afternoon behind heavy curtains on cool fresh sheets with starched hard pillows and used each other's sore and tender bodies to temporarily silence the unresolved fears of all humanity. We stripped away all the separations between thick skin and deep bone, leaving no space between thought and action, no inside, no out, no me, no you, until pleasure, magnified to oblivion, became separate flesh again and we slept. We lay undisturbed until the early evening when evening cathedral bells rang out six times.

In the early evening, we left our room to find some dinner. First we dropped by the stable to check on our burros and buy them some extra hay. Inside, the stable was full of bags painted purple with a skull and crossbones printed on them.

"What's with the purple paint on the bags?" asked Phyllis

"Don't you remember them from Tilza?" I said. "Those are government seed-corn bags. They are painted with a purple poison to keep people from eating it. It's only good for planting. It produces a bigger yield but you can't replant the next year's crop; the hybrid corn you grow doesn't grow true to seed the following year. The next year you have to buy more seed from the government. Pretty soon, no one's self sufficient."

"What's happening to the world? I don't know how to live *anywhere*. Copalillo was like a dream but it can't hold out forever.

I love New York but people there just go along and live for today. Most of the white people in my town go to Mass and say they love Jesus but they don't want black or brown people to live in their neighborhoods. They are afraid there isn't enough *stuff* to go around and someone will take *theirs* away. When you and I have babies, how are they going to live in this world? You took me over the wall into the old world, how can we just climb back over it and live like nothing happened there?"

Warm blood flushed through capillaries all over my body. "Wait a minute. Did you say you want to have babies with me?"

"Don't you?"

"Yes," I stammered. "I do. When do we get started?"

"Don't be funny. I'm saying I'm all mixed up. I love you but I always feel like an outsider in the world, whether I'm home in the USA or here in the mountains. Where do we belong? Where is our community? The world is going to come to Copalillo eventually and ruin it. They'll put in freeways and shopping malls. Do we stay here? Are our kids going to grow up around Tilzapotla? All the other kids and their parents have gone north to work. Where do we fit in?"

"Okay, look. Where we belong is with each other. What did Don Pablo from Copalillo say? *The whole world has to be exposed to the failures of this world before a new one can start.* And the old man in Santa Fe? *Only believe, all things are possible, only believe.* I think we need to go home to America, have lots of babies and let them be a part of whatever that change is. We can do whatever we can from inside the world we were born in. Our kids will know more than we do. What does Joseph Campbell say? *If you can see your own path laid out in front of you, you know it's not your own path.*"

"*Andale, mi amor,* you always have all the answers. Let's go home."

CHAPTER NINETEEN

BELIEVING IN POSSIBILITIES,
ALLOWING FOR MIRACLES

No there's nothin' you can send me, my own true love
There's nothin' I'm wishin' to be ownin'
Just carry yourself back to me unspoiled
From across that lonesome ocean.

       —Bob Dylan, "Boots of Spanish Leather"

Wednesday, September 14, 2011, 4:16 a.m. Coma Day 210.

Phyllis and I are living together in a double room at Health-South Rehab Hospital. The nurses have become friends and don't turn me in for staying overnight and never book another patient in our room. Our life together goes on, oblivious to the outside world.

Phyllis works very hard at this rehabilitation but isn't very impressed with herself. As always, it's hard to know (for her or me) what's going on in her head. Physically, she's moving ahead with her upper body, having progressed to a recumbent bicycle machine and other more complex stretching exercises. She can navigate on two legs but only with a walker and someone to hold her up with a belt from behind. Her leg strength remains her nemesis, though clearly it's growing.

The last few days since all her family left, I've noticed a new straightness to her spine; she no longer lists to one side when she sits. Her physical therapist, Craig, says she will be ready soon to try the *Big A* machine, a space-age, high-tech auto-ambulatory treadmill that resembles a giant robot. It holds you up so you can walk without bearing your full weight and moves your body in a normal stride so your brain can watch and your muscles adapt. As you progress, your muscles take over more and more of the weight-bearing.

It is hard for both of us to accept how much functionality Phyllis lost while she was immobilized in a coma. She does the work with a grim, relentless commitment that is amazing but it isn't joyful. I wish I could get her outside so she could be tempted by normal life outside. The natural world has always been so therapeutic for her; I believe getting her outdoors will rekindle her sense of *belonging*. The taste of salt on the tongue as you swim in the ocean, the sound of geese honking as they wing southward in the fall, the warmth of sunshine as you sit by a murmuring stream in the mountains, the breathtaking surprise at a close-up encounter with a young doe, all these and more are what we experienced together over the years in delirious wonder at the unexplainable peace of being *home* on Planet Earth.

We will have to bide our time until the moment is right to feel that again. As we did forty years ago, we will have to be brave enough to wander back out into the real world around us and remember where we belong.

I remember Phyllis and me in Mexico learning to soak and grind the corn, forming rounds of masa and greeting the day with the miracle of a simple gordita puffing up on the comal with the encouragement of ancient charcoal, a world where material for your shelter and sustenance for your body were free for the taking if you would work, a world where most of your day could be given over to the creative joy of living the miracle that we are *here*.

Sunday, September 18, 2011. Coma Day 214.

Today is a chilly, rainy day. After the blast furnace of the summer we've had, a cold, wet day is something glorious. Phyllis woke up early in the morning, stayed fully awake until evening, a miraculous feat, given the last seven months of her semi-consciousness.

Since I live with Phyllis now at HealthSouth, I have let go of most of my support network. I no longer have a network of angels sitting by her side throughout the day. For the last seven months, devoted friends have come in two-hour shifts throughout the day and into the night which has allowed me to live my life outside in some semblance of freedom. Sometimes it was just the freedom to go home to the ritual of letting out the dog and reading the paper in bed. But every taste of that freedom only made me want to have *her* to share it with; so I ran back to look for the next clue to Phyllis's awakening.

Now that I'm here living with Phyllis in the hospital as she pushes her body and mind back into movement, there are restrictions. A lot of people live in one space here and they all have their own demons to conquer. There is virtually no privacy and movement is restricted even while you are being trained how to move. I am here to learn how I can free Phyllis and myself from living in a restricted world. Nobody can exactly answer that question since no one knows exactly what "disabilities," physical or otherwise, she will retain or for how long. Ultimately, Phyllis has to answer the question for herself. So I am here in training. For the last week or two, I've made it my mission to take over the staff functions that are necessary for safety and survival, as if we were living in our own home. I have learned the art of "transfer," getting her up and down, into and out of beds, bathrooms, showers, chairs, and states of wakefulness. At the same time, her independence and strength are expanding, so that we are learning together how to expand the limits of her world.

The big question on everyone's mind these days about Phyllis is how much longer will she be in rehab and what then? As usual, I have no answers, only questions. The hospital case manager mentioned a date of three weeks recently but she's not really a hands-on observer, so she's not that aware of Phyllis's actual condition. But what if she's right about leaving in three weeks, then what? How do I take over what a complete hospital staff is doing now? I see twenty tasks a day that staff members carry out that I don't know how to perform.

As always when I'm confused I ask *what do I know?* One lesson I have learned from this experience is that human existence is about movement. We evolved into the creatures we are by *moving*: out of the ocean, away from the glaciers, across the mountains, out of bed, off to work. It's all about movement and when we stop moving, we become a fossil drying in the mud for someone else to study. But movement for humans isn't just about physical movement any more than Phyllis's freeing herself from the confinement of this hospital is just about walking. Humans have evolved this super-conscious brain that moves in all kinds of realms other than physical. So Phyllis and I also have to evolve in order to have a life beyond here. Humans yearn to break free. At the same time, in the dark of night, I'm afraid that I'm not up to the job. Guess that's a good reason to get out in the light. Maybe that's what Leonard Cohen meant in his song "Boogie Street."

> *So come my friends, be not afraid, we are so lightly here*
> *It is in love that we are made, in love we disappear.*
> *Though all the maps of blood and flesh are posted on the door*
> *There's no one who has told us yet what, Boogie Street is for.*

Wednesday, September 21, 2011, 5:02 a.m. Coma Day 217.

Tuesday was the start of Phyllis's sixth week at HealthSouth Hospital. The progress she has made here is dizzying. She has gone from sleeping half the day to being awake all day. She can move her arms, legs and torso in hundreds of small ways you wouldn't imagine unless you had lost control of them. She's aware of her surroundings and can carry on a conversation by phone, even dial a number from memory. On the other hand, she frequently forgets the way back to her room. She repeats the same mistake in how to exit her wheelchair. She's not sure where I go when I go to work. She has only vague memories of the last seven months' struggles or even of the advances of the last three weeks. Without a memory of life's daily victories over adversity, she's stuck in a kind of Groundhog Day reenactment of her impairment.

Saturday, September 24, 2011, 10:58 p.m. Day 220.

The hospital case manager informed me today through a letter left in the room that Phyllis has stopped improving and that our insurance would only pay for two more weeks. I know this isn't true so why does she want to push us out? I am seeing red, feeling the blood fill my face as I experience anger at this woman. This is the same case manager who didn't want to give Phyllis a pass to go out for her birthday party. Suddenly, I am in a frenzy imagining a place to live with Phyllis in her current condition. I have to speak with this bureaucrat who, I suspect, wants us gone because the insurance company pays less per day for long-term stays. I walk down the corridor to see this woman—who probably doesn't even know I'm living here—and knock on her door, then open it, uninvited.

"Can I speak with you?"

"I'm very busy at the moment. What do you need?"

"I want to talk to you about your letter evicting my wife from the care she needs."

"Oh you must be Mr. Head. I am just doing my job, sir. I'm sorry if that is hard for you to accept."

"What I can't accept is that you make decisions without consulting me or my insurance case manager. All of Phyllis's physicians find her case quite unique and agree with me that she needs more treatment."

"I've been doing this job for fifteen years. I believe I know when people need to move on. My husband was here as a patient last year after a stroke; he had to move home as well."

We were still going in circles but suddenly I saw this woman as human. This was personal, not just a bureaucratic machine in my way. I thanked her for her time and left. Still I wondered how *anyone* gets through the maze of health care on their own?

Monday, September 26, 2011. Coma Day 222.

8 a.m. Monday comes and goes; nobody comes to give Phyllis her weekly schedule. I go looking for Craig, the physical therapist. I find that two of Phyllis's three therapy sessions were canceled because of confusion in the scheduling. Twenty new patients were admitted over the weekend according to one of the nurses and they are scrambling to get them all settled. Phyllis has been here so long, she's becoming invisible.

The thought occurs to me: maybe *it is time* to move on from here. On top of that news, my nurse/spy tells me that Craig, our super-star physical therapist, is leaving for an extended paternity leave as soon as his wife gives birth to their second son who is due any day now. Understandable and he certainly deserves it but it means Phyllis will be tossed around between therapists unfamiliar with her needs.

At lunch, the case supervisor finds me and brings me up to date. She coolly suggests we schedule a "home evaluation" visit to our house to assess barriers to Phyllis living at home.

The day ended with news of a terrible tragedy. Our friend of twenty-five years, John, husband of Darla, a loyal Team Phyllis helper, died of a heart attack yesterday morning. He had just gone out for a bike ride with his dog. A multi-talented writer, accountant and business-recovery consultant, John was very physically active, riding miles a day on his bike. He died at the emergency room just a block away from our room at Health-South. Our love and prayers for peace and strength went out to Darla and her children. Nothing one can say about death takes away its sting. One moment we are here, conscious, vibrant and curious and then we are not. How is that possible? And why do some fall and not others?

Wednesday, September 28, 2011, 1 p.m. Day 224.

In the afternoon, Craig shows me the "car transfer" move which is the same as "bed transfer" or any other transfer. But I have to be approved for this maneuver for her to leave the facility. Phyllis does the work, standing up from her wheelchair, locking her knees, taking a few steps with support and then, sitting down in the car, after which I swing her legs inside. Craig approves my skill maneuver and gives us a two-hour pass! Next thing we know, *we are free*, on our way in the car *by ourselves* to a doctor's appointment to see why she's having so many Urinary Tract Infections (UTIs). *Everything in life is relative*, I realize. An action as simple as riding in your car with your partner to the doctor, when you have lost the freedom to do it and then get it back, is pure joy.

The doctor tells us that Phyllis has had a low-grade urinary infection for months that was below the radar of the tests they were doing and probably affected her wakefulness. The doctor has a plan to eliminate the recurring UTIs. We are back in the car and take a ride around town, around our neighborhood, passing by our house. Phyllis is totally aware and oriented, knows every street we take and which friend lives in which house—*much more aware than when she's trapped in the hospital.*

Before returning to the hospital, Phyllis and I attend our friend John's funeral. The ceremony is at the Jewish temple that his wife Darla helped to create and prosper and I manage to get Phyllis into her wheelchair and inside for the services. The building of this temple attracted national attention, aided as it was by a local Muslim builder/ philanthropist. We feel a special connection here as so many of our friends attend the temple. It is a beautiful day in the Ozarks, the place John adopted as home. I hope he knew how much he was admired and appreciated. The size and diversity of the audience is a fitting tribute to a life well-lived.

Thursday, September 29, 2011, 1 p.m. Coma Day 225.

Today we went with Craig and two other therapists-in-training to evaluate our house for "accessibility." Until now I have resisted the possibility of living at home after rehab. I am just plain scared to do it alone. I even made a deposit on a handicap-accessible apartment for us to live in when insurance will no longer pay for hospitals. Our house has three stories with steps everywhere, at the front door, between the living room and kitchen, down to the laundry, up to the bedroom. I have been convinced living here would be a disaster. But I trust Craig. He has worked miracles with Phyllis, teaching her to move in myriad ways and directions.

Walking around the house, familiar memories of our years raising six kids here flood my brain. It is as if our home is talking to us, welcoming us home. A voice in my head speaks to me:

Frank, I think you can do this. If you build a ramp to get her wheelchair in the front door, the access is pretty good. Then you make this TV room into a bedroom, put some handrails in the bathroom and you're home free.

Looking at our house layout through Craig's eyes, I begin to gain new hope. We measure and her wheelchair will squeeze through the door into the bathroom; the shower has just enough room for a seat. *We can do this,* I start to repeat as I wheel her from room to room in the house where we have lived since 1983.

Phyllis asks to sit in a living-room chair and four students lean in to help but Craig motions for me to do the transfer alone.

Phyllis smiles broadly as I help her into her own chair in her own living room. I take Craig aside and put the question to him:

"Craig, if this was your wife, what would you do?" I asked.

"What are your options?"

"I feel like I'm being manipulated by the hospital case worker. I refuse to make choices for Phyllis's care based on what insurance will or won't pay for or what the hospital needs in its patient mix. I don't want her doctors making decisions based on insurance, either. It makes no sense to me. I want to know what the very best medical decision is to treat her ailment. Period. Then I'll find a way to get that care. Everyone in this whole medical show runs around pleasing the insurance companies. Who is in charge of reviewing my wife's complete profile and suggesting treatment? Nobody, except me, of course! Anyway, Craig, I'm ranting. I want to know what you would do."

"If it was my wife, I would bring her home, no question. Forget about the hospital's issues. It's a distraction. I've seen it over and over with brain injury patients. They spend so much time confined to bed before they even start therapy. Then they have to do this grueling work but they do it. Then they get to a point where it's just torture. Going home, when it's possible, gives them a whole new lease on life. This doesn't mean the end of treatment; she's not there yet. It means you can consider the next step from a place where you and she feel most centered. You'll get home health visits for now. They'll send a therapist three days a week at your home. Then when she's ready, do outpatient therapy. Come back to HealthSouth or go to a specialized Neurological Rehab if you find one you like. She'll have ten times the energy to put into it. I totally believe she's going to walk and be fine. I just think she needs to be home for a while."

Craig left. What a saint. Phyllis and I were *home alone*. No one told us how long we could be away from the hospital that day, even though I knew the administrator would be fuming if I stayed too long. We made the schlepp back to the car and Phyllis and I dropped in unannounced on some friends, Moshe and Hamsa, for a visit. We considered going out for dinner (a joy just to imagine the possibility) but Phyllis was too close to exhaustion. *Normal* never felt so wonderful. We checked ourselves back into the hospital room and got ready for bed.

"Do you think going home is the best thing to do?" I asked.

"I know it is," she said.

"Then we'll figure out how to do it."

Friday, September 30, 2011, 1 p.m. Coma Day 226.

I met again with our case worker.

"Mr. Head, as you know, the team thinks that Mrs. Head has reached a plateau," said the case supervisor. "She doesn't have her heart in rehab and your insurance will not extend coverage unless she is improving."

"I'm not resisting anymore," I said. "Let's do the discharge. Do you have a date in mind?"

"We set it up for Saturday," she said.

"This Saturday?" I asked, incredulously. "Tomorrow, you mean?"

"Yes, the team feels it is best," she said.

"You realize I don't have a ramp built into my house or anyone hired to be with her all day?" I asked.

"I'm sure she's going to be fine," the case supervisor said.

"You know what?" I said. "Never mind. Saturday will be perfect. Can you get me a summary of the home evaluation that Craig did and the specifications for the ramp?"

"Of course," she said. "Would you like me to come in and pray with her?"

"No thank you," I said. What kind of prayer would someone make who was oblivious to our needs? "You are welcome to do that yourself, privately."

Phyllis woke in the night and I helped her with the wheelchair to the bathroom. She was asleep again as soon as she hit the bed. As I lay in the dark, I did a mental exercise of separating the voices competing in my head for air time.

One voice was really angry at the case supervisor for sending us home. *She wants to pray for Phyllis? Why doesn't she pray for herself to wake up tomorrow and do her job right?*

Another voice says, *It's not her fault. She's just caught up in a system that cranks people through healthcare like it was a huge car repair shop. No time to understand a complicated case; she's got twenty new arrivals today and twenty reports to file to insurance.*

Next I look at my own fear of not measuring up to the task at hand. How exactly do I plan to get the bathroom at the house converted, a ramp built, all the medical supplies ordered, a hospital bed set up and someone hired to be with her in one day? How do I expect to wake up at any time of the night for her but never give my body enough sleep to catch up during the day when she really needs me? We're going to need staff trained to transfer her from chair to bed to bathroom and back. I can't expect fifteen volunteers to do that on two-hour shifts. I need to hire somebody at least six hours a day during the week. And I still have a forty-hour a week job doing immigration law.

How will I get it all done? *One step at a time*, I answer. We're going *home*, remember? This is the moment I've been working toward for eight months. Phyllis has been living in hospital rooms a mile away from home all this time. This is *our* neighborhood, *our* community, *our* life. We'll be fine; we'll figure it out. We'll make the house work for now. We've slept in strange places before; now we'll sleep at home. We're going to sleep *together* in *our* bed. I have a list of trained caretakers; I can hire the core help for workdays. So there's pressure? Pressure makes you sharp; helps you summon the energy for the long haul. Look where we've come from; imagine where we'll be. *Only Believe. All Things Are Possible.* How lucky am I to have her alive after five brain surgeries, much less to be well enough to go home?

September 30, 2011, Friday, 6 p.m. Coma Day 226.

My phone rang as Phyllis and I sat in her hospital room for the last night.

"Mr. Head, this is Brett, your insurance company manager. Did you get everything worked out with the hospital?"

"The hospital told me you wouldn't cover Phyllis anymore because she had reached a plateau," I said. "They've given me a Saturday discharge."

"This Saturday?" he asked. "Tomorrow? We never denied coverage. I've been waiting on the hospital case manager to call me back. Do you want me to call her and insist that you be allowed to stay?"

"Thanks, Brett, but no," I said. "You know, I really think going home now *is* the best medicine. I was pretty pissed at how they handled the process. But I'd have to be really arrogant to complain at all. They treated her like a queen for two months. They let me move in for free. The therapy she got was life-saving. And I believe Craig, the therapist, when he says this is going to bring the next big leap in healing for her."

"Well, hang in there," he said. "And tell your volunteers that they are the reason she's back with you today. Let me know if you have trouble setting up home health."

Phyllis's therapy team, Craig, Erin and Walt, spent the day showing me exercises she can do at home to continue her progress. She can get herself from sitting on a bench to standing by slowly leaning forward enough to let gravity kick in, then grabbing the sides of a walker and straightening up to standing. Scary as hell but also exhilarating. Once she is standing, she can reach objects on her far left and right and put them on a shelf. She can take steps with the walker but she needs a lot of work on finding her balance. Craig showed me how she has to hinge forward at the waist in an exaggerated manner until the brain feels its balance and then straighten up. Of course, she has to wear a safety strap for all of this with a handle on her back that I can hold as a safety precaution. Eventually the brain will let her go from sitting to a balanced standing position in one move but first she has to break it into all its parts and practice each one. She already can catch a weighted basketball while she's sitting and throw it back.

October 1, 2011, Saturday, 10 a.m. Coma Day 227.

Home! After a ten-minute drive to our house, we are greeted by my son Joey and two family friends, Ralph and his son Ben who offer to help carry Phyllis up the three front steps. Instead she insists she can climb them herself. I thought *no way* but I let her try. Sure enough, with great effort, she picked up her legs, one at a time, and climbed the steps. Thirty-two weeks after she fell unconscious and we took her out of the house in a stretcher, she is home on her own terms. A caravan of friends followed with two carloads of clothes, flowers, pictures and bric-a-brac from 227 days in hospital rooms.

Inside the house, there were miracles too. The hospital case supervisor had arranged for delivery of a hospital bed, a wheelchair and a retrofit to the bathroom with bars and handles. As we walked in, the phone rang. It was my friend, Geshe-la, a Tibetan Buddhist monk who recently brought the Dalai Lama to Fayetteville. He knew a lady with experience in nursing who was ready to go to work on Monday. The pace things are falling into place is making me dizzy! The rest of the day, friends brought fresh-cooked food and I unpacked. Ginny's husband, Steve, agreed to start building a ramp on Monday and our friend Judith insisted on helping him with the labor. Settled into our downstairs den with a hospital bed and leather couch, we soon fall into a deep sleep and dream of other paths and other journeys. What a long, strange trip it's been.

Only Believe! Only Believe! All things are possible, only believe.

EPILOGUE

Everything changes and the only certain route is the one we have already traveled. A decade has passed since Phyllis recovered from her coma in 2011 and we returned home from the hospital. Five decades have elapsed since 1972, when Phyllis and I began our pilgrimage through the Sierra Madre of Guerrero, Mexico and came home to America.

Don Lauro died in Tilzapotla in 1974, an unsung Mexican revolutionary hero. Augustina lived on in the house we gave her in Tilzapotla until her death in 1998. Before she died, she came to visit us in Arkansas for a month. We had forgotten how short she was, less than five feet. In our memories, she towers over us all. Our good friend Veronica, Augustina's granddaughter, who lived with us as a child in Tilza, married Martin from Tilzapotla. They live in Chicago, are both American citizens and are the proud parents of three sons, two of whom are officers in the American military.

In 1983, the Mexican government built a new toll road from Mexico City to Acapulco and chose the Paso Morelos route through the Sierra, passing within a few miles of our wilderness trek to Copalillo. Tilzapotla is now a passing blur on the toll road. Change can be so painful. The same superhighway currently passes by Atenango Del Rio with an exit for Copalillo. A new concrete bridge hangs over the Rio Amacuzac. Copalillo itself has electric lines marring the view—at least Google tells me so. What took us a month to carefully explore on foot fifty years ago can now be driven in two and a half hours.

Good things did happen. The Amacuzac River valley, the town of Atenango Del Rio and the surrounding ancient civilization was saved from a government plan to dam the river by an archeological discovery a few years after Phyllis and I passed through. While building the super-highway past Copalillo in 1983, construction was halted temporarily when the crews uncovered an ancient temple, ten miles south of Copalillo, directly on the route Phyllis and I walked, very close to where we drank bad water and got sick.

A Mexican archaeologist, Doctora Guadalupe Martínez Donjuán, explored the area around Copalillo at the request of the government. Following Indian reports of artifact finds, Doctora Martinez discovered an ancient Olmec temple outside Copalillo on the trail leading to Tlalcozotitlán, very near where Phyllis and I crossed the Rio Balsas. Carbon-dating puts the temple's date of construction at *fourteen centuries before Christ*, one of the oldest locations of advanced civilization on our continent. Doctora Martinez gave it the name Teopantecuan-itlán, which translates "the Temple of the Jaguar God." Thanks to these discoveries, the Amacuzac was not dammed; plans to build a giant lake submerging the region never came about and most of the wilderness where Phyllis and I walked has now been protected as a Biosphere Reserve.

But overall, the end of the 20th century was a victory for the forces of darkness. In 1992, the North American Free Trade Association (NAFTA) was signed, allowing cheap American hybridized corn to be imported, undercutting the livelihood of millions of Mexican indigenous farmers. The Mexican government used the occasion to undermine protection for the *ejido* rural agricultural system which, for fifty years, had allowed for self-rule and collective ownership by indigenous communities, governing the vast majority of rural Mexico. Both Tilzapotla and Copalillo, as *ejido* villages, had been allowed to stay independent since the Mexican Revolution.

Thanks to NAFTA's dismantling the *ejido* system, ten million land-deprived Mexican farmers would subsequently illegally migrate North to survive. Drug cartels used the new ease of cross-border transportation and lack of rural protection to take over the Mexican countryside and convert it to a mega-meth-exporting machine. A small-time drug lord now claims Tilzapotla as his own. American politicians used the plight of desperate Mexican immigrants to rant against aliens while accepting donations from laundered drug money. Our friend David from Copalillo was murdered as he traveled north to sell his family hammocks, caught in crossfire between rival drug gangs.

As much as I long to, I haven't been able to make myself go back to Guerrero. I wonder what became of the dugout canoes that braved the mighty river? Do families in Copalillo still walk daily to their ancient wells to bathe? But who am I to judge how it has changed? Phyllis and I had the privilege to return to modern corporatized America to make our own way; our hosts there did not. As Don Pablo enlightened us in Copalillo, humans can't evolve until enough of them go down the wrong trail and their survivors find a new path.

And yes, Phyllis had a miraculous and complete recovery of consciousness. After returning to our Fayetteville, Arkansas home in October of 2011, she gradually re-learned to walk, run and climb stairs. A year after our return from rehab in 2011, we moved back upstairs to our bedroom on the third floor, which means she had to walk up and down two sets of stairs to get to the laundry room. Four years after her coma, in 2015, Phyllis and I traveled around southern Europe for a month by train, bus and on foot. We visited her late mother's hometown on the Amalfi coast, climbed seemingly endless stone steps from the ocean to the mountaintops and down again.

Until February of 2020, we lived in the same home where we raised our six children, a three-story stucco house near the university in Fayetteville. Phyllis still has the brain shunt that was inserted in March of 2011; you can feel the bump on the top of her head where the drain tube fits between bone and skin, pulling spent cerebrospinal fluid to the surface from deep in the base of the brain, down her neck unnoticed, draining the clear, life-preserving liquid, like everyone else's, into the abdominal cavity.

There were other bumps along the way. In January of 2012, four months after coming home, Phyllis lost her balance opening the refrigerator, fell and broke her hip. That meant hip surgery and back to the rehab hospital for a week. I felt like we had both fallen down a familiar deep well and I was full of fear. But Phyllis was lionhearted and continued her healing. Then the following July, she went on an outing with friends to the shore of a nearby lake. She slipped out of a beach chair, hit a rock and broke her collarbone, having to be transported up a hill on a makeshift stretcher. None of these events stopped her from a relentless march to the restoration of her ability to move.

Recently, in 2020, Phyllis went for an annual check-up with her neurologist. I took the opportunity to review her doctor's notes from when the coma began:

March 6, 2011:

"Patient was admitted a week and a half ago with a bacterial shunt infection. Since then she doesn't show any signs of mental functioning. She is mostly withdrawing from flexor posturing and of course cannot speak."

March 15, 2011:

"Patient does not appear to respond when I call her name. She doesn't follow any commands to move. Her brain ventricles remain enlarged despite external drain. Multiple tests do not reveal any explanation for the patient's continued comatose stature. She is now brought back to the operating room for implantation of a complete new shunt system."

Miracles do happen and Phyllis is living proof that "all things are possible." We are well aware that not everyone is so lucky. Phyllis encourages others to keep hope alive and to be participants in their own healing. I will never forget when the top neurosurgeon at Barnes-Jewish Hospital in St. Louis told me in late April 2011 that "she may never get any better than this." Faith, love and a community across an infinite universe proved him wrong.

When I read today's news headlines demonizing immigrants escaping hardships and oppression in their own countries, I often remember the hospitality the Indians in Morelos and Guerrero showed Phyllis and me so many years ago. I think about the Olmec who built water canals, dams and temples in those very lands 3,000 years earlier and live on now in the faces of the immigrant children attending Arkansas schools. I also think with deep gratitude of my parents, who inspired me to live life as if everything has meaning—because it does.

Since March of 2020, Phyllis and I are living full time in the Ozark Mountains at the edge of one of the largest areas of biodiversity in the United States. The Ozark mountains have been continuously inhabitable for 300 million years, an amazing refuge throughout the ages for all living beings. We have spent the age of Covid-19 rediscovering our roots, living close to the ground, eating simply, gardening and introducing ourselves to the larger community of wild animals as well as the forest: lichens, moss, and fungi that connect to every tree as if they and every one of us were just part of one giant, living being. It feels a lot like we've come home.

We pray that the current era of worldwide suffering, mistrust and chaos will lead to a new renewal of the spirit, an evolution of our human species that allows us a more complete understanding of the sacred interdependence of all life and a resurgence of joy in the journey.

Looking ahead, the kind of change you pray for seems to happen so slowly, almost imperceptibly and takes so much patience. But looking back, the time seems to have passed so quickly and the change was in fact breathtakingly fast. The trails that we followed which seemed so random then, seem now, if not predestined, at least, *prepared* for us to follow. By living each day as if it were a gift, Phyllis and I got our life back. Maybe that's what the relativity of time is all about. The future seems much too far away and the past went by all too fast.

Guess we'll have to settle for joy in the present. Only believe.

ACKNOWLEDGMENTS

Almost by definition, a memoir itself is an acknowledgment of all those who influenced its writing. So for all those mentioned in the book itself, especially Ginny Masullo and Barbara Dillon, who organized the coma volunteers, please know how deeply grateful, how beyond words I find myself, to express the gratitude I feel for what you gave us. You are part of our family and without you, there would have been no story to tell. To the love of my life, my wife Phyllis, for whom the book was written and who helped write and edit it, I will let the story speak for itself. From that union has come six children, their loving partners and six grandchildren, all of whom are part of the daily oxygen I breathe.

As to those who directly contributed to the writing of the book, first I have to thank my late father, Frank W. Head Sr., who always encouraged me to write and blessed me with his great imagination. Then, of course, my mother, Betsy Head, who not only gave me life but surrounded me with unconditional love and an understanding of life and death as one continuous spiritual adventure. My three older sisters, in order of birth, Eleanor, Charlotte and Elizabeth and their families who each in their own way gave me so much love and support that I owe them many lifetimes in return.

In the time immediately before I met Phyllis in 1972, I was

encouraged and kept sane by a group of friends who don't appear in the book but played an essential role: Joe Stokes, a fellow conspirator since high school; Judith Horton, deep soul and true friend, Jim and Mary Crook, lifelong friends since college; the late Greer Taylor and the late Ivan Illich.

The book would never have been compiled without my first editor, Houston Hughes. My most recent team, Nicole Gregory, editor extraordinaire, and Karen Richardson, independent publishing guru, have brought this project from "almost complete" to "dream realized". You're the greatest.

To the late Ralph Nesson, my friend for the next couple of lifetimes, and his brother Bob, my fondest love. To Carole and Kerry Price, and Chaka and Robert Varley, our special angels, and to all those who I've forgotten to thank, mille grazie.

ABOUT THE AUTHOR

Frank Head was born in Houston, Texas in 1947. He attended Vanderbilt University and then graduated from the University of Texas at Austin in 1969. He worked in a great variety of occupations, from itinerant fruit picker to Director of Arkansas Catholic Charities Immigration Services from which he retired in 2019.

He married Phyllis Petrella Head in 1973. From then until 1982, they lived in various locations, including central Mexico, Vermont, Austin and Houston, Texas. Since 1982, they have lived in Fayetteville, Arkansas with their six children and six grandchildren. Since 2019, Frank and Phyllis have lived on their fifty acres of Ozark wilderness bordering the Little Buffalo River.